# SHROPSHIRE

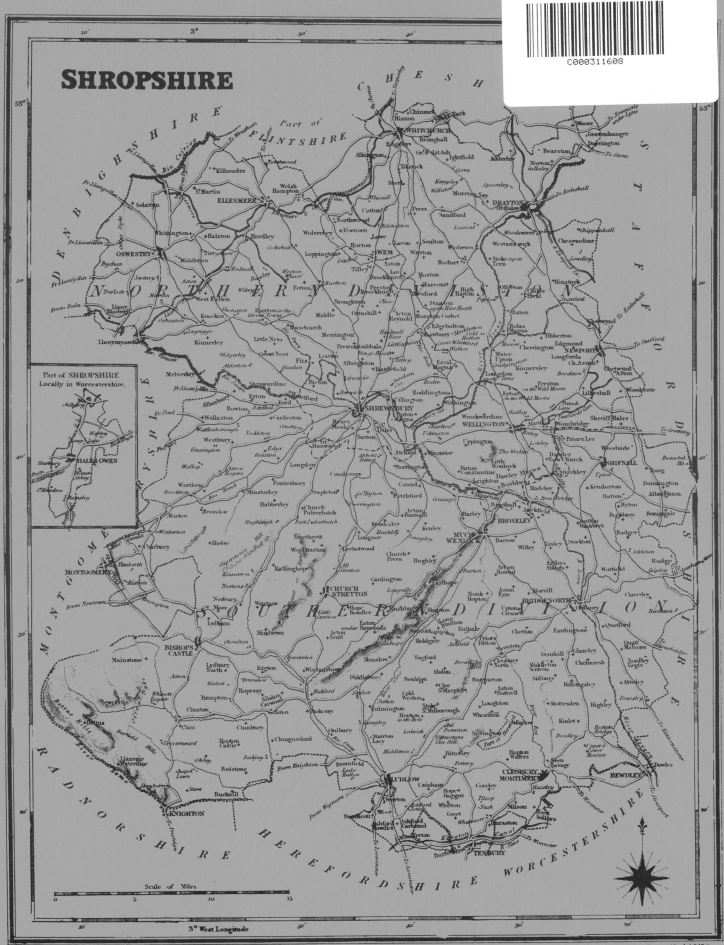

Part of SHROPSHIRE
Locally in Worcestershire.

Scale of Miles

3° West Longitude

Drawn by R. Creighton.      DRAWN AND ENGRAVED FOR LEWIS' TOPOGRAPHICAL DICTIONARY.      Engraved by J. & C. Walker.

C000311608

# BURKE'S AND SAVILLS GUIDE TO COUNTRY HOUSES

VOLUME II

HEREFORDSHIRE · SHROPSHIRE
WARWICKSHIRE · WORCESTERSHIRE

Peter Reid

LONDON
BURKE'S PEERAGE LTD
MCMLXXX

*For Richard Murton and Amy Tritton*

© Burke's Peerage Ltd, 1980
All rights reserved. Except for normal review purposes
no part of this book may be reproduced or utilized in any form
or by any means, electronic or mechanical, including photocopying, recording or
by any information storage and retrieval system without permission
of the Publishers

PUBLISHERS' NOTE
Every care was taken to check the information supplied for this edition
but the Publishers cannot accept responsibility for mis-statements,
omissions or other inaccuracies which may appear in this work

ISBN (Standard Edn) 0 85011 031 9
ISBN (Collectors Edn) 0 85011 032 7

This book has been set in Imprint by
Santype Ltd of Salisbury, Wiltshire
printed and bound by Garden City Press Ltd of Letchworth, Herts
for the Publishers, Burke's Peerage Ltd
(Registered office: 42 Curzon Street, London W1
Publishing offices: 56 Walton Street, London SW3)

Designed by Humphrey Stone and Jonathan Tetley

# Contents

*125 years experience of Estates,
Country Houses and Agricultural Property
throughout the United Kingdom*

# SAVILLS

Residential, Agricultural and Commercial Surveyors

**20 Grosvenor Hill, Berkeley Square, London W1X 0HQ.  Tel: 01-499 8644  Telex: 263796**
**Country Residential department: 5 Mount Street, Berkeley Square, London W1Y 6AQ**
**Tel: 01-499 8644**

**London Banbury Beccles Brechin Cambridge Chelmsford Croydon Hereford**
**Lincoln Norwich Salisbury Wimborne York Paris Amsterdam**
**Associates in North West England and Scotland**

# Editor's Preface

THIS IS the second volume of a series that is attempting to record the family seats, standing and demolished, of the British Isles. The first volume, covering Ireland, appeared in 1978 to a generous reception from the press. In her review for *The Times*, Mary Cosh noted that *Burke's Guide to Country Houses* "takes as criterion the 'illustrious obscure' houses neglected by most books, not all architecturally excellent, but, even more than the well-known Statelies, a British speciality whose increasing loss is a real threat to our history. This is a first-rate idea . . . it seems eminently reasonable to discuss these houses, as here, in relation to the families who made them."

Since settling down in earnest to the task of covering England, Scotland and Wales it has become clear that the series will now run to at least ten volumes, featuring perhaps 10,000 seats. Already further volumes are in preparation on East Anglia, the North West, South West and South East of England, with plans afoot for volumes on the remainder of the Midlands, Cotswolds to Chilterns, North East, Wales and Scotland. It should be stated at the outset that we are sticking to the old counties as they used to be.

Some 600 seats in Herefordshire, Shropshire, Warwickshire and Worcestershire are dealt with in this volume. The entries take the usual form of a photograph or two, an architectural commentary, a brief history of the property and its devolution, together with the odd anecdote and human touch, plus bibliographical references of note. As well as houses that have been owned by families appearing in *Burke's Peerage & Baronetage*, *Landed Gentry*, etc (the codes used for the Burke's series are explained in the "Principal Bibliography" which follows the individual introduction to each county section), most other seats find a place.

In addition to writing the text, Peter Reid has assembled a rare and richly evocative collection of photographs, achieving a notably high percentage of illustrations per entry. Mr Reid has had a lifelong interest and concern for country houses; he is peculiarly well qualified to contribute to this series for his knowledge of seats is as comprehensive as his grasp of genealogy. It is fair to say that he has probably done more than anyone to make permanent visual records of country houses. He initiated the search for photographs of vanished houses and much of his work in this direction helped lay the foundation of the memorable "Destruction of the Country House" exhibition at the Victoria & Albert Museum in 1974.

Although Mr Reid has devoted care and attention to detail far beyond the call of duty, no one is more keenly aware of the work's imperfections than he. It should, of course, be borne in mind that this is essentially a pioneering study—there has never been a fully illustrated survey of family seats like this before—and it is therefore inevitable that the results must be uneven.

The practical problems of putting together such an ambitious project should not be underestimated. From the publishing point of view the production costs have risen alarmingly since the Irish volume came out. Indeed, were it not for the welcome intervention of Savills, the estate agents and surveyors, the publishers would have been obliged to charge almost double the final cover price for this volume. We are most grateful to Savills for their generous patronage and pleased that they should be associated with Burke's in the title of this book. "The fitness of the new partnership hardly needs stating", observed "Nimrod" in *The Field*. "No one knows their country houses better than Savills."

The author's own acknowledgements follow overleaf; here we would particularly like to thank Howard Colvin, John Harris, Mark Bence-Jones, James Lees-Milne, Michael Sayer, David Watkin, Hugh Weldon and Andrew Wells for their helpful editorial advice in framing this series.

HUGH MONTGOMERY-MASSINGBERD
General Editor *Burke's Guide to Country Houses*
September 1980

# Sotheby's
### FOUNDED 1744

## The world's leading auction house

A Chelsea figure of a Jewish Pedlar after a Meissen original, *c.* 1752-56, sold in May 1980 for £4,000.

*The Resurrection* by Dievic Bouts, sold in April 1980 for £1,700,000

A William and Mary marquetry cabinet on stand, sold in May 1980 for £7,800.

*Juliet and her Nurse* by J. M. W. Turner, sold in New York in May 1980 for £2,689,076

*A Portrait of Joseph Smyth, Esq.* by George Stubbs, sold in July 1980 for £100,000

- **Auction sales held in thirteen countries**
- **Forty-eight auction rooms and offices throughout world**
- **Valuations for Insurance and Probate**
- **Taxation Advisory Service**

A James II 'Chinoiserie' porringer and cover, sold in July 1980 for £21,000.

**Sotheby Parke Bernet & Co.,
34-35 New Bond Street,
London W1A 2AA**
*Telephone:* **(01) 493 8080**
*Telegrams:* **Abinitio, London**
*Telex:* **24454 SPBLONG**

Salerooms and offices in: Amsterdam, Boston, Bournemouth, Brussels, Buenos Aires, Cambridge, Cheltenham, Chester, Chicago, Danbury, Dublin, Edinburgh, Florence, Frankfurt, Geneva, Hamburg, Harrogate, Hong Kong, Honolulu, Houston, Johannesburg, London, Los Angeles, Madrid, Melbourne, Milan, Monto Carlo, Munich, New York, Palm Beach, Paris, Philadelphia, Pulborough, Rio de Janeiro, Rome, San Francisco, Sao Paulo, Stockholm, Taunton, Tokyo, Toronto, Torquay, Vancouver, Zurich.

# Author's Note and Acknowledgments

IT WAS my intention to present a comprehensive survey of all seats in the counties of Herefordshire, Shropshire, Warwickshire and Worcestershire. But research on this scale requires substantial sums to support it and I have had to create a book with financial limitations. In spite of this, here for the first time is an illustrated survey concerning most of the country houses in the West Midlands. It was my wish to create a much-needed quick-reference book—and I feel it has not fallen far short of its target. Most important are the photographs which show the rich and diversified houses together for the first time. The majority of these houses are unknown and much country house tragedy can be laid down to ignorance of the houses concerned.

On the spot research has proved impossible in many cases and, as a consequence, some of the text may appear inadequate. I have had to rely heavily on printed sources such as Sir Nikolaus Pevsner's unrivalled *Buildings of England* volumes, the *Victoria County Histories* of Warwickshire and Worcestershire and the Royal Commission on Historical Monuments' three handsome volumes on Herefordshire. I must stress that the bibliography for each house is far from complete, but I have endeavoured to include the more important sources, *e.g. Country Life* articles.

As far as photographs are concerned, I have above all to record my warmest thanks to the National Monuments Record. For many years they have patiently copied the numerous photographs and miscellaneous visual records of hundreds of lost houses I have unearthed. Mr Eric Mercer, Director of the NMR, has been tolerant of this present venture and I thank him for his support. Mr Stephen Croad has guided photographic printing operations to successful conclusions and has been most helpful with suggestions and worthwhile comments which have been gratefully received. Mr Ian Leith has sought out the obscure from the inner recesses of the NMR and has provided his own personal photographs in several cases. My deepest thanks as well to the photo-graphic department for the consistently outstanding quality of their work both on copying and in the prints they have provided for this book. That quality was much appreciated by the designers, Humphrey Stone and Jonathan Tetley, who responded in the best possible way with the layout.

Many people have kindly helped with photographs and work in Herefordshire has brought to light two outstanding amateur photographers—Sir Geers Henry Cotterell, 3rd Bt (1834–1900), and William Hartland Banks (1867–1930), creator of Herefordshire's finest garden at Hergest Croft, Kington. Samples of their work are found in the following pages with photographs of The Byletts, Compton Verney, Eastnor Castle, Garnons and Knill Court.

Numerous owners of houses have answered questions, allowed me to take or borrow photographs and indeed have provided sustenance to help me on my way. I must thank them as well as friends, Record Offices, etc, in alphabetical order: Andrew League Trust, Mr D. L. Arkwright, Mr Simon Bailey, Messrs R. A. & W. L. Banks, Miss P. G. Barker, Mrs Egbert Barnes, Sir Adrian Beecham, Bt, Mr & Mrs M. A. Bellville, Hon Lady Betjeman, Amy Lady Biddulph, Hon Edward Biddulph, Mr J. N. R. N. Bishop, Mrs L. F. P. Bletchly, Mr John Bold, Miss Priscilla Boniface, Mr Richard Booth, Mrs G. H. Bray, Mr George Bray, Mr & Mrs J. Brazier, Brockhampton Park Hotel, Mrs G. E. Burbidge, Mrs Grayston Burgess, Miss Bythell, Brig & Mrs E. B. W. Cardiff, Dr I. A. Bewley Cathie, Mr William Chichester, Mr P. L. Clarke, Mr G. M. Clive, Lady Mary Clive, Mr Gerald Cobb, Mr C. E. Colbourn, Mr R. J. Collins, Mrs C. R. T. Congreve, Col & Mrs Uvedale Corbett, Sir John Cotterell, Bt, Mr Michael Cottrill, Mrs E. Snead-Cox, Mr J. R. Snead-Cox, Mr G. E. Cresswell, Major D. J. C. Davenport, Mrs L. A. Davenport, Betty Countess of Denbigh, Mr Richard Dennis, Mr & Mrs John Dorrell, Sir William Dugdale, Bt, Capt & Mrs Thomas Dunne, Mr J. K. Farrow, Mr

A. T. Foley, Mr Richard Green, Mrs Rupert Lycett Green, Mr Eric Halsall, Mr M. A. Hammon, Miss E. H. Harding, Mr E. H. V. Harington, Mr C. C. Harley, Mr Leigh Harrison, Mr & Mrs Jeffrey Haworth, Hereford Record Office, Hereford & Worcester Record Office, Major & Mrs R. J. Hereford, Mr Bernard Higgins, Major H. R. Holden, Mr C. B. Holman, Mr & Mrs T. S. Hone, Mrs L. N. Hope, Mr & Mrs Simon Hopton, Mr F. G. Howell, Dr W. Logan Jack, Mr & Mrs T. H. Jay, Miss Nora Keane, Mr Francis Kelly, Miss Bridget Lakin, Miss A. W. Lambert, the Latvian Home, Mr Peter T. Leach, Mr Denis Lennox, Lt-Col J. E. Little, Longworth Hall Hotel, Mrs G. D. Manley, Mr H. E. J. Marriott, Mr Michael Marshall, Hon Mrs A. E. Bromley-Martin, Dr K. Miller, Mr Nicholas Moore, Sir Jasper More, Mrs E. Morgan, Mr Victor Morris, Mr & Mrs A. C. Mortimore, the Misses Mumford, the Musicians Benevolent Fund, Mr & Mrs D. F. Naughton, Lord Norton, Mrs D. Oglander, Mrs J. H. Oram, Lord Ormathwaite, Mr Trevor Parker, Pengethley Hotel, Mrs E. O. B. Turville-Petre, Mr Malcolm Pinhorn, the Earl of Plymouth, Vice-Adm Sir Ernle & Lady Kyrle Pope, Mr Richard Porter, Hon Diana Pritchard, Mr & Mrs J. Price, Mr D. Prophet, Pudleston Court School, Mrs P. R. de Q. Quincey, Mr M. V. Robinson, Miss P. M. Rogers, Mr C. M. T. Smith-Ryland, St Mary's School, St Richard's School, Mr Derek Sherborn, Shropshire Record Office, Lt-Cmdr & Mrs R. M. Simpson, Mr J. T. Smith, Sir Edward Thompson, Major J. H. N. Thompson, Mr Nicholas Thompson, Mr John Thorne, Mr William Townsend, Mr J. Powell-Tuck, Brig H. Vaughan, Mrs M. L. C. Vaughan, Sir David & Lady Wakeman, Lt-Col M. H. Warriner, Warwick County Record Office, Mr E. R. Poore-Saurin-Watts, Mr C. D. Webster, Wessington Court School, Whitbourne Hall Community Ltd, Mr & Mrs J. P. Wilkerson, Mrs J. Williams, Mr Antony Wilson, Mr C. J. the late Mrs H. P. Wood and Mr & Mrs J. G. Wordsworth.

Lastly, I must pay tribute to Hugh Montgomery-Massingberd for his constant advice and great patience.

*London SW1*                                    PETER REID

# HEREFORDSHIRE

HEREFORDSHIRE is a land of extraordinary beauty and the land of the farmer. It is a broad territory and the majority of country houses spread over it are essentially squires' houses. Even today industrialization is virtually unknown.

The proximity to Wales and the danger of border warfare invested some of the earliest houses with some form of fortification. Kentchurch Court, Treago and Croft Castle still show evidences of 14th-century defence. Herefordshire to the layman means half-timbered houses and the county is rich in them. In many cases it is difficult to elucidate the difference between a grand yeoman's dwelling and a gentry house. But Lower Brockhampton and Rudhall certainly fall within the latter class while Brinsop Court and Burton Court, Eardisland are examples of 14th-century stone houses with magnificent great halls with timber roofs.

The 16th and 17th centuries produced a rash of new building in the county—many with notable plaster ceilings and chimneypieces. Michaelchurch Court, Fawley Court, Hellens and The Rodd are a few of the outstanding ones. Moving into the later 17th century we are met with Holme Lacy, the first really grand house employing reticent classical facades. Behind these bland exteriors were some of the richest rooms of their date in England. To the last years of the 17th century and the first years of the 18th century belonged Stoke Edith, arguably the most beautiful house in the county, with its magnificent painted hall by Thornhill.

The 18th century, generally accepted as the highpoint of country house building, provided Herefordshire with a fair number of new houses, but most of them suited to a remote and seemingly secret part of the world. Reticence was the watchword for the Prices' Foxley built in 1717—later to become the seat of Sir Uvedale Price who, with Richard Payne Knight of Downton Castle, became high priests of the Picturesque movement. Foxley has gone—so too have Tyberton Court (1728), with its interior by Wood of Bath; Aramstone (*ca* 1730); and Rotherwas (1732), probably by Gibbs.

Later in the century Anthony Keck gave us Moccas Court and Canon Frome Court—agreeable but not outstanding houses. The later 18th century, however, did provide two houses of national importance—Downton Castle and Berrington Hall. Of 18th-century landscape parks two of the best to survive are Garnons and Sufton—both by Humphry Repton.

Into the 19th century we are met with the Greek and the Gothic. There is Smirke's Haffield of 1818 and the much later Whitbourne Hall (1862) by Elmslie—one of the most important Victorian Classical houses in England. Nash's dim Garnstone, Smirke's Norman Eastnor and Blore's extravagant and eccentric Goodrich paved the way to the tragic remodelling of Hampton Court in the 1830s by an amateur, Charles Hanbury-Tracy, later 1st Lord Sudeley.

One notable Victorian house which has gone and which is virtually unknown to architectural history was Broxwood Court—an extraordinary building with an odd combination of architects: Hansom and Stokes. The 20th century has seen appalling losses in the county and between 1948 and 1958 almost 20 houses—including some of the best—were demolished. Cubberley, built in 1971, stands as a lone new house in the county.

As in most counties, there are relatively few long-established families. The Crofts, in spite of their loss and regain of Croft Castle in 1746 and 1923, outdo all other families for continuous tenure in the male line of their ancient holding. The Mynors of Treago, the Greenlys of Titley, Herefords of Sufton and Scudamores of Kentchurch represent the original families only through the female line. Vaughans held Courtfield from the 16th century until the 20th century; Kyrles and their descendants have remained at Much Marcle since the 16th century too; whereas Foleys have held Stoke Edith since the 17th century.

# Principal Bibliography

CL — *Country Life*

Colvin — Colvin, H. M.: *A Biographical Dictionary of British Architects 1600–1840* (1978)

DEP — *Burke's Dormant and Extinct Peerages* (1883)

Duncumb — Duncumb, John: *Collections towards the History and Antiquities of the County of Hereford*, Vols I, II (1804–12); Vols III, IV by W. H. Cooke (1882–92); Vols V, VI (1887 and 1913)

EDB — *Burke's Extinct and Dormant Baronetcies* (1841)

IFR — *Burke's Irish Family Records* (1976)

LG — *Burke's Landed Gentry*, 18 edns (1833/37–1972)

PB — *Burke's Peerage and Baronetage*, 105 edns (1826–1970)

Pevsner — Pevsner, Nikolaus: *Herefordshire* (1958)

RCHM — *Royal Commission on Historical Monuments*, Vols I–III (1931, 1932 and 1934)

Robinson — Robinson, Rev C. J.: *Mansions and Manors of Herefordshire* (1872)

VSA — Burke, Sir Bernard: *A Visitation of Seats and Arms of the Noblemen and Gentlemen of Great Britain and Ireland*, 2 vols (1852–53); 2nd series, 2 vols (1854–55)

WCF — *Walford's County Families*

**Allensmore Court, Allensmore.** The building was composed of 2 distinct parts at right angles to each other. The original section, 1714, contained a C17 panelling from an older house. But to this, in the late C18, was added a long, 2-storey block of brick relieved only by a fat bow—in which the entrance door was situated. Unexecuted drawings by Anthony Keck, for the house, are in the RIBA Drawings Collection. The interior of the house boasted a fine staircase. Allensmore was bought by the Pateshall family 1725 and it remained in their possession until the 1940s when it passed to the Parkers. The Georgian block was demolished July 1958. PATESHALL/LG1937; PARKER *formerly of Clopton Hall*/LG1952; RCHM I; *Colvin; Robinson.*

*Allensmore Court*

*Aramstone House*

**Aramstone House, King's Caple.** The most important house of its date in the county. A 7 bay, 3 storey building of brick with top balustrade, urns and segmental headed windows. The 3 centre bays formed a slight projection and there was a handsome doorcase of Doric columns supporting an entablature. The interior was of high quality with a fine wooden staircase of turned balusters and marble chimneypieces flanked by pilasters. There remains a clock tower, early C19 stable block and an old cider mill which, with the house, formed a charming and dignified group. Francis Woodhouse was the client for whom the house was built *ca* 1730 and it descended to the Smiths. J. W. W. Smith still owned the house 1929. After much protest, the house was demolished 1959 and it has been replaced by a small brick dwelling. SMITH/WCF; *Angus*; *Robinson*.

*Ballingham Hall*

*Aramstone House: staircase*

*Belmont House: entrance front*

*Aramstone House: hall*

*Belmont: garden front*

**Ballingham Hall, Ballingham.** Now a farmhouse, but the inscription above the porch, "William Scudemore, 1602", probably indicates the date of the building as well as its builder. "T"-shaped now, it was possibly "E"-shaped when built. Walls are stone with ashlar dressings and the fenestration is C18 replacing mullioned windows of which the hood-moulds still exist. In the gables are blank panels with ovals, generally a sign of *ca* 1660–70. Some original panelling and chamfered beams inside. The Scudamores of Ballingham received a Baronetcy 1644, but on the death of the 3rd Bt in the early C18, the title became extinct. The last Bt sold the house, 1704, to his cousin 3rd Viscount Scudamore and it descended with the Holme Lacy property (*qv*) thereafter. SCUDAMORE, Bt/EDB; SCUDAMORE, V/DEP; *Pevsner*; *Robinson*; RCHM.

**Barton Court, Colwall.** Georgian, of red brick with a hipped roof. It is of 6 bays with a pediment over the 3rd bay. There is a lunette window and a Venetian window below it. The house is on an older site and it is said to have been built for Henry Lambert *ca* 1790. In 1870s, Major T. Griffith Peyton, descended from Lambert's sister, owned Barton; but by the end of 1920s it belonged to A. H. Bright. PEYTON/WCF; *Pevsner*; *Robinson*.

**Belmont House, Clehonger.** In place of the seat of the Aubrey family destroyed by fire 1785, Col John Matthews built a new house 1788–90 to the designs of James Wyatt. Perched above the Wye, it was originally a 3 bay, 3 storey block with a bow on the river front. But in the 1860s F. R. Wegg-Prosser commissioned A. W. Pugin to rebuild the house in Early English Gothic style, so it now appears as a tall Victorian house with gables and a porte-cochère; but not to the river side where Wyatt's elegant front of Bath stone survives untouched. Pugin's work inside the building was as thorough as the exterior, and, apart from the Georgian drawing-room, no evidence of Wyatt's hand remains. Stout Pugin staircase with heavy balusters. Col Matthews died 1826 and Belmont was purchased by Dr Richard Prosser. He bequeathed it to his grand-nephew, F. R. Wegg-Prosser, who created and endowed the nearby Benedictine St Michael's Abbey in 1850s. Once Pugin had finished with the Abbey, he turned his attention to the benefactor's house. Now the property of Mr William Chichester who inherited through his mother. MATTHEWS *of Hereford*/LG 1863; WEGG-PROSSER/LG 1952; CHICHESTER *formerly of Calverleigh*/LG 1965; *Robinson*.

**Bernithan Court, Llangarron.** Built by the Hoskyns family late C17 (the date 1695 appears on a barn), it remained in their possession until late C18. A Mr Phillips, of Worcester, bought it *ca* 1830 and a hundred years later it belonged to Lt-Col Ernald Barnardiston (*d* 1944). It is very much in the style of neighbouring Langstone Court. Bernithan, too, has 5 bays (with wooden cross-windows preserved), is of 2 storeys and has a hipped roof with 2 symmetrical chimney-stacks. The similarity does not stop there. There are gatepiers with vases and iron gates and a staircase with dumbbell balusters; a sharp pediment above the doorway is here too. The Royal Commission

*Bernithan Court*

*Bernithan Court : staircase*

reports plasterwork with fleurs-de-lis, pomegranates and grapes in one room. HOSKYNS, Bt/PB; BARNARDISTON *of The Ryes*/LG 1952; *Pevsner*; *Robinson*; RCHM.

**Berrington Hall, Eye.** Of reddish ashlar sandstone quarried nearby, the house consists of a rectangular block with 3 office pavilions which form a courtyard at the rear. The building is one of the triumphs of its architect, Henry Holland. Begun 1778, it was designed for Hon Thomas Harley, yr son of 3rd Earl of Oxford and Mortimer. Harley had had a remarkable career as banker and government contractor and was Lord Mayor of London 1767. It is likely that the site of the house was chosen by Capability Brown as he is known to have visited Berrington, with Harley, whilst the latter was staying with his brother, the 4th Earl of Oxford and Mortimer, at Eywood (*qv*). But it was not until 1780 that Brown supplied a

proper landscape plan for Berrington. The entrance front of the house is of 7 bays and 2 storeys, with a giant tetrastyle portico which now contains a lunette window in its pediment, but which formerly contained a carving of the Harley escutcheon. Round-headed windows are to be found on the first floor and there is a top balustrade. The courtyard elevation is more chaste with a pediment over the three centre bays which break slightly forward. Inside the house, one is astonished by the richness of the decoration which remains virtually unaltered since it was built. The entrance hall has a ceiling which appears as a saucer dome, but the centre is actually flat. Roundels of armorial trophies appear above the 6 doorcases and the doors themselves are of fine Spanish mahogany. The drawing-room has a superb chimneypiece of Carrara marble and a delicate ceiling with roundels which are reputed to be by Biagio Rebecca who designed panels for Holland at the Brighton Pavilion. One of the most charming rooms, the boudoir, leads from the drawing-room. It has a barrel ceiling and a wide alcove with fan-shaped semi-dome behind a screen of scagliola columns of lapis lazuli blue. The centre of the building is taken up by the great staircase hall which is top-lit by a glass-domed lantern. The room is a masterpiece, with a great coffered arch carrying the landing and facing the steady rise of the stone stairs with the balustrading of lyres and reversed lyres. Scagliola columns form screens to 3 of the galleries at 1st-floor level. The library has inset bookcases with pediments and a pediment becomes part of the wall decoration above the chimneypiece. Over the woodwork in the corners of the room are panel paintings of the Muses in grisaille. These are said to be by Rebecca, who is also supposed to have been responsible for the ceiling medallions representing English men of letters. The ceiling design of the library bears a close resemblance to that of Lord Clive's dressing-room at Claremont, Surrey, also by Holland in partnership with his father-in-law Capability Brown. One of the main features of Brown's landscape is the pool which is in reality a lake of 14 acres. The approach to the house is by way of a triumphal arch which is topped by a balustrade. Harley's daughter married 2nd Lord Rodney; and Berrington

*Berrington Hall*

*Bosbury House*

remained the seat of that family until 7th Lord Rodney sold it 1900 to Frederick Cawley, later 1st Lord Cawley. The house became the property of the National Trust 1957. HARLEY, *sub* OXFORD, E/DEP; RODNEY, B/PB; CAWLEY, B/PB; *Colvin*; *Pevsner*; *Robinson*; Hussey, *English Country Houses: Mid-Georgian* (1956); Stroud, *Henry Holland* (1966); Stroud, *Capability Brown* (1975); CL 2,9&16 Dec 1954.

*Berrington Hall: staircase*

**Bircher Hall, Yarpole.** Of C18 and C19 date, Bircher is chiefly remarkable for its long side elevation. The entrance front is of 5 bays with a porch on Doric columns. Adam Ward (*d* 1772) built the oldest part of the house; the daughter of his niece brought it to the Dunnes of Gatley Park (*qv*). In 1920s, F. A. Morris lived in the house, and Hon Bridget Devereux sold it in late 1960s to the 3rd and present Lord Cawley. DUNNE *of Gatley Park*/LG 1965; DEVEREUX, *sub* HEREFORD, V/PB; CAWLEY, B/PB; *Robinson*.

**Bosbury House, Bosbury.** The Georgian house was built by the Stedmans, but it was purchased from them by the Higgins family 1828. Rev Edward Higgins made additions, in the Italian style, 1873. As it stands, the house is of 7 by 5 bays with brick and stone dressings. There is a big balustrade and a porch on pairs of Tuscan columns. Mrs Robert Buchanan owned the house 1929; it was then bought by the Hones and now belongs to Mr T. S. Hone. HIGGINS/LG 1875; HONE/IFR; *Pevsner*; *Robinson*.

*Brainge*

**Brainge, Putley.** Handsome brick house of 5 by 3 bays with quoins and hipped roof. C19 wing at the rear and C19 porch at one side. There is handsome doorcase with scrolly pediment on the main front and it is approached by a short flight of steps. A keystone of a doorway to the basement bears the initials and date "I. and M.G. 1703". This probably indicates the builder and his wife Sir John and Lady Gwillim. Pavement of black and white marble squares in the hall, bolection-moulded panelling in south-east room and a staircase (probably moved) with twisted balusters. The house is now owned by Mr J. B. Daly. DALY (*Co Galway: Dunsandle*)/IFR; *Pevsner*; RCHM II.

**Brampton Bryan Hall, Brampton Bryan.** The Harley family, who own the house today, are said to be a younger branch of the Harleys, Earls of Oxford and Mortimer, former owners of the place. It was in 1872, when Jane, Lady Langdale (co-heiress of her brother, the 6th and last Earl) died, that R. W. D. Harley succeeded to the Oxford estates. The house, which has been reduced, is large and of brick with stone dressings. The south and main front is 7 bays, 3 storeys, with a pedimented 3-bay projection. There is a porch of Roman Doric columns on the west front. In the drawing-room there is a remarkable Victorian chimneypiece of white marble from the other Oxford house, Eywood (*qv*), demolished 1954. Ruins of Brampton Bryan Castle lie close to the house. There is evidence of C13, C14 and C16 work in them. HARLEY, OXFORD, E/DEP; HARLEY *of Brampton Bryan*/LG1969; *Pevsner*; *Robinson*.

**Bredenbury Court, Bredenbury.** The earlier part of this big square Italianate house of red sandstone was rebuilt 1873 by T. H. Wyatt. Sir Guy Dawber added more 1902 and even more was added 1924. Formerly seat of the Greswolde-Williams family; now a school. GRESWOLDE-WILLIAMS/LG1921; *Pevsner*; J. M. Robinson, *The Wyatts* (1980).

**Brinsop Court.** Important as an example of a large C14 moated manor house, Brinsop is of red sandstone with some later timber-framed work. Its present fine condition is due to the extensive restoration 1913 for H. D. Astley. At that time the east wing of narrowly set timber-framing was added for offices; Avray Tipping presided over the remodelling. The north range is of C14 with original 2 light windows and at the west end of this range there is a large 2-light window with transom. Following the north range there is some C16 timber-framing and after that timber-framing of *ca* 1700. And the south range is the hall range with some ogee-headed windows. The C18 is represented by the west range which is Georgian and brick-faced. The most impressive interior is the hall with its magnificent open roof of cambered tie-beams and kingposts. Foiled 4 way struts make pointed trefoil shapes which, with the foiled principals, are typical of the West Country. Stone window seats and a fireplace with shouldered lintel add to the original beauty of this outstanding room. More stone window seats are to be found in the north-west room on the 1st floor. Another room has a Jacobean overmantel taken from Mildmay House, Clerkenwell, London. The various ranges of the house enclose a rectangular courtyard and the countryside about is of great natural beauty. The earliest known owners of Brinsop were the Tirrells and from them it passed to the Danseys who held it until 1820. The purchaser in that year was David Ricardo of Gatcombe Park, Gloucestershire (now the home of HRH

*Brampton Bryan Hall*

*Bredenbury Court*

*Brinsop Court*

The Princess Anne), son of the celebrated political economist. Ricardo let the house to William Wordsworth's brother-in-law, Hutchinson; it is known that the poet made his first visit here 1827 and the last 1845. During those visits they were often joined by the poet's favourite sister, Dorothy, and his son-in-law

Edward Quillinan. Robert Southey came as a visitor too. Wordsworth planted a cedar at the south-west corner of the house and this survived until it was blown down on Boxing Day 1916. Rev Francis Kilvert recalls his visit to the house in his diary for March 1879. After the Hutchinson tenancy came that of Dearman

*Brinsop Court: hall*

Edwards and he eventually bought the place *ca* 1909. Both Hutchinson and Edwards were farmers and the house was in a parlous state when purchased by the Astleys *ca* 1912. The Astleys were still here between the wars, but for some years now Brinsop has been the property of Sir Derrick Bailey, 3rd Bt. DANSEY *formerly of Butterley*/LG1952; RICARDO *formerly of Gatcombe Park*/LG1972; ASTLEY, *sub* HASTINGS, B/PB; BAILEY, Bt/PB; *Pevsner; Robinson;* RCHM II; CL 22 May 1909 & 7, 14 Nov 1914; *Kilvert's Diary* 1879.

**Broadfield Court, Bodenham.** Two separate buildings possibly make up the present large and composite house. A doorway with ballflower decoration on the arch and a window with reticulated tracery date the house back to the first half of C14. The ranges of the building form a very shallow "V"-shape and the mixture of window styles and openings forms a picturesque whole. C17 panelling survives in some rooms inside. Thomas Hayton sold the house 1770 to Thomas Phillipps whose son sold it to John Burchall. F. C. Romilly bought Broadfield in 1920s; it now belongs to Mr Keith James. ROMILLY/LG1965; *Pevsner; Robinson;* RCHM II.

*Broadward Hall*

**Broadward Hall, Leominster.** Behind a very attractive wall of Chinese Chippendale fencing is this handsome brick house, a mid-Georgian building of 5 bays and 2 storeys with a 3-bay pediment. There is a doorcase with Tuscan pilasters and a pediment. A handsome Venetian window enlivens the facade on the 1st floor. In the grounds there is a square 2 storey pigeon house with a pretty hexagonal lantern. The burnt inscription "HH 1652" appears on a door-lintel. James Edwards is recorded as owner of Broadward 1929. *Pevsner;* RCHM.

**Brockhampton Court, Brockhampton-by-Ross.** For Arthur Wellesley Foster and his rich American wife, Faulkner Armitage of Manchester created a huge house in the neo-Tudor style. There is a main tower and seemingly endless gables and mullioned windows. Most of what one sees is dated 1893; but Middleton and Sars designed another part of the house 1879. All has grown from a modest late C18 rectory which is still embedded in the present building. An imitation-Jacobean lodge looks towards the notable church by W. R. Lethaby which was built 1902 in memory of Mrs Foster's parents, Mr & Mrs Eben Dyer

*Broadfield Court*

*Brockhampton Court*

Jordan. Now owned by the Clay family, there
has been an hotel at Brockhampton for many
years.  FOSTER *formerly of Hornby
Castle*/LG1965; CLAY *of Piercefield*/LG1965;
*Pevsner.*

*Brockhampton Court: lodge*

*Brockhampton Park*

*Brockhampton Park: lodge*

**Brockhampton Park, Brockhampton-by-
Bromyard.** For Bartholomew Barneby this
house of the mid-C18 is virtually a duplicate of
Hatton Grange, Salop (*qv*) and, on this
similarity, can be attributed to Thomas
Farnolls Pritchard. The house has 7 bays and
has a 3 bay pediment. There is an entrance door
with pediment on corbels and the window
above it has side volutes. The house retains
some original panelling, but it was altered in its
details *ca* 1860. There is a handsome lodge on
the Worcester road. This has a temple front of
4 slender Tuscan columns with a pediment.
The Barnebys became Barneby-Lutleys and it
was left by them to the National Trust 1946.
The house is let and not open to the public.
BARNEBY *of Llanerch-y-Coed formerly of
Brockhampton*/LG1972; Harris, *Architectural
History* Vol 11; *Colvin; Pevsner; Robinson.*

**Bromtrees Hall, Bishop's Frome.** Red
brick and of 3 storeys, Bromtrees was built for
the Stephens family toward mid-C18; it later
passed to the Nicholetts. But the main block
was tacked on to a low kitchen wing built in
early C17. Inside C17 wing there were exposed
ceiling-beams and a staircase with late C17
turned balusters. Some panelling, of the same
date, appeared in C18 block. A portrait of
Queen Anne, said to have been given to Col
Nicholetts, was preserved in the house which
by *ca* 1870 belonged to Richard Browne.
Bromtrees was demolished, with its early C18
octagonal pigeon-house, *post* World War II. It
has been replaced by a medium-sized house
which belongs to Mr W. Pudge. *Robinson*;
RCHM II.

*Bromtrees Hall*

*Broxwood Court*

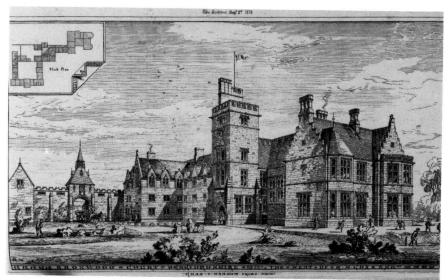

*Broxwood Court: Hansom's original design*

**Broxwood Court, Broxwood.** Richard Snead Cox commissioned C. F. Hansom, 1858 to build a large house in the Gothic style. Hansom had already designed a small RC church, at Broxwood, for his client, but he suddenly died and, on his death, only a Gothic stable-range and service wing were complete. Cox then developed new ideas and much later (1891) he called in Leonard Stokes to erect a free Tudor-style mansion tacked onto his predecessors service wing. The result was one of Stokes's best works. His range was aligned on a great avenue of trees over a mile long (planted by Nesfield 1850s). The combination of Hansom's Gothic work with the Tudor work by Stokes was entirely successful. The interiors, which were rich in heavy wooden ceilings and oppressive fireplaces, were less so.

The house was demolished 1955 and replaced by a small and even freer Tudor house. SNEAD-COX/LG1952; *Robinson.*

**Bryngwyn, Much Dewchurch.** On a different site, but replacing an earlier house of the Bodenhams and Phillipps families, Sir James Rankin, 1st Bt, built the present seat to the designs of Kempson 1868. It is large and uninspired Tudor. Of stone and gabled with an asymmetrical front, it seems suited to its present role of factory-cum-flats. RANKIN, Bt/PB; *Pevsner; Robinson.*

**Buckenhill Manor, Bromyard.** Packington Tomkyns refronted an older house *ca* 1730 and created the long 9 bay, 2 storey front which we see today. The house is of brick and has a doorway with segmental pediment on 2 stone columns with Corinthian capitals. The gables and finials are probably early Victorian. The Tomkynses continued here until 1804 when they sold it to Robert Higginson, ancestor of the Higginsons of Saltmarshe Castle (*qv*). By inheritance the Barneby-Lutleys owned the place late C19; it is now owned by Mrs K. H. Young and Mr K. J. Stewart. BARNEBY-LUTLEY, *sub* BARNEBY *of Llanerch-y-Coed formerly of Brockhampton*/LG1972; *Pevsner; Robinson.*

**Burghill Court, Burghill.** A rather bright red brick house standing somewhat aloof from the

*Bryngwyn*

*Buckenhill Manor*

*Burghill Court*

village of Burghill. It is late-Georgian, of 7 bays and 3 storeys with a 3-bay pediment. There is a porch of 2 pairs of Greek Doric columns. Col H. G. C. Swayne owned the house 1937; it is now owned by Mr D. V. N. Adams and Mr T. A. C. Collins. *Pevsner.*

**Burghope House, Wellington.** An engraving in the *Gentleman's Magazine* (Sept 1791) shows the house as a square building with 3 straight gables on each front. Projecting bays appear on the entrance side and there are mullioned windows. Burghope is said to have been built for George More in early C17. In due course, it was bought by the Gooderes who gained a Baronetcy 1707. Sir John Goodere, 2nd Bt, an unmarried man, was on bad terms with his younger brother for many years and threatened to disinherit him in favour of their nephew, John Foote, brother of Samuel Foote the dramatist. This so alarmed Samuel Goodere, a sea captain, that he arranged for his elder brother's murder aboard his ship 1741. This unscrupulous deed was immediately discovered and the captain, who had succeeded as 3rd Bt on his brother's death, was tried at Bristol and executed April 1741. Sir James Peachey, 4th Bt (later 1st Lord Selsey) bought the house *ca* 1770 and later it passed to a Mr Turberville who sold it for the materials as the house had acquired the reputation of being haunted as a result of the unfortunate occurrence related above. GOODERE, Bt/EDB; PEACHEY, SELSEY, B/DEP; *Robinson*; *Gentleman's Magazine* Sept 1791.

*Burton Court, Eardisland*

**Burton Court, Eardisland.** One is greeted by the free Tudor front of Sir Clough Williams-Ellis—an early work as it dates from *ca* 1913. This was commissioned by P. L. Clowes. The shallow bow, the porch and the giant window to the right of it are all Williams-Ellis's work. But inside there is the surprising survival of an early C14 hall, open to the roof. The roof has arched braces up to collar-beams. The collars are cusped, and there are 2 tiers of cusped wind-braces. A Georgian dining-room survives as well as a circular C18 stairwell, but the staircase itself is part of the Victorian going-over by Kempson 1865. Burton passed through the ownership of the St Owen, Downton, Cotes and Brewster families before being sold to the Clowes family 1863. A branch of the Croft family occupied the house in C17. Burton is now the property of Lt-Cmdr & Mrs R. M. Simpson. CLOWES *of Norbury formerly of Broughton*/LG1969; CROFT, Bt, *of Croft Castle*/PB; RCHM; *Pevsner*; *Robinson*.

*Burton Court, Eardisland: before removal of pointed gables*

*Byford Court*

*The Byletts*

**Burton Court, Linton-by-Ross.** The house was probably built for William Matthews whose grandson, John Matthews, commissioned James Wyatt to build Belmont (*qv*). As it stands, it is a brick-faced stone house of 5 bays and 2 storeys. It has segment-headed windows. A steep 3-bay pediment contains lunette windows. The builder of Belmont inherited the house and subsequently sold it to Joseph White, from whom it was purchased by Alexander Baring, 1st Lord Ashburton. By 1929 it was the home of Kathleen, widow of 9th Earl of Harrington. MATTHEWS *of Hereford*/LG1863; BARING, ASHBURTON, B/PB; STANHOPE, *sub* HARRINGTON, E/PB; *Pevsner*; *Robinson*.

**Byford Court, Byford.** Highly picturesque: partly timber-framed and partly of stone. It has 3 gables—the left and right ones being the ends of cross-wings of a C16 house. The stone-faced centre represents the hall-block which was extended to line up with the ends of the cross-wings in early C17. It contains 2 large 6 light transomed windows. The doorway has a semi-elliptical head, above which are 3 shields including one with the arms of Gomond—the family seated at Byford from at least mid-C15. The principal apartment inside the house is the hall which retains its original ceiling. The room is lined with early C17 panelling, formerly at Marsh Court, Bridge Sollers, which was demolished *ca* 1910. The house contains an inserted staircase with early C18 turned balusters. Outside in the grounds is to be found an attractive timber-framed late C17 dovecote, which has a lantern. At the end of C17 the Gomond estates passed into the possession of the Geers family and thus descended to the present owner, Sir John Cotterell, 6th Bt. COTTERELL, Bt/PB; *Pevsner*; *Robinson*; RCHM III.

**Byletts (The), Pembridge.** Spiky Victorian Gothic. A rebuilding of 1879 by John Bowle Evans, whose family had owned the estate since 1754. The Lochard and Hill families had owned it before that. The previous house, parts of which are embedded in the present building, was supposed to be large, irregular and Elizabethan. Ownership by the Evans family continued well into C20, but it was let to Lt-Gen Sir Charles Macpherson Dobell 1929. Now owned by Herefordshire County Council. EVANS/WCF; *Robinson*; RCHM III.

*Cagebrook*

**Cagebrook, Eaton Bishop.** C18, all brick and in English bond. Of 5 bays and 2½ storeys with a later Georgian addition on the left. The Moore Green family were here in C18 and their heiress conveyed it to J. S. Gowland. Later in C19, it belonged to Adm Reginald Yorke.

*Canon Frome Court*

Major G. E. B. Stephens has been the principal owner in this century. YORKE, *sub* HARDWICKE, E/PB; STEPHENS *of Church House*/LG1952; *Pevsner; Robinson.*

**Canon Frome Court, Canon Frome.** Attributed convincingly to Anthony Keck the house was built 1786 for Richard Cope Hopton. It replaced a C17 building called The Gable House. Of 7 bays and 3 storeys, a blank arch comprises the tripartite doorway, the Venetian window on the 1st floor and the centre window on the top storey. There is a 3 bay pediment and the porch was added 1874. Both entrance and garden fronts were identical. The entrance hall retains a double screen of scagliola columns with Corinthian capitals. These lead through to a delicate wooden staircase with carved tread ends. Apart from one or two doorcases, this is virtually all that survives of the original interior decoration which was intact until 1948. In that year the Hoptons sold the estate to the Rochester Bridge Trust who split up the land. In 1952 the Herefordshire County Council bought the house with a few acres and a secondary school was opened here 1954. Four years later most of the chimneypieces were removed and sold, and the chimneys themselves were taken away. The 1914 Music Room added to the west side of the building— where Dame Myra Hess and Sir John Barbirolli performed—became the school hall and gymnasium. The splendid organ is now in Coventry and the library has lost its fine C18 bookcases. In 1929 a garden house was built with bricks from demolished Rotherwas (*qv*). The Swiss Cottage, said to be a replica of the

*Canon Frome: library*

*Canon Frome: dining room*

*Caradoc Court*

one at Osborne, is derelict and the very important C17 overmantel in the former billiard room has lost its architectural perspectives in the blank arches. Sold to a housing association 1979. HOPTON/LG1937; *Colvin*; *Pevsner*; *Robinson*; *Frome Cannonica* (privately printed, 1903); RCHM II.

**Caradoc Court, Sellack.** Large, much-altered and in a commanding position above the Wye. There is black and white of the C16, parts of stone *ca* 1620 and many alterations C19 and C20. On the entrance front, the shaped gables, bay window and porch are Victorian; and the roof did, at one time, boast an enormous C19 lantern which was totally incongruous. But the grand bay window on the rear elevation is original. Many mullioned and transomed windows. There is a grand oak-panelled hall and the Royal Commission reports painted C17 decoration in the room at the north end of the west wing—large flower scrolls and landscapes. Once a seat of the extinct Viscounts Scudamore, it passed to the Digbys 1716. From them it was purchased 1864 by Elisha Caddick. Lt-Col George Basil Heywood is recorded as owner 1929. The house has recently changed hands again. SCUDAMORE, V/DEP; DIGBY, DIGBY, B/PB; HEYWOOD/LG1937; *Pevsner*; *Robinson*; RCHM.

*Cheyney Court: north front*

**Chase (The), Ross-on-Wye.** Rectangular box of *ca* 1815 built for John Cooke. 3 by 4 bays with stringcourse and porch. Rendered. Later additions. Passed to the Strong family; now an hotel. STRONG/LG1898; VSA; *Robinson*.

**Cheyney Court, Bishop's Frome.** Probably early C17. A large house with an irregular front showing both mullioned and mullioned and transomed windows. Long wings stretched forward from the main building to a chapel on one side and a tall tower with a cupola on the other. *Ca* 1870 F. R. Kempson added a large block, in Tudor style, back to back with the main range of the old house. This new block faced north and became the entrance front. The house contained a room of considerable interest called The Sibyls Room. This had a Jacobean chimneypiece with paired columns above and below and, above the oak panelling, inset paintings representing 13 sibyls and 18 prophets. The Slaughters built the house, but by 1739 it belonged to Richard Gardiner. His representatives sold Cheyney 1854 to John Jones and he disposed of it 1867 to James Moilliet of Abberley Hall, Worcs (*qv*). It was leased in 1880s by A. J. Monson who ran a school there; but in 1888 the house was mysteriously destroyed by fire. A few years later, Monson faced a murder charge as a result of a drowning in a Scottish loch. What remains today is the chapel of the house—now used as a barn. SLAUGHTER *formerly of Slaughter*/LG1937; MOILLIET *of Abbotsleigh*/LG1898; MONSON, *sub* MONSON, B/PB; *Pevsner*; *Robinson*; RCHM II.

*Cheyney Court: south front*

**Clater Park, Bromyard.** The Paunceforts built this house *ante* 1760. Of 3 widely-spaced bays and 3 storeys, Clater is a seat of moderate size. The building has been rendered and the rooms inside contain no notable architectural features. After the Paunceforts came the Danseys and they married into the Barnebys. It descended thereafter with Saltmarshe Castle (*qv*). Now the property of Mr D. Watkins. BARNEBY *of Saltmarshe Castle*/ LG1952; *Robinson*.

**Coddington Court, Coddington.** A small and elegant facade. Mid-Georgian, brick, of 5 bays and 2¹/₂ storeys with a low hipped roof. There is a 3-bay pediment. A blank arch comprises the doorway and the window above. Built by the Holders, it passed to the Hales and Homes families before being purchased *ca* 1860 by Henry Edward Vale. In the late 1920s the house was owned by Mrs Buck; it is now the property of the Poore-Saurin-Watts family. POORE-SAURIN-WATTS, *sub* POORE, Bt/PB; *Pevsner*; *Robinson*.

**Combe House, Combe.** An irregular house of *ca* 1830 which was, at one time, the home of the Misses Coats. But by 1929 it was the property of Thomas Morgan who let it to Hon Reginald Walsh (later 5th Lord Ormathwaite). Now reduced, it forms separate houses. WALSH, ORMATHWAITE, B/PB.

**Court of Noke, Staunton-on-Arrow.** Early C18, of red brick and of 7 bays and 2 storeys. Pediment over centre bays which break slightly forward. Later porch on slender columns. Centre 3 bays recessed on rear elevation. Handsome staircase with turned balusters and carved tread ends. Oak room with fielded panels and giant pilasters on chimney breast. Canals in grounds are possibly remains of an old garden layout. The

*Clater Park*

*Combe House*

*Court of Noke*

house was built as a dower house to Staunton Park (*qv*), which was the seat of the Stanley family in C18. The King family bought Staunton *ca* 1770 and thereafter Noke was used as a farmhouse and evidences of that occupation remain. In the 1920s the house belonged to the Glover and Evans families, but it was finally purchased 1927 by P. R. de Q. Quincey whose widow owns it today. Mr Quincey was the great-great-great nephew of Thomas de Quincey, the essayist and miscellaneous writer. KING-KING/LG1972; *Pevsner*; *Robinson*; RCHM III.

**Courtfield, Welsh Bicknor.** The great Roman Catholic family of Vaughan came here 1575 and their old house was demolished in early C19 to make way for the present Regency building which is rectangular and of 7 bays and 2 storeys. Central pediment, pilasters on the first floor above a semi-circular porch. The windows on the ground floor are in blank arches and a long link composed of blank arches joins house to stables. The site, on a knoll in a loop of the Wye, is magnificent. When John Vaughan died 1780, his brother Richard was excluded from the succession to Courtfield because he had been outlawed for fighting with the Duke of Perth's division at Culloden; he later became a Lt-Gen in the Spanish Army. Richard's great-great-grandson, who became squire of Courtfield 1880–1903, was Cardinal Herbert Vaughan. Major J. H. Vaughan sold the house and grounds to St Joseph's Society for Foreign Missions 1950 but retained the estate. His yr son, Oliver, founded Juliana's Discotheque. Courtfield is now a school, run by the Fathers of Mill Hill who have made extensive additions behind the original block. VAUGHAN/LG1972; *Robinson*.

*Courtfield*

*Cowarne Court*

**Cowarne Court, Much Cowarne.** Built in 1870s for the Bourne family, it was a Tudor style house with stepped gables. Piecemeal demolition then took place, but it was not until the 1960s that the entire building had gone. A circular dovecote, possibly medieval, survives from an earlier house on the site. Prof G. C. Bourne, the anatomist, was the last of the family here. BOURNE *formerly of Symondsbury*/LG1972; RCHM II; *Pevsner*.

**Credenhill Court, Credenhill.** Formerly the seat of the Hardwicks, one of whom was Philip Hardwick, RA, the architect (1792–1870), the house was built 1760. Originally it stood as a 5 bay, 3 storey block of red brick. A Venetian window is at the centre of the 1st floor and there is a parapet and giant angle pilasters. Later and lower extensions,

*Credenhill Court*

with bays, are attached to mid-C18 house. In the late C19, the house was purchased by the Ecroyd family who held it until the mid-1940s. It is now a refugee home. ECROYD/LG1969; *Pevsner*; *Robinson*.

**Croft Castle, Croft.** Crofts are known to have been here in Domesday, and, apart from a break between 1746 and 1923 they have remained here ever since—although the National Trust has owned the estate since 1957. The building is a large and irregular quadrangular castle with four corner towers. It can be dated as late C14 or early C15. A few mullion and transom type windows remain which are of the late C16 or C17. John Leland described Croft, in 1538, as '. . . sett on the browe of a hill, somewhat rokky, dychid and waulled castle like". But the house is mostly sashed, due no doubt to the general going over of the building in C18. At that time, *ca* 1765, the east side (which was possibly open originally) was rebuilt for Thomas Johnes by Thomas Farnolls Pritchard, the Shrewsbury architect. Johnes had married the daughter of Richard Knight (of the Downton Castle (*qv*) family), who gained possession of Croft 1746. The charming Gothickry throughout the castle today is undoubtedly due to Pritchard. He designed chimneypieces, door friezes, pier frames and the delightful staircase with its walls and ceiling in panels of varying Gothick shapes. The Blue Room has Jacobean panelling from Stanage Park, Powys, with painted C18 gilded rosettes in the centre of each panel to give a *trompe l'oeil* effect. The Oak Room has panelling and chimneypiece of late C17, but an attractive ceiling incorporating a vine pattern is C18. The dining-room is comparatively modern having been formed 1913 in the old West Hall of the house. Some of the Georgian decoration in it is genuine, but the screen at the north end of the room is C20. The drawing-room has painted early Georgian panelling. Until 1913, when the house was let to Major Atherley, the south side of the castle had battlements and crow-stepped gables. The east side had a show of

*Croft Castle: Pritchard's staircase hall*

battlements too. Atherley removed these battlements and added an entrance porch and the pediment on the parapet. The north front of the house is the least altered and remains generally C17 in aspect. From this front there extended a long "L"-shaped wing, possibly a C17 reconstruction, but this was demolished 1937 in order to make the house more manageable. The grounds at Croft contain a great Spanish chestnut avenue *ca* 350 years old and over half a mile long and there are ancient oaks of immense girth. Nestling close to the house is the C14 and C15 Church of St Michael, which has box pews and the splendid altar tomb of Sir Richard Croft (*d* 1509). A Gothick archway to the grounds looks like a fragment of curtain walling with tower. The Crofts received a Baronetcy in 1671 and Sir Herbert Croft, 1st Bt, married a sister of Thomas Archer, the Baroque architect. Sir Archer Croft, 2nd Bt, mortgaged Croft and so lost it to Richard Knight 1746. After the Johnes family inherited Croft, the younger Thomas Johnes, creator of Hafod, Dyfed, disposed of the castle 1785 to Somerset Davies, ancestor of the Kevill-Davies family who owned it until bought back by the Crofts 1923. CROFT, Bt, *of Croft Castle*/PB; KNIGHT *of Wolverley*/LG1937; LLOYD-JOHNES *of Dolaucothy*/LG1965; LACON (*formerly* KEVILL-DAVIES) *of Wigmore and Ormesby Hall*/LG1972; *Colvin*; *Pevsner*; *Robinson*; RCHM III; Harris, *Architectural History* (1968); CL 28 April & 5 May 1950.

*Croft Castle: left-hand wing demolished 1937*

*Croft Castle: ante 1913*

*Cubberley*

**Cubberley, Walford-on-Wye.** The newest country house in Herefordshire, built 1971 for 4th and present Lord Greville, its architect was Hon Claud Phillimore. "L"-shaped and Regency in appearance, it is stuccoed. The principal room is the drawing-room with dentil cornice and great coved ceiling; it is 2 storeys high and has a Venetian window at one end. On the garden front, the roof boasts a lantern and there is a chimney with a touch of Voysey about it. The gardens were laid out at the same time and from an arch by the house there is a long rose walk. GREVILLE, GREVILLE, B/PB.

*Derndale*

**Derndale, Canon Pyon.** For 300 years the Jays have been associated with this place. The present irregular but charming building is composed of parts which date from C17, C18 and C19—the last being represented by the large drawing-room of *ca* 1810. Most of the remainder of the house has rooms of a charm and intimacy which is particularly appealing in the last quarter of C20. Derndale now belongs to Mr T. H. Jay. JAY/WCF; *Robinson.*

*Dingwood Park*

**Dingwood Park, Ledbury.** Exceedingly pretty house of *ca* 1700. Of warm red brick, 5 bays wide and of 2 storeys with a hipped roof. Windows are now sashed, but their form, with stone crosses, survives at the back and side. Between the 1st-floor windows are 2 stone cartouches of arms. The greatest delight, however, is the interior. Here there are rooms with charming stucco ceilings. In the dining-room there are 3 main panels with a central wreath of fruit and flowers and floral sprays in the angles, plus branches of oak and bay. The compact study and a 1st-floor room display notable plasterwork too. On the ground floor, there are corner fireplaces in each of the rooms. Long the property of the Biddulphs of nearby Ledbury Park (*qv*), it was sold to the Gunter-Jones family and now belongs to Mr Mendel. BIDDULPH, *sub* BIDDULPH, B/PB; *Pevsner*; RCHM II.

*Dinmore Manor*

**Dinmore Manor, Dinmore.** House and chapel face each other across a lawn. They are the remains of a preceptory of the Knights of St John of Jerusalem and the position high in a remote wooded valley is both beautiful and secretive. The oldest part of the house appears to be *ca* 1600, but it stands on medieval foundations and there are some reset C14 doorways. Then there is a block of *ca* 1700 linking the oldest part of the building to the newest—and most startling. This is the west wing built 1932–36 and designed by Bettington & Son and R. A. Ford. It consists of a huge baronial hall called the Music Room and adjoining cloisters which contain remarkable traceried windows and an octagonal room which has a grotto. Panelling of C16, C17 and C18 is to be found in the house. The chapel is C12 and C14 and contains late C19 stained glass and a pipe organ, dated 1786, by Samuel Green. The organ was formerly at Moccas Court (*qv*). The Order of the Hospitallers held the place until the dissolution 1540. The Wolrych family obtained their grant of Dinmore 1559, but it is likely that they leased the place before that date. Wolrychs remained until early C18 when the estate passed to the Flemings of Sibdon Castle, Salop (*qv*). Their marriage into the St Johns 1788 brought Dinmore into that family and so it stayed until purchase 1927 by R. H. Murray whose son, G. H. Murray, owns it today. WOLRICH, Bt/EDB; ST JOHN, *sub* ST JOHN OF BLETSO, B/PB; MURRAY/LG1952; *Pevsner*; *Robinson*; RCHM II.

*Donnington Hall*

**Donnington Hall, Donnington.** Much of the existing house was built 1909 by an architect named Ogilvy for Adm Sir Arthur Dalrymple Fanshawe, but the building is said to be basically C18. Bossi chimneypiece in drawing-room. Screen of marbled columns in hall. Bought 1979 by Mr Richard Marcon; previously the seat of the Spence-Colby family and of Mr Mark Hellyer. FANSHAWE *formerly of Donnington Hall*/LG1965; SPENCE-COLBY/LG1952; *Pevsner*.

**Dormington Court, Dormington.** Lying back from the road and close to the church, Dormington is a house of considerable charm. The central block is of brick and was built early in C18. It is of 3 bays and 2 storeys. Attached to this block are 2 lower wings—one of early C17 date and the other of late C17. The former shows some timber-framing. The

*Dormington Court*

main interior feature is the early C18 dog-legged staircase with turned balusters. G. H. Bray owned the property 1929; it is now an hotel. *Pevsner*; RCHM II.

**Downton Castle, Downton.** One of the first examples of a house built to be picturesque on a consciously asymmetrical plan, Downton is a straggling house composed of square, octagonal and circular towers. All is set down in a wild and romantic park above the Teme.

The author of this building of national importance was Richard Payne Knight, neo-Classical antiquary, virtuoso, archaeologist and sponsor with his neighbour, Uvedale Price of Foxley (*qv*), of Picturesque aesthetic theory. Knight is said to have been his own architect, but one wonders if he was really capable of the splendid classical interior—the most outstanding apartment of which is the high pantheon-type dining-room in the centre of the building. Begun 1772, the house in C18

*Downton Castle*

*Downton: dining room*

had a somewhat different appearance to that today. It was altered 1850 (its sash windows were replaced by stone mullioned casements) and S. Pountney Smith made further alterations 1861. But long before this there is evidence that the Shrewsbury architect T. F. Pritchard was concerned with the building and it is even suggested that John Nash might have had a hand in the design. The parade of Classical rooms ranges from the splendid dining-room, with its coffered dome and niches in the wall screened by columns (these niches contain painted Coade stone figures), onwards through the morning-room (the old entrance hall) to the drawing-room, with genuine antique porphyry columns, and the library, which contains a fine chimneypiece, as do the previous 3 rooms. The Victorians added one of the round entrance towers; a chapel; a ballroom in Victorian Gothic; and a Tudor Gothic staircase; as well as a substantial addition at the east end of the building. Knight's catholic but discriminating collection of pictures still hung in the house well into C20. There were outstanding examples by Rembrandt, Ruysdael, Vandyck, Turner and Salvator Rosa. And there was the celebrated series of watercolours by T. Hearn which depicted the wooded and craggy gorge below the castle. Knight rejected Capability Brown's natural landscape sweeping up to the walls of a house and he favoured a terrace so it served as a basement for the building to stand on. There is no evidence, though, that the battlemented terrace along the south front was there in Knight's day. He did, however, erect a number of garden furnishings such as the castle and forge bridges, a cave with windows hewn out of rock, and Roman baths with vaulted chambers. Richard Payne Knight made over Downton to his brother, Thomas Andrew Knight, whose daughter married Sir William Edward Rouse Boughton, 10th Bt. Their 2nd son, A. J. Rouse-Boughton-Knight (*d* 1909) inherited the property and left it to his eldest son. In due course it was inherited by Major W. M. Peareth Kincaid Lennox, grandson of A. J. Rouse-Boughton-Knight; the latter's grandson, D. P. H. Lennox, disposed of Downton to Bryanston Ltd 1979. KNIGHT *of Wolverley*/LG1937; ROUSE BOUGHTON/PB1963; PEARETH KINCAID LENNOX/LG1952; CL 14 July 1917; *Colvin*; *Pevsner*; *Robinson*; *Neale* III (2nd ser); Hussey, *English Country Houses: Mid-Georgian* (1956); Rowan, 'Downton Castle' in *The Country Seat* (ed. Colvin & Harris, 1970).

**Dulas Court, Dulas.** A high Victorian Gothic house built by Lt-Col Robert Feilden *ca* 1860, incorporating an older building. *Post* World War II the house was owned by the Barker family who later ran it as an hotel. Now the property of the Musicians Benevolent Fund. FEILDEN/LG1921; BARKER/LG1952; *Robinson*.

**Eardisley Park, Eardisley.** At the end of a lonely road, Eardisley is a 5 bay, early C18 house of 3 storeys, the top one being a late C18 addition. Inside, there is an early C18 staircase and bold pilasters flank the chimneypiece in the drawing-room. A square dovecote, cider-house and other outbuildings lend strength to its present role as a farmhouse in the possession of Mr John Thorne. The house was built by the Cokes whose memorials are found in the church. RCHM; *Robinson*; *Pevsner*.

*Dulas Court: original front*

*Dulas Court: chimneypiece in drawing room*

*Eardisley Park*

*Easton Court*

**Eastnor Castle, Eastnor.** This enormous toy-fort set high above water is one of the most startling inventions of Sir Robert Smirke, who designed the building for 1st Earl Somers. Eastnor was begun 1812 and replaced an older house called Castleditch, seat of the Cocks family since late C16. The quatrefoil towers at the corners and the raised centre point to an early example of serious Norman revival, but the porte-cochère on the entrance front and canted bay windows brought medievalism up-to-date. The castle is approached by a low gatehouse, with tough round towers which spans the drive. The late Georgian castle, however, contains a variety of Victorian interior styles. The main chamber within is a great hall 60 ft long and 65 ft high. This has wall decoration in the medieval style by G. E. Fox, said to have been copied from woven material at Toulouse, and windows by G. G. Scott. An octagonal room at the end of the hall overlooks the lake. The drawing-room, formerly the dining-room, was designed and furnished by A. W. N. Pugin (*ca* 1850). It boasts a grand chimneypiece, a coved ceiling on fan-vaults and a splendid 2 tiered Gothic chandelier. There are 2 libraries (*ca* 1866); G. E. Fox designed the larger one in the Italian Renaissance style, and the smaller one contains woodwork from Siena which is dated 1646. Jacobean panelling and stained glass of *ca* 1875 are to be found in the chapel on the 1st floor. In the grounds there is an obelisk in memory of Hon E. C. Cocks, son of the 1st Earl, who fell at Burgos 1812. The castle rests on a castellated terrace above the lake and there is good planting in the park. Eastnor became well-known as "Omnium Castle", seat of the Duke of Omnium, in the BBC television series *The Pallisers* based on Trollope's novels. When the 6th Lord Somers died 1944, the estate passed to his only child, Elizabeth, who married Major B. A. F. Hervey-Bathurst. SOMERS COCKS, SOMERS, B/PB; HERVEY-BATHURST, Bt/PB; *Colvin*; *Pevsner*; *Robinson*; CL 7, 14 & 21 March 1968; *Neale* (Ser I, Vol II, 1819).

**Easton Court, Little Hereford.** Early C19, rendered, and with a main block of 3 widely-spaced bays, the centre one being recessed, with a porch on Tuscan columns. Side elevation of 5 bays divided by pilaster strips. A long service wing tails away to the left of the entrance. Rectangular hall within, giving way to a long corridor which terminates with the simple wrought-iron staircase. The Danseys built this house replacing an earlier building of which the handsome C18 stables survive. Sir Joseph Bailey, 1st Bt, bought Easton *ca* 1840 and his grandson, 1st Lord Glanusk, owned the property into C20. In 1909 it was bought by Col R. H. W. Cardiff, whose eldest son owns it today. Easton suffered a bad fire 1959, but was re-roofed immediately. DANSEY *formerly of Butterley*/LG1952; BAILEY, GLANUSK, B/PB; CARDIFF/LG1972; *Robinson*.

**Elton Hall, Elton.** The house is in remote and beautiful country near Ludlow. A master builder, perhaps from Worcester, probably rebuilt Elton, with its charming front in the Gothick taste, *ca* 1760. It is of 6 bays and 2 storeys, a hipped roof and a steep pedimental gable with circular window. But the house was undoubtedly a half-timbered C17 building, typical of the regional architecture. Evidences of this are the C17 gables on the garden front,

*Eastnor Castle*

*Elton Hall*

now bricked over, and the beams plastered over in the entrance hall—which runs from the front door to the simple late c18 staircase at the back. Range of half-timbered stables and a granary or dovecote adjoining the entrance front. From the reign of Charles II the manor belonged to the Salwey family; it was Rev Thomas Salwey who rebuilt the house in c18. His great-granddaughter, Harriet Charlotte,

married Rev C. W. N. Custance 1862; their grandson, Brig E. C. N. Custance, owns the house today. In late c18, Thomas Andrew Knight, brother of Richard Payne Knight of Downton Castle (*qv*), lived at Elton and began his experiments in raising new varieties of fruit (Elton Cherries) there. SALWEY/LG1952; CUSTANCE/LG1972; CL 5 Oct 1945; *Pevsner*; *Robinson*; RCHM III.

**Evesbatch Court, Evesbatch.** Thomas Symonds, an architect who worked in Hereford until his death 1791, probably designed this house for Robert Dobyns 1757. The Dobyns family had owned the estate since 1627. Following a marriage with a member of the Yate family of Gloucestershire, the surname became Dobyns-Yate. But they sold it about 1800 and during c19 it changed hands

*Evesbatch Court*

*Eye Manor*

several times and, it is said, its status had reached that of a farmhouse when it was destroyed by fire. In 1898 Joseph Rowlands purchased what remained and rebuilt the house. A link joins the present house with an C18 stable-block. Mr Rowlands was succeeded by Capt English; in 1934 it was bought by the Porter family, of whom Mr Richard Porter is the present owner. DOBYNS/LG1833/7; *Colvin*; *Robinson*.

**Eye Manor, Eye.** Built for Ferdinando Gorges, a Barbados trader in sugar and slaves, *ca* 1680. The house, of 5 bays and 2 storeys with dormers and a late C18 porch, is unassuming outside. The interior, though, contains plaster ceilings of the highest quality. They are of the kind in panels of all shapes with garlands of almost detached fruit, flowers, figures, animals, etc. There is a staircase with twisted balusters and pilasters on the upper landing. For many years the house served as the Vicarage, but the Misses Carver owned it 1929. More recently it was bought by Mr Christopher Sandford, founder of The Golden Cockerel Press and father of the writer Mr Jeremy Sandford. GORGES *formerly of Wraxall*/LG1965; *Pevsner*; *Robinson*; RCHM; Cornforth & Hill, *English Country Houses*: *Caroline* (1966); CL 15 Sept 1955.

**Eywood, Titley.** Seat of the Harleys, Earls of Oxford and Mortimer, Eywood was a large house said to have been begun 1705 for Edward Harley, brother of the great Robert Harley, 1st Earl, who was Secretary of State and Chancellor of the Exchequer. Built around a central courtyard, it was a rambling building of 3 storeys, rendered, with a main front of 9 bays—the middle 5 of which projected and which were crowned by a top

*Eye Manor: hall*

balustrade. The projection had a rusticated ground floor with central doorcase carrying a segmental pediment and the upper storeys showed Ionic pilasters supporting the entablature and balustrade. Sir Robert Smirke was the architect responsible for the partial remodelling of the Queen Anne house for the 5th Earl 1805–07. It was his intention to remodel the entire structure. The side elevations were of 9 bays, too, and the porch must have been Smirke's, as well as the refacing of the large service wings which were set back either side of the house. A small Grecian orangery was built at the same time. In 1898, an architect named Milne reduced the side elevations to 2 storeys and refaced the whole building with brick. Huge quoins were added to the angles. Milne virtually rebuilt the

*Eywood: ante 1898*

*Eywood:* post *1898*

*Eywood: dining room*

entire interior, but obviously re-used some old fittings. The staircase, which looked early C18, was also by Milne. All that remains now of the house, which was taken down 1954, is a range of C18 stables with a cupola surmounting the entrance arch. The house overlooked Titley Pool and Capability Brown is known to have visited Eywood in Aug 1775. The park certainly contained planting reminiscent of

him and, in spite of recent depredations, it still bears traces of its former beauty. When the 6th and last Earl died 1853, the estate passed, with that of Brampton Bryan Hall (*qv*), to his eldest sister, Lady Langdale. On her death 1872, it went to another sister, Lady Charlotte Bacon, widow of Gen Anthony Bacon; but in due course it was sold to 2nd Lord Ormathwaite. The Gwyers purchased Eywood 1892 and

they held it until 1950. The eldest daughter of C. J. Gwyer married 1915 the late Major J. R. H. Harley of Brampton Bryan Hall— renewing ancient ties between the two estates. Mr Vowells was the last owner before demolition. HARLEY, OXFORD, E/DEP; LANGDALE, LANGDALE, B/DEP; BACON/LG1898; WALSH, ORMATHWAITE, B/PB; *Colvin, Robinson*; Stroud, *Capability Brown* (1975); RCHM III.

**Fawley Court, Fawley.** Eminently picturesque, close to the country road and standing behind large gatepiers which support heraldic beasts formerly on the porch of nearby Brockhampton Court (*qv*). The early C16 shows itself at the rear of the building, where all is timber-framed with narrowly spaced uprights and diagonals in the main gable. But at the front it is stone and *ca* 1630. The house appears nearly symmetrical, but at the beginning of C20, a half-timbered wing was attached at right angles to the main front. The arched windows proclaim Henry VIII rather than Charles I, and this is a curiosity of the building. Canted bays, 3 light transomed windows and a porch, with the upper floor mullioned windows, are the ingredients of the entrance front as it now exists. The entrance hall has a very large fireplace with a moulded surround and a wooden overmantel—a combination of *ca* 1630 and *ca* 1750 motifs. One room retains good panelling and the staircase has turned balusters. The house was possibly built by the Gwillim family, but it was sold in C17 to Sir John Kyrle, Bt, and from him it descended, with other estates, to the Money-Kyrles. It was bought by G. L. Clay 1931 and now belongs to his son. MONEY-KYRLE *of Whetham*/LG1965; CLAY *of Piercefield*/LG1965; *Pevsner*; *Robinson*; RCHM II.

*Fownhope Court*

**Fownhope Court, Fownhope.** Large and basically Jacobean, but the Victorians made extensive alterations which all but obliterated the C17 building. According to the Royal Commission, there is even evidence of a medieval semi-circular turret on the west side of the house and a C13 niche with refoiled head reset in the garden. Seat of the younger branch of the Worcestershire family of Lechmere until C20. Now owned by Mr M. V. Robinson. LECHMERE/LG1952; *Pevsner*; *Robinson*; RCHM II.

**Foxley, Yazor.** Seat of Sir Uvedale Price, 1st Bt, who inherited the brick 9 bay, 3 storey house 1761. It had been built by his family 1717 and was sober and dignified in the style of the Smith family of architects of Warwick. The 3 centre bays formed a breakfront and there were 4 bays on the side elevations. It was at Foxley that Price developed his ideas on garden landscape and wrote *An Essay on the Picturesque*, in which he argued in favour of natural beauty. Scott declared "he converted the age to his views". Price laid out his estate in accordance with his principles and had begun as early as 1743 when he returned from the Grand Tour and built Ragged Castle—one of the earliest Gothick garden buildings. The Price family retained Foxley until 1856 when John Davenport, dilettante son of the founder of the pottery firm, bought it. This ushered in a period of great change to the house. It was tricked up with balustrades, canted bays and a porte-cochère. Extensions were built and the house was rendered. Inside, there was a virtual rebuilding and only an occasional C18 chimneypiece was suffered to remain. In the 1920s, there was an attempt to tidy up the building and the canted bays were removed along with one or two of the extensions. World War II brought the soldiery who damaged the house and put concrete roads and Nissen huts in Price's beautiful park. Foxley was demolished 1948, but Ragged Castle and glimpses of Price's planting remain. PRICE, Bt/PB1857; DAVENPORT/LG1952; *Robinson*.

*Fawley Court in late C19*

*Foxley*

*Freen's Court*

*Gaines*

**Freen's Court, Sutton.** This former seat of the Unett family had become 3 tenements by the time the Royal Commission published their volume on the area 1932. It was 2 storeys, timber-framed and was probably built by the Lingen family in c15 on an "H"-shaped plan. The RCHM reported that the central or Hall-block had been destroyed and replaced by a modern passage. The west wing had been extended northwards, probably in late c16, and the east wing was extended in the same direction, probably in c17. A south-west wing had 2 mullion and transom windows and a stone chimney-stack with diagonal shafts of brick was on the east side of the east wing. But inside, apart from some original roof trusses and a late c16 or early c17 door, all panelling, fireplaces, heraldic glass, etc, had been removed. Fragments of the moat which formerly surrounded the house still existed in the early 1930s. Freen's was finally demolished *ca* 1955. UNETT/LG1863; *Robinson*; RCHM II.

**Gaines, Whitbourne.** The large irregular red-brick house of 11 bays masks an interior with fine late c18 decoration by Thomas Farnolls Pritchard. Chimneypieces and Gothick columns were part of his work. There is a large room with graceful Gothick revival and there is stucco work in the Adam style in other rooms. Many chimneypieces were removed recently. An oval glazed dome lights a small staircase. There are c19 parts to the house as well. Bellingham Freeman acquired the estate *ca* 1683 and it remained in that family until 1921. Later in the 1920s, Gaines was owned by Harry Wheelock; it is now in institutional use. FREEMAN (*formerly* CHILDE-FREEMAN)/LG1952; *Colvin*; Harris, *Architectural History* II; *Pevsner*; *Robinson*.

*Garnons*

*Garnons: Blomfield's library*

*Garnons: Atkinson's hall*

**Garnons, Mansell Gamage.** A gabled Elizabethan or Jacobean building, formerly the seat of the Geers family, stood on this site 1791 when Humphry Repton was commissioned to prepare a Red Book for John Geers Cotterell (later 1st Bt). Most of Repton's recommendations were carried out: today, the beauty of the landscape from the long ridge on which the house stands is merely enhanced by the sweeping vista towards the Black Mountains. In the Red Book, James Wyatt is suggested as the architect of a new castellated house, but the ideas for the new building were postponed and, when put into action, it was William Atkinson who gained the commission 1815. The earlier house remained to the west and Atkinson designed a castellated range consisting of a tall broad tower and 3 bays to the right of it. Francis Bernasconi and son were responsible for the Gothic plasterwork within. This later part was reduced 1958 to ground-floor level and now forms a loggia and conservatory. Originally there was Gothic fenestration throughout the house, but *ca* 1908 Sir Reginald Blomfield altered this to sash windows and the Gothic interiors of the Atkinson range gave way to mid-c18-type interiors. Of these, the library was the most successful room. A number of fine chimneypieces of c18 were introduced at the same time. What remains of the truncated house today, in addition to the stunted Atkinson building, is the *ca* 1855 replacement,

*Garnons: Atkinson's library*

*Garnstone*

designed by Thomas Blashill, of the original house. This consists of an ashlar-faced castellated range of a 1 bay tower with 6 bays to the right of it. All is mounted on a grand terrace which sets it high in the park. William Wilkins, the elder, prepared drawings for an impressive entrance lodge, etc, in the Gothic style, 1792; and C. H. Tatham exhibited a design for the house at the Royal Academy 1802. Neither of these designs was carried out. A cottage ornée on the estate might have been designed by Robert Ebbels who submitted designs for such buildings. Garnons is now the seat of Sir John Cotterell, 6th Bt. COTTERELL, Bt/PB; *Colvin*; *Neale* (Ser. II, iv); *Pevsner*; *Robinson*; Stroud, *Humphry Repton* (1962).

**Garnstone, Weobley.** The awkward massing of square, round and octagonal towers resulted in this wholly unsuccessful attempt to create a romantic Gothic castle. Surely Garnstone was the least happy of Nash's country houses—for it was he who designed the house *ca* 1806 for Samuel Peploe. There was a spacious staircase hall lit by a great lantern, but the Victorians had done over most of the other rooms leaving them dull and lifeless. Parts of an older house (a 3 storey "U"-shaped building of C17) were incorporated in the service quarters. When seen from a distance, the house sat well in its park, but a last great ball, held in the house to mark its closure before demolition 1959, left few with real regret. Peploes had inherited from the Birch family (one of whom was the unscrupulous Col John Birch, supporter of both Cromwell and Charles II), but they sold out to the Verdin family 1899. PEPLOE/LG1952; VERDIN *of Stoke Hall and Garnstone*/LG1969; *Colvin*; *Robinson*; Summerson, *John Nash* (1935); Terence Davis, *Architecture of John Nash* (1960); *Neale* IV

**Gatley Park, Leinthall Earls.** The house as it stands presents a picture of a sizable Jacobean seat; but, on closer examination, one can detect that much of it, although successful in design, is not old. Basically, Gatley is a house of the 1630s—a farmhouse—and it was inflated to its present dimensions in 1890s and to the designs of C. D. Coleridge 1907. It is of brick, gabled, and of 2 storeys. There are mullioned and transomed windows and a

*Gatley Park* ca *1865*

*Gatley Park*

*Gatley: staircase*

*Gatley: The Folly (built 1963)*

staircase with heavy turned balusters and 2 decorated overmantels. The Dunnes had bought Gatley when it stood as a square farmhouse in late C17. Capt Thomas Dunne owns the house today. In the 1960s the park gained a startling addition in the form of a tall finger-like tower, built as a folly and dower-house, to the design of Raymond Erith; John Fowler decorated the interior. DUNNE/LG1965; *Pevsner; Robinson;* RCHM III.

**Gayton Hall, Upton Bishop.** An early C19 house of 3 widely-spaced bays with a porch on Doric columns. The side elevation was of 5 bays—those on the ground floor being in blank arches. There was a verandah at the side and a parapet. For most of C20 the house was owned by the Marshall family—the last owner being Vice-Adm H. J. T. Marshall. Gayton was demolished 1955. MARSHALL *formerly of Patterdale Hall*/LG1952.

**Gillow Manor, Hentland.** Now a partly-moated farmhouse. The deep gatehouse and south-west front of red sandstone, however, date from late C14. This gatehouse is tunnel-vaulted and there is a 2 light Perpendicular window with transom to the left of it. The way through the gatehouse leads to a small courtyard which was undoubtedly larger in C14. Much rebuilding in the various ranges of the house took place in C17. A late C16 staircase with square newels and flat-shaped balusters is one of the notable features of the interior. The most curious survival within is a life-size effigy, in stone, of *ca* 1430. This figure is in civilian costume and might have been one of several placed on the embattled gatehouse similar to those at Alnwick, Belsay and Raby castles in the north of England. In 1645 Benedict Hall owned the house, but later it became part of The Mynde estate (*qv*). *Pevsner; Robinson;* RCHM I.

**Goodrich Court, Goodrich.** An enormous fantasy house designed by Edward Blore for Dr (later Sir) Samuel Rush Meyrick. Meyrick was an antiquarian and a leading authority on armour (he reorganized the collections at Windsor Castle and the Tower of London) and he wanted a suitable building in which to arrange and display his remarkable accumulation, which ranged from armour to all kinds of objects of antiquarian interest. The house, built 1828–31, was without doubt inspired by the nearby ruins of Goodrich Castle (which Meyrick had attempted to buy in order to rebuild). Even greater inspiration

*Gayton Hall*

*Goodrich: 1889 gates (now at College of Arms)*

*Gillow Manor*

came from castles on the Continent which he had so avidly sketched on his Grand Tour through Europe 1823. The completed building was unlike most of Blore's country houses which were built in the Jacobethan style. Wordsworth called it an impertinent structure. It was a great mass of towers and turrets and had a massive keep—the whole dominated by the huge 100 ft Sussex Tower (named after his friend HRH Duke of Sussex). It was built round a large courtyard and entry was over a drawbridge and through 2 stout towers. Inside, the entrance hall had a ceiling modelled on a chapel in Rochester Cathedral and there were chairs resembling the Coronation Chair at Westminster Abbey. The grand staircase, at the end of the hall, was lit by an oriel window designed by Thomas Willement and it proclaimed in portrait and coats-of-arms the Meyrick ancestry. In the Henry VI Gallery was the famed suit of armour, made for the Duke of Ferrara, which is now in the Wallace Collection. There was a room with Moorish, Hindu and Chinese decoration. The most impressive chamber at Goodrich was the Great Hall, designed to

*Goodrich Court*

evoke the great halls of medieval castles, with its arch-braced roof. The Hastitude Chamber was full of tableaux presenting more suits of armour. The Grand Armoury, 86 ft long, containing the finest items of Meyrick's collection, was a prelude to the Chapel full of ecclesiastical relics. The library had an Italian ceiling from Holland. And there were further rooms furnished in a particular period style. Meyrick died 1848 and left the house and contents to a cousin, Lt-Col A. W. H. Meyrick, who made alterations which principally involved subdividing some of the larger rooms. In 1868, after refusing an offer from the South Kensington Museum, the great collection of armour was sold and the house followed 1871, when its purchaser was George Moffatt. He and his son were keen antiquarians and they altered the house to the south and west in the Elizabethan style. Many new rooms were created, the most remarkable being a new Great Hall with hammerbeam roof closely resembling that at Hampton Court Palace. In this hall the huge chimney-breast commemorated the coronation of Edward VII and Queen Alexandra. At the same time, Moffatt removed the old stables, made a new entrance on the south side and created a forecourt with railings and a wrought-iron gate (now at the College of Arms in Queen Victoria Street, London). Moffatt's daughter married into the Trafford family of nearby Hill Court (*qv*) and they retained the house until its demolition 1950. The whereabouts of many of the notable fixtures and fittings today are unknown. From 1940 to 1945 Goodrich was in the occupation of Felsted School. The gatehouse, resembling one in Aachen, survives. It has round towers and a false portcullis. MEYRICK/LG1875; TRAFFORD (*formerly* MOFFATT)/LG1952; VSA; *Colvin*; *Robinson*; Hugh Mellor, *Transactions of the Woolhope Naturalists Field Club*, Vol XLII (1977) II.

**Great Brampton House, Madley.** Regency house, on the site of an older structure, probably built for John Pye who sold it 1825 to Charles Ballinger. The Murray-Aynsleys bought it 1853 and probably made the alterations which leave the house as it is today. The central 3 bay block recessed between wings with canted bays was, until 1950s, of 3 storeys. The Italianate arcade linking the two wings was probably built at the same time as the interiors were Frenchified. *Post* World War I it was the seat of Major L. Beaumont-Thomas, who broke up the estate in the 1930s. Since World War II it has changed hands 4 times; the present owner is Mr F. G. Howell who bought it 1969. He uses it as both home and premises for his antiques business. MURRAY-AYNSLEY *of Hall Court*/LG1921; BEAUMONT-THOMAS/LG1937; *Robinson*.

*Great Brampton House*

*Haffield House*

*Hagley Court*

*The Green*

**Green (The), Bacton.** Basically a farmhouse of 1628. But 2 additions, one of *ca* 1860 and the second of *ca* 1900, made it into the large, rambling structure it is today. Inside, there is an air of solid Victorian comfort with generous use of woods in the staircase, doors and fireplaces. The Hamp family owned the property *ca* 1730 and from them it passed to the Partridges, who married into the Manley family, its present owners, in 1902. PARTRIDGE/LG1921; MANLEY/LG1952.

**Haffield House, Donnington.** One of the more inventive designs by Sir Robert Smirke. A white house of 7 bays and 2 storeys. There is a portico of 6 attenuated Greek Doric columns; another 2 with 2 pillars flank the side entrance. A splendid mid-c18 chimneypiece, from Bowood, Wilts, was brought here when the principal part of that house was demolished in 1950s. The house was erected 1817–18 by William Gordon, but by the 1880s it belonged to W. C. Henry, MD; Sir John Mitchell owned the house 1929 and the present owner, Mr Alan Cadbury, came here in 1960s. GORDON *of Abergeldie*/LG1969; *Colvin*; *Pevsner*; *Robinson*.

**Hagley Court, Lugwardine.** Two periods are represented side by side. An early C18 3 storey range, of stone, is tacked on to an early C19 range with pilasters. Onetime home of a branch of the Hoptons, it is now divided into 2 houses owned by Mr J. Dorrell and Mr G. H. Shore. HOPTON *of Canon Frome*/LG1937; *Robinson*.

**Halesend (The), Cradley.** Essentially an early C19 building of "L"-shape wrapped around an older 3 storey house. Decoration is sparing without as well as within. A long entrance hall has an arch which leads through to a simple wrought-iron staircase. The Yapp family was here in the mid and late C19; by the end of the 1920s it was the seat of Lt-Col S. H. Enderby. A/M Sir Bertine Sutton bought the property *ca* 1937 and he was succeeded by Mr Leonard Lord (later 1st and last Lord Lambury) 1942. Mr Bernard Higgins, the present owner, came here 1954. YAPP/WCF; ENDERBY/WCF; LORD, LAMBURY, B/PB1967; *Robinson*.

*Hall Court*

**Hall Court, Much Marcle.** A notable example of a complete timber-framed building of its period, Hall Court was built *ca* 1608 for John (later Sir John) Coke and is of half "H"-shaped plan. It is possible that parts of an earlier building were re-used. The main front is of 5 unequal bays and the porch is original. Inside, the best room is the dining-room at the south end—all lined with original panelling. It has a notable frieze and the walls are divided by fluted Ionic pilasters. Several rooms in the house retain original fittings. Hall Court recently belonged to Mr R. D. Marcon. RCHM II.

**Hampton Court, Hope-under-Dinmore.** Basically one of the largest medieval manor houses in England. Licence to crenellate was granted to Sir Rowland Lenthall 1435 and he erected a quadrangular, partly fortified manor house. In 1510 it was bought by the Coningsbys (whose name Disraeli used for the hero of his eponymous novel) and their descendant, Thomas, future 1st Earl of Coningsby, brought great changes to the building. A man obsessed with the lineage of his family, he re-enacted it all in heraldry, portraiture and tournament. Even as a minor, he began alterations at Hampton *ca* 1680; these are reflected in the views of the house by Knyff and Stevens. Between 1706 and 1710 he regularized the C15 facade and employed

*Hampton Court*

George London to lay out the great gardens. Throughout all Coningsby's alterations, he maintained respect for the medieval gate tower and the chapel and this same respect was shown in the almost total rebuilding of the 1830s and 1840s. After Coningsby's death 1729, the house remained in the family and eventually passed through marriage into the possession of Viscount Malden (later 5th Earl of Essex) 1781. Immediately fresh alterations were put in hand and views of the south front, at the end of C18, show extensive changes in the Gothick style, possibly to the design of James Wyatt who was restoring Hereford Cathedral at the time and who was working at Lord Essex's principal seat, Cassiobury, Herts, *ante* 1803. J. M. W. Turner visited Hampton at the end of C18 and executed soft, evocative watercolours of great beauty. These show the great stone house, with sashed and pointed windows, in its final period of mellowness. But the most drastic alterations were to come. In 1810, the house was bought by John Arkwright, grandson of the industrialist Sir Richard Arkwright, inventor of the spinning frame. And in the 1830s began the great transformation (formerly attributed to Wyatville) of the house due, in the most part, to an amateur architect Charles Hanbury-Tracy, later 1st Lord Sudeley. However, it is not entirely clear how great a part was played by the architects William and John Atkinson—a cache of whose drawings for Hampton came to light in recent years. The Atkinsons certainly advised Arkwright, but Hanbury-Tracy, more than anyone, had his way and virtually rebuilt the whole house. Only on the north entrance side was restraint shown and the great medieval entrance tower remains substantially that of Lenthall's time and the C15 chapel is also untouched. Hanbury-Tracy's internal alterations were severe. He created a great hall in the north range, in place of the old one on the south side of the house. And this new hall, called Coningsby Hall, contains the most important relic of the Coningsby building—a great chimneypiece which appears to be of the early C18. Drawing-room, dining-room, staircase and the heavy-ribbed cloisters are all very much Hanbury-Tracy—a heavy, unattractive Gothic which has been possibly toned down since building. The Arkwrights continued at Hampton until 1912 when it was sold to Mrs Burrell and she, in turn, sold it to Viscountess Hereford (wife of the 17th Viscount) 1924. The present Viscount (holder of the premier viscountcy of England) disposed of the property 1972 to Capt Hon Philip Smith (brother of 4th Viscount Hambleden). Mr George Hughes purchased Hampton 1975 and has completely restored it. CONINGSBY, CONINGSBY, E/DEP; CAPELL, ESSEX, E/PB; ARKWRIGHT *of Kinsham Court*/LG1965; DEVEREUX, HEREFORD, V/PB; SMITH, *sub* HAMBLEDEN, V/PB; *Colvin*; *Pevsner*; *Robinson*; RCHM III; *Torrington, Diaries*; CL 25 June 1901, 22 Feb, 1 & 8 March 1973; *Farington, Diary*; *Neale* III (2nd ser); *Campbell, Vitruvius Britannicus* II; *Morris, Seats* II; *Copper, late Magazine* III: *Kip*, 1716, 1717; *Nash, Mansions of England . . . III* (1841).

*Harewood Park*

**Harewood Park, Harewood.** Bought 1654 by Bennet Hoskyns, Harewood remained in the hands of his descendants until C20. The old house was said to be a Tudor structure with a tower at one corner. But the building which was demolished 1952 was part C18 and mostly of early C19 when a great deal of rebuilding was done by Sir Hungerford Hoskyns, 7th Bt. The garden front was of 11 bays and a pediment with a circular window crowned the central 5-bay projection. It was only of 2 storeys whereas the entrance front was of 3. On this front the central 5 bays were recessed between 2 bay wings. There was a porch with paired Tuscan columns. The interior of the house demonstrated the thoroughness of the early C19 rebuilding and rooms were large and generally undistinguished. It is known that someone named W. A. Mar provided a design for a Grecian library chimneypiece for 7th Bt. Entrance to the stableyard was through an arch in a cube-shaped building with a pyramidal roof. This was flanked by the pedimented ends of the stable ranges. Now the remains of the estate are confined to the pedimented gate lodge with a portico of two pairs of Tuscan columns and the small Church of St Denis, erected 1864, with an Early English front and Norman east end. Between the wars Harewood was the property of the trustees of J. H. Parry and it was the residence of Capt. W. F. Campbell. HOSKYNS, Bt/PB; *Pevsner*; *Robinson*.

*Hatfield Court*

**Hatfield Court, Hatfield.** All gone now; but earlier this century the sizeable ruins of a late C16 house. The main elevation had 3 projecting and gabled bays the full height of the house. All gables were crow-stepped. It was of 3 storeys and the external walls had

lozenge-diapering in black bricks. Chimney-stacks of grouped diagonal and square shafts. Some panelling from this house is found in the new Hatfield Court which was the seat earlier this century of Major Arthur Chambers. The old house was attached to a 2 storey Georgian farmhouse which still remains. The Colles family was probably responsible for the original late C16 building. Later it passed to the Geers and Cotterell families before being sold C19 to Thomas Ashton. COTTERELL, Bt/PB; *Pevsner*; *Robinson*; RCHM III.

**Haywood Lodge, Haywood.** The fine wrought-iron gates and screen fronting a high quality brick facade of *ca* 1710 create the impression of a professional man's town house removed to the country. There are 7 bays and 2 storeys with a hipped roof. An open scrolly pediment, of lush carving, surmounts the

*Haywood Lodge*

*Heath House*

doorway with pilasters. Narrow windows flank the door. Within there is a staircase of high quality with carved tread-ends and feather inlay on some of the steps. There are curiously shaped turned balusters. This house was probably built by the Whitmore family. They sold it 1783 to George Livius and he, in turn, disposed of it to Col Matthews, builder of Belmont (*qv*) 1810. It has descended with Belmont since that time and its role became that of a farmhouse in C20. MATTHEWS/LG 1863; WEGG-PROSSER *of Belmont*/LG1952; *Pevsner*; *Robinson*; RCHM.

*Hellens*

*Heath House: staircase*

**Heath House, Leintwardine.** Probably mid-C17. Of brick, with 2 projecting wings to the north. Hipped roof with dormers. The south side of the house is flat and of 8 bays and 2 storeys. There are wooden cross-type windows. Inside, there is an imported or re-used staircase assembly and a room with fine mid-C17 panelling on the 1st floor. Lady Ripley lived in the house 1929 and it was just saved from demolition by the architect Simon Dale thirty years later. RIPLEY, Bt/PB; RCHM III.

**Hellens, Much Marcle.** An ancient house, but what one sees today is predominantly Jacobean. It is principally of brick with mullioned and transomed windows, but at one time there was much more of it. The tower, in the courtyard, has a stone newel staircase and this probably belongs to the original building which was possibly late C15 or early C16. But reconstruction took place in the late C16 or early C17 and, at that time, Hellens extended farther to the south and west. Certainly it was reduced in size 1641 and in late C18. More evidence of Jacobean alteration is seen in a 2nd staircase of wood with sturdy balusters, an overmantel with blank arches in the staircase hall and a rich plaster frieze in a ground-floor room. On the 1st floor there is a big chimneypiece with coupled Ionic columns and smaller Corinthian coupled columns above. There is a pendant with patterns of thin ribs in another room on the 1st floor and this could possibly date from Mary Tudor's day. In the grounds there is an interesting octagonal brick dovecote with the date 1641 and the initials "F. and M.W." on it. Hellens was long a seat of the Walwyns and in the mid-C19 it had descended to R. D. Cooke; but more recently it was restored by the wife of the writer Axel Munthe and now belongs to the Pennington-Mellor-Munthe family. WALWYN *formerly of Longford*/LG1972; MUNTHE, *sub* REA, B/PB; *Pevsner*; *Robinson*; RCHM II.

*Hennor House*

**Hennor House, Hamnish Clifford.** A front of *ca* 1775 with Adamish porch masks an older house with 2 stone wings at the back. One of these wings is dated 1679. Inside, there are 2 rooms with fine decoration of late C18. There are chimneypieces with reliefs and one has a delicate frieze as well. The late C18 refronting was carried out by William Poole of Homend (*qv*) and his descendant, a Major Stephenson, was living in the house in 1880s. Early in C20 it was owned by Arthur William Walker. Now owned by Mrs C. R. T. Congreve. CONGREVE *of Congreve*/LG1969; *Robinson*; RCHM III.

**Henwood, Dilwyn.** The house has an Irish air. Lacon Lambe, whose family had lived at nearby Bidney (now a farmhouse) since 1661,

*Henwood*

erected Henwood in 1770s. The centre block boasts a wide bow and like the flanking pavilions, it is faced with stone. One of these pavilions masks a range of farm buildings. Inside, there is a simple wooden staircase lit by a tall round-headed window. In the dining-room there is a good c17 overmantel from Bidney with paired columns above and below. The house was owned by the Lambes until *ca* 1900 when the Verdins gained possession of it. But since the 1860s it has been lived in by the Bray family and it was the present owner's father, Cmdr A. J. Windebank, who bought it from the Verdins 1933 and presented it to his daughter Mrs G. H. Bray. LAMBE *of Bidney and Henwood*/LG1862; VERDIN *of Stoke Hall and Garnstone*/LG1969; *Robinson.*

*Hergest Court*

**Hergest Court, Kington.** The old seat of the Vaughans; in its truncated state, a farm belonging to the Ridgebourne estate (*qv*), property of the Banks family. 2 ranges: one of closely-set timbering; the other of stone. Hergest is said to have been built c1430 for Thomas, 2nd son of Sir Roger Vaughan on the site of an earlier house. It has been described as having 8 strong buildings, but *ca* 1750 the dilapidated parts and minor buildings were demolished. Inside, there is evidence of c17 work mainly in the staircase with its flat shaped and pierced balusters. Panelling of the same period too. There are remains of c16 colour decoration and the kitchen has a stone fireplace of *ca* 1500. BANKS/WCF; *Pevsner*; *Robinson*; RCHM III.

*Hill Court*

**Hill Court, Walford-on-Wye.** From entrance gates to the great gatepiers of the forecourt, there is a long straight avenue flanked by lines of oak and lime. It is a large building representing three periods of work—the late c17, 1732 and 1750s. The original rectangular block had a hipped roof, balustrade, cupola and a large segmental pediment over the three centre bays. It has the usual double-pile plan of the time with entrance hall at the front and stairs behind and it was built 1698–1705 for Richard Clarke of a family formerly of yeoman stock. There is a splendid early c18 staircase of walnut and yew, with inlaid half-landings, twisted balusters and carved tread-ends. A fine plaster ceiling with a wreath of fruit and flowers presides over it. In the hall there is wainscot of the same period and there are contemporary panelled rooms. The most noteworthy of these is the

Painted Bedroom with panels of browns, creams and reds simulating rockwork. On rails and stiles are chinoiserie scenes simulating lacquer and two ruin pieces in grisaille which might be from the hand of Isaac Bayly who worked in the hall of Stoke Edith (*qv*). This old block had cross-type windows, one of which survives at the back of the house where there is also a handsome doorway with open scrolly pediment. In 1730s 1 bay wings with Venetian windows and lower links to the main building, were added. One of these wings contains a large drawing-room with a fine chimney-piece of *ca* 1760. In the 1750s, a major undertaking at Hill took place, probably under the direction of the Shrewsbury architect Thomas Farnolls Pritchard. Now the original house was given an extra half-storey and refaced with quoins at the angles etc. A part-balustrade, part-parapet was built either side

of a pediment whose tympanum contains the crisply-carved arms of Clarke. The wings were given pediments as well. Pritchard's original intention was to heighten the entire building with 3 storey canted bays on either side of the old block. There have been later alterations by successive owners, but these have tended to be minor. The links have been heightened to 2 storeys. A dog-gate of *ca* 1700, originally at the bottom of the principal stairs, is now in the south corridor of the first floor, the late owner, Mr J. L. Trafford, commissioned painted trophies by Mr Hugh Robson for the morning-room as well as making other internal alterations and additions. Mr Trafford also built a number of eccentric garden buildings—notably a summer house with huge onion dome and a Chinese Pavilion overlooking a small pool. Ranges of yew hedges are spread through the

*Hill Court: hall*

*Hill Court: staircase ceiling*

*Hill Court: summerhouse and pavilion*

extensive gardens and views to the ruins of Goodrich Castle are cut through at regular intervals. The walled garden boasts a parterre and gatepiers like those of the forecourt with huge exuberant urns. There is also an octag-onal brick dovecote of *ca* 1700 with a lantern. The Clarkes left the property, 1806, to the Evans family and they, in turn, left it to the Powers 1851. Major Lionel Trafford bought the house 1888 and it now belongs to his nephew's cousin, Mr N. J. Moore. POWER *of the Hill Court*/LG1863; TRAFFORD *of Hill Court/* LG1972; *Colvin; Pevsner; Robinson;* CL 27 Jan, 3, 10 Feb 1966; J. Harris, "Pritchard Redi-vivus" *Architectural History* (1968); RCHM II.

*Holme Lacy House*

**Holme Lacy House, Holme Lacy.** In an area of great natural beauty lies the huge house of the Scudamores—one of the largest in the county and preserved in its use as a hospital by the Herefordshire County Council. Holme Lacy was built for 2nd Viscount Scudamore after his marriage 1672. It is known that Anthony Deane was the builder, but the contract mentions Hugh May, in case of need for arbitration, so he may possibly have provided the basic designs. The contract also states that many of the details were to be copied from Sir John Duncombe's now vanished home at Battlesden, Beds. Before Sir Robert Lucas-Tooth, 1st Bt, bought the house 1910 and made alterations (which included a ballroom, a new principal staircase and extensive service quarters), it had 4 main facades. The west side (where the ballroom was inserted) was the old main entrance flanked by outbuildings which were swept away. The building is of sandstone ashlar with Bath stone dressings and the porch and balustrades (which altered the roofs) were added to the designs of William Atkinson 1828–31. The house is roughly "H"-shaped and its facades are reticent and virtually repeat each other. It is possible that parts of an older house are embedded in the present structure. The bland facades do not prepare one for the outstanding interiors. No less than 9 rooms have plaster ceilings which are among the finest of their date in England. The principal apartment is the saloon which occupies the 2 storeys in the centre of the east range. The elaborate plaster ceiling surmounts a higher plaster cove enriched with cartouches-of-arms of the Scudamore and Cecil families (Lord Scudamore had married the daughter of

*Holme Lacy: saloon ceiling*

John Cecil, 4th Earl of Exeter). All about there are branches of oak and laurel leaves, festoons of fruit, leaves and flowers and, in the end panels, cartouches with coronets and branches. In addition to this exuberant display of plasterwork there were, in the dining-room, library and saloon, magnificent wooden garlands and trophies forming part of the overmantels. These have all the delicacy and refinement associated with Grinling Gibbons and are generally accepted as being by him. Much of this carved woodwork left the house soon after Lucas-Tooth's purchase of

the property and is now in the Metropolitan Museum, New York, and at Kentchurch Court (*qv*). The gardens, which were extensive, show great ranges of yew. An attractive orangery of brick, with 5 round-headed windows and a parapet, is found on the old terrace walk. After the death of the 3rd and last Viscount Scudamore 1716, Holme Lacy descended through female lines to Capt Sir Edwyn Scudamore-Stanhope, 2nd Bt (*d* 1874). His eldest son succeeded a kinsman as 9th Earl of Chesterfield 1883. It was 10th Earl who disposed of the property 1910 breaking the hereditary link of the Scudamores. SCUDAMORE, SCUDAMORE, V/DEP; SCUDAMORE-STANHOPE, *sub* CHESTERFIELD AND STANHOPE, E/PB1967; MUNRO-LUCAS-TOOTH, Bt/PB; *Colvin; Pevsner; Robinson*; RCHM I; CL 12 & 19 June 1909.

**Homend (The), Stretton Grandison.** To a half-timbered house of C17, Edward Poole built an addition which forms the entrance front now. This occurred during the years 1814–21 and his architect was Sir Robert Smirke. Of 5 bays and 2 storeys, but the centre is of 2½ storeys. All the ground-floor windows are round-headed and on the short sides there is one window each flanked by coupled Tuscan pilasters. Augustus William Gadesden owned the house 1929. In 1973, the estate was split up and the house divided into several dwellings. There is a beautiful park. *Colvin; Pevsner*.

**Homme House, Much Marcle.** Francis Kilvert, in his *Diary* for Sept 1874, records how he came here for the wedding of his friend Rev Andrew Pope to Miss Harriet Money-

*The Homend*

*Homme House*

Kyrle. He refers to a large dinner-party in the house and how the magnificent presents were laid out on tables in the library. There was photography on the front steps and dancing with the tenants on the lawn. The Popes did eventually come into the ownership of the place and the present owner is Vice-Adm Sir Ernle Kyrle Pope. Kyrles were here first, but they were eventually succeeded by the Money family; there were several generations of Money-Kyrles at Homme and monuments to both families fill the Church. The house is of two parts, meeting at right angles. The older part appears to be *ca* 1500 and has a low tower with a canted oriel window and battlements. There is an attached C19 gateway. The other part of the house is late Georgian, of 6 bays and 2 storeys. There is a porch of 2 pairs of Tuscan columns and round the corner a contemporary canted bay window. Inside, there is a handsome curved flying staircase and a room to the left of the hall contains late Jacobean panelling and a monumental wooden chimneypiece. There is a Queen Anne range behind the early Tudor part of the house. In the grounds is an octagonal summerhouse of the seventeenth and eighteenth centuries. MONEY-KYRLE *of Whetham*/LG1965; POPE *of Part-y-Seal*/LG1952; VSA; *Pevsner*; *Robinson*; RCHM II.

*Hope End*

*How Caple Court*

**Hope End, Colwall.** The fantasy country house of the Barretts of Wimpole Street and birthplace of Elizabeth Barrett Browning. An extraordinary eccentric building of pseudo-Moorish design by J. C. Loudon for Edward Moulton-Barrett, father of the poetess. It undoubtedly incorporated the owner's ideas and was completed by 1815. Minarets, and a huge glass dome lighting the central staircase, dominated the exterior. But the offerings inside were even more fantastic. A round-ended drawing-room was decorated by Italian artists and took 7 years to complete; there was a billiard room with Moorish views; a dining-room with crimson flock paper and a Verde antique chimneypiece with columns. The staircase had brass ·balustrades and a mahogany handrail. There was an enclosed vaulted portico with stained glass doors and a noble vestibule with columns. It was possible that Hope End incorporated part of its C17 or early C18 predecessor. Loudon's work included the stables and today there survive posts with ogee tops, minarets and a 2 storey gateway topped by a dome and pinnacles. In 1832, Thomas Heywood, the antiquary, bought the property and it remained in his family until 1867. C. A. Hewitt purchased it in that year, but he pulled down the house 1873 and erected a Tudor-style residence higher up the valley. MOULTON-BARRETT, *sub* ALTHAM *formerly of Timbercombe*/LG1972; HEYWOOD *formerly of Hatley St George*/LG1937; VSA; *Colvin*; CL 19 Sept 1968; *Pevsner*; *Robinson*.

**How Caple Court, How Caple.** Much of this sizeable house on its elevated site above the charming park is C19 or early C20 rebuilding. Of ashlar and rubble it is of 3 storeys and the centre of the principal front is late C17 or early C18—the kitchen wing is also C17. An early C17 overmantel has been reset in south-west wing. Onetime seat of the Gregorys it has belonged to the Lees, who inherited from the MacLellans, for much of C20. LEE/LG1972; RCHM II.

**Huntington Court, Huntington (nr Hereford).** Close to Yazor Brook. A late Georgian house of 4 bays with a hipped roof and attractive cast-iron porch. 2 storeys. The home of Mr Peter Temple-Morris, MP. *Pevsner.*

**Huntington Court, Huntington.** To an C18 building there was added in early C19 a villa-type addition of 3 bays with a verandah. The drawing-room, inside the later part, boasts what might be an earlier chimneypiece. James Cheese, only surviving son of Edmund Cheese of Ridgebourne (*qv*), lived here in the mid-C19 and his grandchild, Anne Geraldine, who married, 2ndly, Lt-Gen A. B. Crosbie, owned the house in early C20. In the 1920s Huntington became the property of Dr C. D. Edwards and, on his death 1954, it passed to Dr W. Logan Jack. The house was formerly the centre of an extensive estate. CHEESE/LG1863; *Robinson.*

**Huntington Park, Huntington.** A late Georgian house of red brick; 5 bays, 2 storeys with Victorian additions. Probably a simple farmhouse enlarged to its undistinguished appearance by the Romilly family who bought the house from the Walshams 1802. Childhood home of Esmond Romilly, the nephew of Sir Winston Churchill, who eloped to the Spanish Civil War with Jessica Mitford; latterly the seat of his brother Mr Giles Romilly, the journalist. Derelict by the early 1960s and demolished 1966. WALSHAM, Bt/PB; ROMILLY/LG1965.

**Kentchurch Court, Kentchurch.** Scuda-mores have been here for more than 600 years and the castellated and rambling house lies in a cleft of the hills. There is an all-pervading feeling of an ancient holding. Basically a C14 fortified manor house—and approached through an entrance arch of that date—with some evidence of C16 work, the present appearance is almost entirely due to a thorough recasting beginning 1795 under the authorship of John Nash and continuing in 1820s under Thomas Tudor, the agent to the estate. Nash heightened the dominant north-west tower (onetime hide-out of Owen Glendower); refaced the former great hall (refaced again, in ashlar, by Tudor); and windows, battlements and chimneys, typical of him, appear on the east wing of the north range. Round the corner, on the north side, there is a huge 2 storey Gothic window called the chapel, but it lights nothing more than the final upper stage of the long traverse corridor within the house. Faint neo-Norman touches between the ashlar-faced hall and the medieval north range are repeated inside in the library, where there is a screen of arches with dog-tooth ornament. These are alterations of the 1820s. Decoration inside the building is generally restrained. The drawing-room has a fine late C18 chimneypiece and hints of Gothic enliven the main corridor and its corresponding gallery above. Some Swiss stained glass is to be found in the great window and there is luscious carved woodwork from Holme Lacy (*qv*) in the dining-room and the terrace room, which is convincingly attributed to Grinling Gibbons. These came as heirlooms to Lady Patricia Scudamore-Stanhope, the last of that family and only daughter of 12th Earl of Chesterfield, who was representative of the extinct Viscounts Scudamore. Lady Patricia married her distant cousin Mr J. H. S. Lucas-Scudamore, of Kentchurch 1947 and their only son Mr J. E. S. Lucas-Scudamore is the present owner. LUCAS-SCUDAMORE/LG1972; *Colvin*; *Pevsner*; *Robinson*; RCHM I; CL 15, 22 & 29 Dec 1966; Summerson, *John Nash* (1935); Davis, *Architecture of John Nash* (1960).

*Huntington Court*

*Huntington Park*

**Kinnersley Castle, Kinnersley.** One comes upon Kinnersley unexpectedly and its great height is a total surprise. A lofty embattled tower stands in the angle of 2 ranges running from it to the south and east. It was supposed to have been built for Roger Vaughan in late C16, but it is probably a remodelling of an older and real castle. Certainly there was a larger building here as vaulted brick cellars extend beyond the east end. Noteworthy Elizabethan features are the north doorway, some mullioned windows and the stepped brick

*Kentchurch Court*

*Kinnersley Castle*

*Kinnersley: drawing room*

gables which were fashionable at the time, but unusual in this county. Inside, there is an Elizabethan plaster ceiling and frieze in the upper south-west room and cornucopias, sea serpents, etc, abound. Again, in this room, there is the fine chimneypiece with Ionic-type columns, the Vaughan arms and an oak branch spreading over the whole overmantel. Other overmantels of Elizabethan and Jacobean date are found in the house. The C18 saw remodelling in the north-west room on the ground floor. The Victorians made minor additions and alterations, *eg* the porch, 2 storey bay window, etc. Vaughans were succeeded by Smallmans and their heir sold it to Sir John Morgan, 2nd Bt. Kinnersley remained with the Morgans until the death of the last Bt 1767 when it was inherited by the Cluttons who sold it. In the C19, it was bought by the Reavelys who retained it until well into C20. The castle was let frequently and tenants included G. W. Davey and 1st Lord Brocket. It is now a home for the elderly run by the Herefordshire County Council. MORGAN, Bt, *of Llangattock*/EDB; REAVELY/LG1937; NALL-CAIN, BROCKET, B/PB; *Pevsner*; *Robinson*; RCHM III.

*Kinsham Court*

**Kinsham Court, Kinsham.** The Dower House of Brampton Bryan (*qv*), seat of the Harleys, Earls of Oxford. An C18 building much done over in C19, but still containing several of Thomas Farnolls Pritchard's fine chimneypieces. It was a favourite residence of Bishop Harley (*d* 1788). In the C20 the house was bought by the Arkwright family who formerly owned Hampton Court, nr Leominster (*qv*). The house was, at one time, the residence of the family of Florence

Nightingale; Lord Byron also stayed here—in fact, he is said to have written *Childe Harold* under a large cedar tree in the grounds. Kinsham stands high in a beautiful position above a dingle. HARLEY, OXFORD, E/DEP; HARLEY *of Brampton Bryan*/LG1969; ARKWRIGHT/ LG1965; Harris, *Architectural History* II, *Colvin*; *Robinson*.

**Knill Court, Knill.** What appeared as a large rambling Victorian house was, in fact, a rebuilding of 1867 by Sir John Walsham, 1st Bt, to the designs of Henry Shrimpton. Parts of the house were possibly of medieval origin. Many gabled, half-timbered with a ground floor of stone, Knill was an archaeologically incorrect building. A small tower with a Gothic arch was the principal feature on an otherwise dull facade. But the interior retained 2 notable C17 overmantels in the library and dining-room. The house was situated in a small, deep valley with tree-clad hills which gave a somewhat gloomy air to the place. Knill was the seat of the Walshams from early C17, but in C20 it was let for long periods. Among the tenants were Cmdr K. R. Walker and a school for girls. It was during the latter's occupancy that the house was destroyed by fire 1943. A fragment of the building survived and this was rehabilitated and made into a small house. Sir Stuart Knill, 3rd Bt, took up residence with his family in this fragment during 1950s, but their stay was a brief one. WALSHAM, Bt/PB; WALKER *of Warden Court*/LG1952; KNILL, Bt/PB; VSA; RCHM III; *Robinson*.

*Langstone Court*

**Langstone Court, Llangarron.** Of brick, 5 bays, 2 storeys with a hipped roof. There is a forecourt, stone piers, iron gates and a clairvoie. A stable-block lines up on the right-hand side. All is presented as a very perfect picture of a small squire's home. Built *ca* 1700 by the Gwillym family, the house possesses a panelled hall and parlour with Caroline-style plaster ceilings and there is a staircase with sturdy balusters. A later bow on the side of the house marks an alteration of 1825 and there is a screen of marbled columns in the room behind the bow. Since 1794 the house has belonged to the Jones family—Mr Colin Jones being the present owner. A small unspoilt park sets off the house to great advantage. In separate ownership is the back and older part of the house. Evidences of its date are confined to a Jacobean plaster ceiling and a staircase with openwork slatted balusters. JONES/WCF; RCHM; *Pevsner*; *Robinson*; Lees-Milne, *English Country Houses: Baroque* (1970); CL 9 Nov 1967.

*Knill Court*

*Langstone: staircase*

*Ledbury Park*

**Ledbury Park, Ledbury.** The extraordinary and rare fusion of town and country house. In the middle of the town, its walls flush to the footpaths, Ledbury is the grandest black and white house in the county—and the only one to match some of the houses in Shrewsbury. The show front has 5 gables and, on 2 floors below, the windows have projecting sills between stop-chamfered posts. All other timbering consists of closely-set verticals. An extension of 1820, at the back of the house, shows itself on the Worcester Road. There are pedimented cross-windows. Extensive brick stables and outbuildings. A large park stretches behind the building and, when seen from that side, it appears as a remote country house. The Hall family built Ledbury Park in late C16 and they intermarried with the Biddulphs in C17.

Prince Rupert made his headquarters at the house April 1646 when he routed Colonel Massey's forces. Biddulphs retained ownership until 1950s when it was sold. Now it has become the headquarters of a papermaking company who maintain it to a high standard. BIDDULPH, B/PB; RCHM; *Pevsner*; *Robinson*.

**Lemore, Eardisley.** The early Victorian appearance of the house is possibly deceptive. As it stands, it appears as a 4 bay block, 2 storeys high, attached to a lower wing. The windows have dripstones. There is an internal porch and staircase with wrought-iron handrail. But it is an ancient seat and the Coke family lived here from 1640 until the house was bought by the Longuevilles in C20. It now belongs to the Brazier family. COKE/LG1900; LONGUEVILLE *formerly of Penylan*/LG1965; *Robinson*.

**Letton Court, Letton.** A long irregular facade of red brick. Robinson states that Samuel Teulon was the architect of the rebuilding in 1863 of this former seat of the Blisset family. The 1863 house was, in fact, destroyed by fire 1925–26 and again rebuilt within the Victorian shell. The Blissets were succeeded by the Dews and Tom Millett Dew owned the house between the wars. BLISSET/ WCF; *Robinson*.

*Lemore*

*Letton Court*

*Longworth*

**Longworth, Lugwardine.** Formerly known as Longford and replacing an older house, seat of the Walwyns (the family now noted for its racehorse trainers). One of Anthony Keck's bland facades: 6 bays and 2 storeys with wide bows wrapping round the corners of the main elevation. Keck built this house for Robert Phillips and that family retained it until 1864 when it was acquired by Edward Smalley Hutchinson. Lady Dillon occupied the house in 1920s when it was the property of the Barneby family; since the 1950s it has been an hotel. Inside, there is much alteration. Two bold lodges of stone with hipped roofs, Gibbs surrounds and windows with Tuscan columns and pediments stand on the Ledbury-Hereford road. They look C20 classical. WALWYN/LG1972; BARNEBY/LG1952; DILLON, Bt/PB; *Colvin*; *Pevsner*; *Robinson*.

*Lower Brockhampton Manor*

**Lower Brockhampton Manor, Brockhampton-by-Bromyard.** Much photographed because it represents all that one expects in a picturesque and ancient timbered house. Its roof appears to ripple slightly and the rare timbered gatehouse leans to one side. All is set down in woods at the end of a small valley and the site itself is nearly surrounded by a moat. The long, low house is late C14, but the gatehouse is late C15. Originally the house was composed of a main range and 2 contemporary cross-wings, but one of these has disappeared. Some of the bargeboards have vine trails and there is an original studded door. The house has an interesting example of a medieval open hall with a spere truss, a cruck truss, several collar beams and a tier of foiled wind braces. Nearby are ruins of C12 chapel. For centuries it formed part of the nearby Brockhampton Park Estate and it was given to the National Trust, with its mid-Georgian neighbour, by Col J. T. Lutley 1948. Barnebys and Lutleys held this estate since at least C16.

*Lower Brockhampton: hall*

BARNEBY and LUTLEY, *sub* BARNEBY *of Llanerch-y-Coed formerly of Brockhampton*/LG1972; *Pevsner*; *Robinson*; RCHM II.

house is stone-faced and commands fine views over the Wye. Built in the 1770s; it was purchased by Sir Herbert Croft, 9th Bt 1865. The Duchess of Hamilton owned the house in 1920s, but by 1929 it was in the ownership of C. R. L. Perkins. A thatched entrance lodge heralds the approach from the Ledbury-Hereford road. The house is now a school. CROFT, Bt, *of Croft Castle*/PB; HAMILTON, D/PB; *Robinson*.

**Luntley Court, Dilwyn.** The *beau ideal* of a timber-framed manor house. Basically Jacobean, but the porch is dated 1674. Of the earlier work there are cusped arched braces in the gables, balusters in the porch and curved brackets and pendants. The extensive outbuildings create the impression of a prosperous farm. The cowhouse has some cusped concave-sided lozenges, but the black and white dovecote, across the tiny road, is outstandingly attractive—particularly when seen in conjunction with the house. Tomkyns, Capel, Whitmore and Ferrer are some of the families who have held this place. From the last-named it passed to Thomas Davies, of Leominster, and his daughter, Margaret Edwards Davies, brought it to the Burlton family late C19. Mr E. M. M. F. Burlton owns the house today. BURLTON/LG1969; RCHM; *Pevsner*; *Robinson*.

*Lower Eaton*

**Lower Eaton, Eaton Bishop.** With lawns sloping to the Wye. The 7 bay, 2 storey brick house was built *post* 1743 by Thomas Phillipps, who had married a Ravenhill heiress of the older house. The Victorians tricked up the Georgian house in an attempt to give it a Gothic air. This left the building with insipid details which disfigure rather than embellish it. In C19 G. Percival Smith sold the house to Joseph Pulley; Sir Charles Thornton Pulley owned it 1929. PULLEY, Bt/PB1901; *Pevsner*; *Robinson*.

**Lugwardine Court, Lugwardine.** A sober facade of 5 bays and 3 storeys with Ionic porch and Venetian window on the 1st floor. The

*Lugwardine Court*

*Luntley Court*

*Lyston Court*

*Manor House, Almeley*

*Michaelchurch Court*

**Lynhales, Lyonshall.** An irregular house, mainly late C19 in appearance. Lynhales incorporates an older building, called The Moor, which was the seat of the Lloyd family. Stephen Robinson bought the property 1860 and his family remained there until C20. Mrs R. F. Hibbert (*d* 1945) owned the house earlier this century. ROBINSON/WCF; HIBBERT *formerly of Birtles and Chalfont*/LG1965; *Robinson*

**Lyston Court, Llanwarne.** Early C19 and 2 storeys. Round-headed windows. Property of Mr J. C. Cheetham 1937; now divided into flats. *Robinson.*

*Mainstone Court*

**Mainstone Court, Pixley.** The red ashlar house of *ca* 1821—5 bays, 2 storeys with a Tuscan porch—fronts an older building and the east block is probably C17. The dining-room has exposed ceiling-beams and has original panelling with a frieze of dolphins, swans and monsters. There are other rooms with exposed ceiling beams. The head of a trefoiled niche has been reset in a garden wall. In C17 a family named Jones lived here and later in C18 it belonged to the Workmans. They were succeeded *ca* 1820 by J. Johnstone, who sold it to Rev John Hopton. C. O. Gallimore lived here 50 years ago; the present owner is Mr W. R. Robinson. HOPTON *of Canon-ffrome*/LG1937; RCHM II; *Pevsner; Robinson.*

**Manor House, Almeley.** It stands close to the road and is timber-framed with brick infilling. A 2 storeyed gabled porch adds to its charm. There is diagonal bracing in the porch and in the gable to the right of it. Inside there are moulded ceiling beams of *ca* 1500 and a little C17 panelling. Basically a house of medieval origin, the east wing and the porch were added *ca* 1500 and the west end was altered in C17. *Pevsner;* RCHM III.

**Michaelchurch Court, Michaelchurch Escley.** High on the hills of the Herefordshire/Monmouthshire border. The house is "L"-shaped. The older C17 part is timber-framed on a stone ground floor. There are 3 gables with narrow uprights and concave-sided lozenges. Old photographs reveal that there was more of the building, this side, until *ca* 1900. The porch, which has the date 1602, contains charming plaster decoration of trails of leaf and berry. The other half of the house is a surprise. It is ambitious and neo-Tudor of *ca* 1870 by an unknown architect. A few years ago, there were plans to demolish this wing. The Trafford family, here since C19, sold the house to Dr Macpherson *ca* 1970. TRAFFORD *of Hill Court*/LG1972; *Pevsner; Robinson;* RCHM.

**Moccas Court, Moccas.** Rather like a town house of considerable sophistication set down in a very beautiful and very remote country park. Anthony Keck was the architect who erected the house 1775–81. It is red brick, of 7 by 5 bays and has 2½ storeys. A 1 storeyed bow, probably later, contains the entrance. There is a Venetian window above. On the river front (it is close to the Wye) a wider bow. Sparing decoration within, but there is a very lovely flying staircase under an oval dome. The

*Monnington Court*

*Moccas Court*

best room is on the river front. It has Pompeian decoration with papered and panelled walls. And there are some very fine chimneypieces as well. The grounds are by Capability Brown, with lodges by Nash. Very large stable-block. The house was the seat of the now-extinct Cornewall Bts, but it was mostly let *post* 1915 and all the contents were dispersed in late 1940s. After the Cornewalls came the Chester-Masters who have opened up many of the dummy windows in the house. CORNEWALL, Bt/PB1959; CHESTER-MASTER *of The Abbey formerly of Knole Park*/LG1965; *Pevsner; Colvin; Robinson*; Stroud, *Capability Brown*; Stroud, *Humphry Repton*; Summerson, *John Nash*; CL18, 25 Nov 1976.

**Monnington Court, Monnington-on-Wye.** House and church make a charming picture. A long somewhat irregular house of *ca* 1600. Part of a screen inside is dated 1656 and the hall ceiling is preserved. Near the house is the famous Monnington Walk laid out by a former owner in C17; it is a mile-long walk to Brobury Scar. The present owner Mr John Bulmer, of the cider family, maintains one of two studs for Morgan Horses here. *Robinson.*

*The Moor*

**Moor (The), Clifford.** A Gothic cloak was flung over an older house in late 1820s. The result was an asymmetrical building topped off by numerous pinnacles. On one side there was a long verandah. In the park there is a water tower of about the same date as well as three obelisks on a hillside. It was all part of the same treatment by George Phillips Manners, City Architect of Bath. The Penoyres had recently lived in that city. The estate has been in the ownership of the family since C16; it remains so today, but the house was pulled down 1952. It was mostly let *post* 1880. PENOYRE/LG1972; *Robinson.*

**Moor Court, Pembridge.** A long avenue of elm trees approaches the site of this house, which was demolished in 1950s. This avenue is

*Moor Court*

said to be one of 4 avenues which formerly converged on the house and there are other remains of what might have been a C17 Dutch-style garden. The house itself is said to have been of C17 origin, but it was heavily rebuilt by James Davies (owner of Ridgebourne (*qv*) and Bronllys Castle, Breconshire) who bought it in the year of Waterloo. Its main elevation consisted of 2 projecting gabled wings standing on either side of a wide 1 storey bow. On the entrance front there was a campanile. The Stead family owned the estate until 1683 when it passed to the James family; from them it was purchased by Davies. Charles A. Benn succeeded the Davies family who had left by the end of World War I. DAVIES/LG1921; VSA; *Robinson*.

*The Mynde*

*Moreton Court*

**Moreton Court, Moreton-on-Lugg.** Kelly states that the large house "in the Elizabethan style" was built by Thomas Evans to the designs of J. H. Knight of Cheltenham. Knight rebuilt the church as well. The house was "L"-shaped, with a tower in the angle, and of stone. It had rows of monotonous mullion-type windows and the tower and parapet sprouted urns of varied shapes and sizes. The house was put up in 1860s and pulled down, like so many other seats, in 1950s. It was an old site and Powell, Keysall and Gwinnett were some of the families who occupied earlier houses. By the late 1920s, Moreton was in the possession of Evans's grandson, Rev Henry Wilmot Hill; the last owner was J. E. Counsell. EVANS/LG1900; COUNSELL/LG1952; *Kelly's Directory* (1929); *Robinson*.

**Mynde (The), Much Dewchurch.** At first sight, a large and plain C18 building; but it hides earlier work as well. The entrance front is rendered and is of 9 bays and 2½ storeys. The porch of 2 pairs of Tuscan columns is early C19. The house is in the shape of a huge "U"—the long arms of which represent the earliest part of the house. It was begun late in C15 or early in C16 with a central hall and cross-wings at the north and south ends. These cross wings were extended in C16 and C17—in the latter century for the purpose of stabling. The greatest change which brought about the present appearance of the structure came in the early Georgian period—probably *ca* 1725. At that time the north, south and east sides of the house assumed new faces; and the interior was given the finest room of its date in the county. A huge room about 60 ft long and 30 ft high, representing the central 5 bays of the ground and 1st floor storeys, is filled with giant Corinthian pilasters and between them large panels exhibiting a rich display of plasterwork showing still-lifes of music, sculpture, painting and architecture. There are splendid doorcases and medallions with busts in profile of King Egbert, King Alfred, William the Conqueror, Edward III and Henry V. Above

the chimneypiece there is a large military trophy. The ceiling is decorated too with a roundel and allegorical figures on clouds. A largish room behind the hall boasts Jacobean chimneypieces at both its north-east and south-east corners. These are unlike each other, but present the usual motifs of their date—2 tiers of blank arches. More work of the date of the hall is found in a room north-west of it; and there is a staircase of slender twisted balusters and carved tread-ends. The grounds were laid out 1798 for Thomas Symons by John Wheeler. The Pyes were the original family here and they reigned for nearly 300 years. They received a Baronetcy and a Jacobite Peerage as Baron Kilpeck. The heiress of the Pyes carried it to the Gorges family and then it was sold in mid-C18 to Richard Symons. From him it descended through female lines to families who immediately adopted the surname of Symons and Mr T. R. Symons still owned the house in C20. At the end of the 1920s Rear-Adm Hon A. L. O. Forbes-Sempill was living in the house; in more recent years it was bought by Mr W. A. Twiston Davies. PYE, Bt, *of Hone*/EDB; GORGES *formerly of Wraxall*/LG1965; SYMONS/LG1921; FORBES-SEMPILL, *sub* SEMPILL, B/PB; TWISTON DAVIES/LG1972; *Colvin*; *Pevsner*; *Robinson*: RCHM I.

*The Mynde: hall*

*Newcourt*

**Newcourt, Lugwardine.** Basically a Georgian house, Gothicized 1808–10 by H. H. Seward for Rev J. Lilly. It presents a picture of a small castle. 5 bays with recessed centre, porch, and turrets—all castellated. In the entrance hall there is a fine coved Rococo plaster ceiling of *ca* 1750. Until 1976 the seat of the Griffiths Burdon family. Now an antique shop. GRIFFITHS BURDON/LG 1972; *Colvin*; *Pevsner*; *Robinson*.

**Newport House, Almeley.** Built 1774, it is of 7 bays and 2 storeys with a pediment. Links to 2 bay pavilions either side and aligned on it; these were built later. The existing house replaced an important C16 and C17 structure which was of stone and half timber. This was the seat of the Pember family who sold it to 1st Lord Foley 1712. From the Foleys the house passed to the Onslows who, in turn, sold it to James Watt Gibson-Watt (grandson of James Watt, the great engineer) 1863. The house, now owned by the Herefordshire County Council, is let to the Latvian Home. FOLEY, B/PB; ONSLOW, ONSLOW, E/PB; GIBSON-WATT *of Doldowlod*/LG 1969; *Robinson*.

**Nun Upton, Little Hereford.** For many years almost derelict after long use as a farmhouse. Very picturesque with big shaped gables and a centre of black and white with a gabled porch. Notable chimney-stacks—one star-shaped, the other with brick rustication. They are *ca* 1700. Much of the house is Jacobean. The house is now owned by Lt-Col H. M. Vere Nicoll. VERE NICOLL/LG 1969; *Pevsner*; RCHM.

*Newport House: entrance front*

*Newport House: garden front*

*Nun Upton before restoration*

*Old Colwall*

*Ocle Court*

**Ocle Court, Ocle Pychard.** The park falls sharply away from the 7 bay, 2 storey block which fronts an older house. This Classical front is probably late-Georgian or even early Victorian. But the rambling structure behind contains a south-east wing which is timber-framed and which can be dated *ca* 1600. Pye, Chamberlain, Walwyn and Brett were some of the families who owned the house before the advent of the Postlethwaites who added the C19 block. Later in C19 it belonged to the Heywoods and, in 1901, came the Cresswells who still own it today. There is C20 internal alteration. WALWYN *formerly of Longford*/LG 1972; CRESSWELL/LG 1937; HEYWOOD/WCF; RCHM II; *Robinson*.

**Old Colwall, Colwall.** Basically early C18 and of 6 bays and 3 storeys; but a later addition has been added to the left-hand side of the main block. A late C18 addition to the right has been demolished recently. The interior decoration belongs mainly to late C18, though the staircase with twisted balusters is original.

*Old Court*

*Pembridge Castle*

*Pencombe Hall*

*Pengethley*

The Brydges family built the house, but *ca* 1800 it was sold to the Martins. Earlier this century it belonged to A. C. Raynor-Wood; it is now the property of Major David Roberts. *Pevsner*; *Robinson*; RCHM II.

**Old Court, Whitchurch.** Built by the Powells in C16 it was altered and enlarged by their descendants, the Gwillims in C17. The entrance is "E"-shaped and long and low. It is of stone with mullioned windows. Evidence of C17 shows more clearly to the garden. An important link with Canada is found here as a Gwillim heiress married Lt-Gen John Graves Simcoe, later Governor of Upper Canada, and his family still owned the property in 1880s. *Pevsner*; *Robinson*; RCHM.

**Pembridge Castle, Welsh Newton.** A small border castle of considerable charm. It is well-preserved and its moat survives in part. The position commands wide-reaching views. Basically C13, the round tower in the north-west corner appears to be the oldest part of the building—it could be pre-1200. The hall is C17, but its outer wall is part of C13 curtain wall. Also C13 is the great gatehouse with its semi-circular towers. Parts of the castle are not well-preserved, while other parts have been the subject of sensitive C20 restoration. The chapel is the most rewarding apartment. It is a C16 building and its tunnel-vaulted undercroft is original, but its furnishings are all brought in. It has a screen from Essex and heraldic stained glass of C17. There are brasses of a knight and a bishop, but it is not known whence they came. At an earlier period it belonged to Sir Walter Pye and it suffered severely during the Civil Wars. A member of the Scudamore family was occupying it 1715 and in C19 it was bought by Sir Joseph Bailey, 2nd Bt (later 1st Lord Glanusk). The castle now belongs to Mr R. A. Cooke. PYE, Bt, *of Hone*/EDB; SCUDAMORE, SCUDAMORE, V/DEP; BAILEY, GLANUSK, B/PB; *Pevsner*; *Robinson*; RCHM I.

**Pencombe Hall, Pencombe.** Built as a very grand rectory, Pencombe is Jacobean in style and its date is perhaps of the 1840s. There are plenty of shaped gables with finials. Latterly owned by the Annesleys, it now belongs to Mr Grayston Burgess. ANNESLEY, ANNESLEY, E/PB.

**Pengethley, Sellack.** Memorials to the Powell and Williams Bts, who owned the Elizabethan house on the site of the present one, fill Sellack Church. One assumes the older building was one of size and considerable importance. On the death of Sir John Williams, 2nd Bt, 1723, the estate passed to his younger daughter who married Thomas Symonds. Descendants of the marriage held Pengethley until well into C20. *Ca* 1826 a new house replaced the older building. It is modest in size and possesses no really notable architectural quality. 3 widely-spaced bays form the entrance front and there is a canted bay around the corner. One room contains good late-Georgian decoration. Pengethley is now an hotel. SYMONDS/LG1937; *Robinson*.

**Pennoxstone Court, King's Caple.** Part C18 and part Victorian, Pennoxstone forms a rambling building of no special architectural distinction. It is agreeable enough, though, and commands a wide prospect. At one time it belonged to John Roberts of the Inner Temple; later it became the property of Sir Edward Cockburn, 8th Bt, and now belongs to Capt J. F. Cockburn. COCKBURN, Bt/PB; *Robinson.*

**Perrystone Court, Foy.** A dull C18 house was transformed into an asymmetrical Elizabethan-style house in 1860s. It was of stone. George Clive, 3rd son of Edward Bolton Clive of Whitfield (*qv*), bought the estate from Col Morgan Clifford 1865. Nearly a hundred years later, in Oct 1959, the house was totally destroyed by a fire in which Lt-Gen Sir Sidney Clive perished. Another house has been built on the site. The Clive-Ponsonby-Fanes of Brympton D'Evercy, Somerset, are a cadet branch of the Clives of Perrystone. CLIFFORD/LGI1879; CLIVE/LGI1965; VSA; *Robinson.*

**Pontrilas Court, Pontrilas.** Gabled stone house of *ca* 1630 with a gabled porch. Round-headed entrance arch. Inside, one room has a plaster ceiling with a geometrical pattern; another plaster ceiling in a room at the back. The house was a seat of the Baskerville family and passed to the families of Jackson and Shiffner. Sir George Shiffner, 3rd Bt, sold it about the time of Waterloo. He was succeeded by a Dr Trenchard until 1840 when it was purchased by Col Scudamore. In the 1870s it

*Perrystone Court, Oct 1959*

served as an inn. D. A. Keown-Boyd now owns Pontrilas. There is a handsome, square, timber-framed dovecote in the grounds, which contain trees planted by George Bentham when he leased the house in mid-C19. SHIFFNER, Bt/PB; LUCAS-SCUDAMORE *of*

Kentchurch/LGI1972; KEOWN-BOYD/LGI886; *Pevsner*; RCHM II; *Robinson.*

**Poston House, Vowchurch.** A casino with ravishing views down the Golden Valley. Built by Sir Edward Boughton, 6th Bt, *ca* 1775 to the

*Pontrilas Court*

designs of Sir William Chambers, it consists of a domed circular room which retains delicate stucco decoration and chimneypiece. There is a small entrance hall as well. Outside, the noble Doric portico remains, but the Georgian temple is, alas, sandwiched between unfortunate Victorian wings of *ca* 1882. Thus, the former shooting-box became a seat. E. L. G. Robinson inherited the place in late C19 and it remained in that family until *ca* 1960— following the death of R. S. Robinson (who married the niece of "Lewis Carroll"). ROUSE BOUGHTON, Bt/PB1963; ROBINSON/LG1972; *Colvin*; *Pevsner*; *Robinson*; Harris, *William Chambers* (1970); *Trans. Woolhope Naturalists' Field Club* (1933, XXIX).

**Pudleston Court, Pudleston.** The house of the Duppa family, who owned the estate until 1846, disappeared long ago and in its place there now lies a simple farmhouse. Elias Chadwick (2nd son of Elias Chadwick of Swinton Hall, Lancs) erected the present large house in the late 1840s and it was still under construction 1852. It is an irregular and castellated building, with towers, bays and a porte-cochère. There are very ambitious east entrance gates with battlements and turreted lodges. The Chadwicks remained here until *ca* 1900; before World War II it was in the ownership of George Malcolm Kent; it is now a boys' school. VSA; CHADWICK/WCF; *Pevsner*; *Robinson*.

**Putley Court, Putley.** Dated 1712, and a very handsome house. Of 5 bays and 3 storeys and a doorway with a curly segmental pediment. There is a parapet and a lower hipped roof and a pretty glazed lantern on top. There is an early C18 summer house with 4 Tuscan columns as well. Formerly the seat of the Riley family, Putley was more recently the property of Norman H. Todd. RILEY *of Brearley House and Putley Court*/LG1921; *Pevsner*; RCHM II.

**Ridgebourne, Kington.** Edmund Cheese had additions made to a half-timbered farmhouse 1806 by John Millward of Hay-on-Wye. This resulted in the present early C19 appearance of the house. It is of 2 storeys with projecting gabled wings. Another gable with a lunette window appears to the west. Minor additions *ca* 1840 and later in C19. Inside there is a screen of marbled columns in the drawing-room and a library with fitted bookcases incorporating desks. Small contemporary stable-block. From the Cheeses the house eventually passed to James Davies, solicitor, banker and entrepreneur (he was involved in Shelley's abortive attempt to rent Nantgwyllt, Powys 1812). Davies's niece married William Banks and that family still owns the house today. William Hartland Banks (1867–1930) built a second house on the estate, Hergest Croft, to the designs of J. Hampden Pratt, 1896. This is of little merit, but it forms the centre of an extensive contemporary garden which contains one of the finest and most thriving collections of exotic trees in the British Isles. Ridgebourne and Hergest Croft now belong to Mr R. A. Banks and his elder son Mr W. L. Banks, who is chairman of the UK ICOMOS Historic Gardens Committee. BANKS/WCF; CL 27 Feb 1975; *Colvin*; Parry, *History of Kington* (1843).

*Poston House: entrance front*

*Poston House: garden front*

*Pudleston Court*

*Putley Court*

*Hergest Croft*

*Ridgebourne*

**Rodd (The), Rodd.** Built by the Rodd family *ca* 1625, it is a stone house with a brick front. "L"-shaped, the right-hand wing projects well forward. There are gables, and mullioned and transomed wooden windows. 3 storeyed gabled porch. The fine stucco ceiling of the 1st floor room in the right-hand wing makes it the best interior in the house. There are notable overmantels in this and other rooms. The staircase has flat balusters. The library was added 1953. By C19 Rodd had become a farmhouse, but still remained in the possession of descendants of the builder. Lt-Col Gilbert Drage resided in the house, then called Rodd Court, 1929; but, in the late 1930s, 1st Lord Rennell, descended from a collateral branch of Rodds, purchased the property. His 3rd son, Peter Rodd (thought to be the model for Evelyn Waugh's "Basil Seal"), was married to Nancy Mitford, the novelist. RODD, RENNELL, B/PB; *Pevsner*; *Robinson*; RCHM.

**Rotherwas, Dinedor.** Stylistically attributed to James Gibbs, the long brick house was built 1732 by Charles Bodenham. It was of 11 bays and 2 storeys, but raised high by a deep basement. The centre 3 bays formed a breakfront which was crowned by a pediment.

*The Rodd*

*Rotherwas*

A great doorcase, with typical Gibbs surround, formed the entrance at piano nobile level. There was a parapet and 8 evenly spaced chimney-stacks. An earlier house formed part of a side wing. This contained panelling and a chimneypiece dated 1611—all of which are now at Amherst College, Massachusetts. The break-up of Rotherwas began 1912 when the panelling, etc, was removed but the house remained, bereft of much of its fine interior,

until 1925 when it was finally demolished. There was even a threat to the nearby Rotherwas Chapel (now a property of Dept of Environment) and its tombs of the Bodenhams. BODENHAM/LGI 1879; *Robinson.*

**Rowden Abbey, Bromyard.** The important late C16 overmantels, now at Canon Frome Court, came from the old house on this site,

which was demolished at the end of C18. The present building, half-timbered and situated at the side of a small valley, dates from 1881. The Hopton family had inherited the old house and they disposed of the estate to the Barnebys of nearby Bredenbury Court (*qv*) 1872. The Victorian replacement was the seat of Col Lewis Birch 1929 and more recently belonged to the Gibbs family. Mr G. Preece is the present owner. HOPTON *of Canon*

*Rudhall*

*Frome*/LG1937; BARNEBY *of Llanerch-y-Coed formerly of Brockhampton*/LG1972; *Robinson*.

**Rudhall, Brampton Abbots.** A complex house with a core of C14 or possibly even earlier. Of the C14 are parts of the original hall-roof and the roof of a cross-wing; both have cusped wind-braces. The most spectacular parts of the building belong to the C16. The west wing has narrowly-set uprights, a deep coving with square panelling and 3 bays above flanked by niches; it has 3 gables too. On its south side, though, this wing presents a Georgian facade with sash windows. The main entrance to the house is by a Jacobean stone 2 storey frontispiece which has coupled Tuscan columns below and thinner coupled columns above. A large Georgian Venetian window

appears to the right of it. This wing, like the west one, has 3 gables and they have decorated bargeboards which look early C16. Inside, the hall has ceiling beams with pendants. They belong to tie-beams with kingposts inserted in C16 below the C14 roof. There is one very attractive chimneypiece of early C17 in a 1st-floor room. It has 2 crisply carved tiers of blank arches. The house is said to have been built for the Rudhall family, but it passed in mid-C17 to the Westphalings who held it until 1830 when it was sold to Alexander Baring, later 1st Lord Ashburton. Earlier this century H. H. Child was living in the house, but Rudhall's most recent owner was Sir Peter Scarlett, the diplomatist, who sold it 1978. BARING, ASHBURTON, B/PB; SCARLETT/LG1969; *Pevsner*; *Robinson*; RCHM II.

**Saltmarshe Castle, Bromyard.** William Higginson built this huge Victorian castle 1840 to the designs of an unknown architect. It was in decorated Gothic style, totally asymmetrical, and decidedly out to impress. The various ranges were dominated by a low tower. Long battlemented walls stretched out into the park in every direction. Inside there were ponderous wooden ceilings in most rooms—the exception being in the great dining-room where there was a high-vaulted one. This room, with its attractive contemporary wallpaper, was the most successful apartment in the house. Saltmarshe was inherited by Higginson's great-nephew, Edmund Barneby, and it continued in that family until demolition 1955. BARNEBY *of Saltmarshe Castle*/LG1952; *Robinson*.

*Saltmarshe Castle*

*Saltmarshe: dining room (formerly picture gallery)*

*Sarnesfield Court*

**Sarnesfield Court, Sarnesfield.** Of brick, 9 bays and 2 storeys with a pediment surmounting the centre 3 bay breakfront. Identical garden front. Dated 1732, but probably incorporating a much older building—parts of which survived in a side wing. The inside was plain—indeed it was enlivened only by the great collection of Chinese armorial porcelain formed by the genealogist and York Herald, G. W. Marshall, who bought the house 1891. This collection was dispersed Oct 1978. Before the Marshalls' ownership, the house had been in the possession of the Monington, Webbe, Weston and Salvin families. Sarnesfield was demolished 1955. SALVIN *of Sutton Place*/LGI898; MARSHALL/LGI937; *Robinson*.

*Sellarsbrooke*

**Sellarsbrooke, Ganarew.** The house appears to be an early c19 refronting of an older building. It is of 5 bays and 2 storeys, and, until a few years ago, this facade showed a 3 bay

pediment on giant pilasters. The pilasters remain, but now all is dwarfed by a huge Ionic portico built *ca* 1970. The interior shows late-c18 chimneypieces and plasterwork. The Marriott family was here in c19; earlier this century the house was owned by Mrs Arthur Woodbyne Parish (*d* 1938). It now belongs to the Linleys. PARISH/LGI969; *Pevsner*; *Robinson*.

**Shobdon Court, Shobdon.** As it stood on its long arcaded terrace until demolition 1933, Shobdon was a largely rebuilt house after a serious fire in mid-c19. At that time, the roofline gained a parapet and a cupola was removed. It was basically a building of Queen Anne's day. Sir James Bateman, sometime Lord Mayor of London, acquired the estate 1705 and the house was built for him in the style of Clarendon House, Piccadilly. Both entrance and garden fronts were similar—9 bays with 2 bay corner projecting wings. The pediments had oval windows and a cartouche with the Bateman arms. Pronounced quoins and heavy dentil cornice. The 11 bay side elevations had segmental pediments over the 3 central bays which were recessed. There was a 2 storey hall with coved ceiling and a gallery on columns—all architectural detail being heavily accentuated. It is known that Henry Flitcroft made internal alterations for 2nd Viscount Bateman 1746 and Edward Haycock made alterations to the house for William Hanbury, later 1st Lord Bateman, 1830–35 with the advice of Sir Jeffry Wyatville. The 1st Viscount Bateman (created 1725) was the son of the Lord Mayor, but the Viscountcy became

*Shobdon Court*

extinct on the death of 2nd Viscount 1802. The estates passed to the Hanburys who received the Barony of Bateman 1837. On the death of the 3rd Baron, 1931, the peerage and the house died with him. An enterprising demolition man made the old service quarters into a handsome self-contained house—with fittings from its vanished parent. This has belonged to the James family and is now the home of Lt-Col Uvedale Corbett. The large C18 stables survive and close by is the celebrated Gothick Shobdon Church (1750s) still in search of an author. BATEMAN, BATEMAN, V/DEP; BATEMAN-HANBURY, BATEMAN, B/PB1931; *Colvin; Pevsner; Robinson;* Lees-Milne, *English Country Houses: Baroque* (1970); Linstrum, *Sir Jeffry Wyatville* (1972); CL 10 Nov 1906; RCHM III; *Vitruvius Britannicus.*

*Stapleton Castle*

**Stapleton Castle, Stapleton.** On the summit of a hill, which appears to have been cut to form a motte, lie the ruins of a C17 stone-built house of 2 storeys. It was still occupied as a farmhouse as late as *ca* 1870 and the Galliers family (ancestors of the novelist Anthony Powell) were tenants there at one time. The Harleys inherited the C17 house 1706, but the original castle belonged to the powerful border families of Say, Mortimer and Cornwall. GALLIERS, *sub* POWELL *of The Chantry*/LG1965. *Pevsner; Robinson;* RCHM III.

**Staunton Park, Staunton-on-Arrow.** By a large lake and late-Georgian in appearance, the house was, in fact, built 1843 by James King to the designs of the sometime County Surveyor, John Gray, of Hampton, nr Leominster. Of brick, with stone dressings, it was of 7 bays and 2 storeys. The trowel used in laying the foundation-stone of the house is still in existence with the explanation of its use clearly recorded on it. There was an older house on the site—probably dating from C18 when the Kings purchased the property. The Parr family (of Parr's Bank) bought Staunton *ante* 1900; but after they sold it 1924, it was demolished. KING-KING/LG1972; PARR *of Mill House*/LG1972; *Colvin; Robinson.*

**Stockton Bury, Kimbolton.** The C18 pedimented, 4 bay brick house was of considerable elegance in spite of its modest size. It was demolished 1960s, but a circular stone dovecote, possibly medieval, survives. The house, on an older site, was probably built by the Harley family, from whom it passed to the Lords Rodney. HARLEY, OXFORD, E/DEP; RODNEY, RODNEY, B/PB; RCHM III; *Pevsner; Robinson.*

**Stoke Edith Park, Stoke Edith.** "Invented by Mr Davies a carpenter"—these words are handwritten on the plate depicting Stoke in the copy of *Vitruvius Britannicus* (1715) belonging to Uvedale Price (for whom Foxley (*qv*) was built—and the grandfather of the famous Sir Uvedale Price). But Colen Campbell, author of *Vitruvius*, states that the house was designed by Speaker Paul Foley, owner of the estate. Perhaps one can assume from Price's handwritten comment that Davies was the unknown builder-carpenter mainly responsible for the design of this beautiful building. Celia Fiennes records progress of Stoke Edith in her *Journeys* and it was certainly being built 1698. A stately house of red brick with a mansard roof, the north front had a stone centrepiece with 4 Corinthian pilasters supporting a pediment.

*Stockton Bury*

*Staunton Park*

*Stoke Edith Park*

*Stoke Edith: saloon*

*Stoke Edith: hall*

*Stoke Edith: garden front—the rebuilt shell prior to demolition*

*Stoke Edith: lodge by Wilkins*

The saloon was decorated in the Adam manner 1771 and C. T. Tatham designed the drawing-room, park gate and cottage *ca* 1800. William Wilkins added lodges at the Hereford and Ledbury entrances 1792. Of the contents of the house, the most notable were probably the contemporary needlework hangings which covered the walls of the Green Velvet Room. These depict an elaborate Dutch-type garden and are supposedly the work of the wives of Thomas Foley, the Speaker's son. They now hang at Montacute, Somerset. The gardens included a great geometrical parterre by Nesfield which was laid out 1854. The year 1927 saw a tragic end to this great house when a fire gutted the entire building. Later on, the shell was built up as it was the intention to restore and live in it once again. But plans were abandoned in 1950s and the shell was taken down at that time. The early C18 stables which adjoined the house still survive. Mr A. T. Foley is the present owner of the estate. FOLEY, *sub* FOLEY, B/PB; VSA; Celia Fiennes, *Journeys* (1947); CL 6 June 1903, 25 Sept 1909 & 24 Dec 1927; *Colvin; Connoisseur* (1907); Latham *In English Homes* III (1909); *Neale* II; RCHM II; *Robinson; Vitruvius Britannicus* I (1715).

**Street Court, Kingsland.** Brick with stone dressings, Street is a C19 house incorporating an earlier one. The estate has had many owners. The Sanders family were here in mid-C19; more recently, John Paton owned it and it was occupied by Major C. T. Jones, MFH. Now owned by Mrs J. Williams who runs it as a community centre. An earlier stable-block survives. SANDERS/LG 1921; *Robinson*.

*Stoke Edith: Nesfield's parterre of 1854*

Its great glory was the interior decoration by Sir James Thornhill. He painted the upper part of the 2 storey hall with mythological figures and it was treated as an open pavilion.

The ceiling of the hall, as well as the ceiling and walls of the staircase, were also by Thornhill. Isaac Bayly painted grotesque rocky landscapes in the lower panels of the hall 1705.

*Street Court*

*Sufton Court*

*Sugwas Court*

*Tedstone Court*

**Sufton Court, Mordiford.** Of Bath stone standing high in a beautiful park by Repton, this seat of the Hereford family is of 5 bays and 2¹/₂ storeys. There is a 1 bay pediment, a Venetian window on the 1st floor and a porch of 4 attached unfluted Ionic columns with a pediment. Inside, there are 2 handsome chimneypieces and a few good doorcases. Family tradition asserts that James Wyatt was the architect of the house (he was engaged on alterations to Hereford Cathedral in 1780s and 1790s), but no documentary evidence to support this is known. Herefords have held the estate since C13 and their original house, Old Sufton, stands over half-a-mile away. It appears to be a half-timbered building of ancient date, but with the civilized hand of the C18 laid upon it. Rather curiously, a C13 coffin-lid with an incised cross forms part of a chimneystack. Nearby is a fat, circular C18 dovecote with lantern. HEREFORD/LG1952; RCHM; *Pevsner*; *Robinson*; Stroud, *Humphry Repton*.

*Old Sufton*

**Sugwas Court, Stretton Sugwas.** The house stands on the foundation of a house of the Bishops of Hereford. There is a remaining Norman archway, now in the stables, which belongs to the wall of a range whose front had traceried windows. The present building is brick and of 5 bays and 2 storeys and is dated 1792. There are broad segment-headed windows and a round-arched centre one. The Ingham family lived here for much of C19 and the early C20; but it was rented by Capt Walter Clarkson Mumford *ca* 1940—his widow lives at Sugwas now. INGHAM/LG1937; *Pevsner*.

**Tedstone Court, Tedstone Delamere.** On a lofty site commanding magnificent views in all directions, the house is an irregular late-Georgian building of considerable size. It is of stone and 3 storeys. The Bellvilles have been seated here since 1909; formerly owned by the Wights. BELLVILLE/LG1965.

*Thinghill*

**Thinghill, Withington.** A house with a short life. In 1870s, Henry Higgins built this house, with its extraordinary frenzy of pointed windows, on a commanding site. It was asymmetrical and spectacular. Burges might have designed it. But, by mid-1920s, it had gone and only an entrance lodge and 2 lonely trees on the hill mark its place. Local gossip says that Higgins was determined to outbuild Moreton Court (*qv*) nearby. Terrys had been previous owners of the Thinghill estate, but they sold out, 1862, to John Morley, father-in-law of Henry Higgins. HIGGINS/WCF; *Robinson*.

*Titley Court*

*Titley: library*

**Titley Court, Titley.** The rambling Victorian exterior masks a much older building. There is a fine stucco ceiling of the later C17 and some Jacobean woodwork. The ceiling has panels enclosing wreaths. One overmantel, dated 1625, is from Upper Mowley, Staunton-on-Arrow. Titley has been the seat of the Greenly family since late C16. GREENLY/LG1972; *Pevsner*; RCHM III.

**Treago, St Weonards.** In a hollow a half-a-mile or so from the church. The Mynors family have been here since the early C15—one of the longest tenures in the county. Yet their house presents no evidence of any work earlier than the late C15. It is really a fortified house: square, of stone, with a tower at each corner and the internal courtyard has been roofed over to provide extra living space. But it still retains its deep well within the courtyard.

*Treago*

Repeated alterations were made in C17, C18 and in 1840. The Georgians put in the sash windows, but there are many Tudor-style windows of 1840 which are based on a mullioned window, near the south-east tower, which looks C16. The top storey of the entrance side is a dummy to match up with the height of the rest of the house. The porch leads into the former screens passage and the great hall which is now the kitchen. A staircase, seemingly of *ca* 1670, is at the end of the screens passage and there is a plaster ceiling of about the same date in the room west of the hall. Of the 4 towers, the south-east one is the most remarkable, as it has a projecting upper storey which was added *ca* 1770 for use as a smoking room. This room has delightful Gothick decoration. The house is now shared between Sir Humphrey Mynors, Bt, and his brother Prof Sir Roger Mynors. MYNORS, Bt/PB; *Pevsner*; *Robinson*; RCHM I.

*Trelough*

**Trelough, St Devereux.** The house, as it appears, is of the early C18 and of brick; 3 by 5 bays with a hipped roof. Originally Trelough was a moated house and was probably built for William Garnons. A north-west room inside is lined with original panelling and the ceiling has simple geometrical panels. A north-east room has some re-used C17 panelling The staircase has turned balusters and square newels. Annabella Garnons married Thomas Williams, Dean of Llandaff, and he sold it to E. B. Clive (*d* 1845) of Whitfield (*qv*). Rev R. S. Pelly lived at Trelough 1929; by 1937 it was the home of Col. H. C. B. Hopkinson. CLIVE *of Whitfield*/ LG1965: HOPKINSON *of Llanvihangel Court*/LG1952; *Pevsner*; *Robinson*; RCHM I.

**Tyberton Court, Tyberton.** The chief significance of Tyberton lies in its connexion with John Wood of Bath. He designed the interior of this uninspiring house for William Brydges 1728. Wood was only 24 at the time and it must, therefore, be considered as a major building of his early career. A plain brick structure of 7 by 5 bays, and of 3 storeys, it had shallow brick arched windows and a balustrade. It was enlivened only by its monumental Ionic doorcase. No visual record of the interior is known, but it is reported that there was a fine wooden staircase and noble drawing-room. Anne Brydges married 1808 Rev Daniel Henry Lee-Warner and that family retained it until *ca* 1950 when it was bought by Mr David Yeomans. The house was demolished 1952. A dull stable-block, also C18, survives. Wood tricked up Tyberton Church at the same time as the house and the splendid altar screen is certainly by him. LEE-WARNER/LG1972; *Robinson*.

*Tyberton Court: entrance front*

**Under Down, Ledbury.** One glimpses the elegant bows of this house from the Ledbury-Cheltenham road. It is a mid-Georgian house, grey, and of 2½ storeys—the bows rise the whole height of the building. It was part of the extensive property of the Skynners and descended to their heir T. W. Miles who held it in the 1880s. Spencer Henry Bickham lived here between the wars; it is now the home of the Hon Edward Biddulph. BIDDULPH, B/PB; *Pevsner*; *Robinson*.

**Urishay Castle, Peterchurch.** Delahays were here for at least 500 years, without ever aspiring to be more than quiet country gentlemen. Their house, high on a hill with far-reaching views, was essentially a fortified or semi-fortified border manor house. A building mostly of the C17 and C18 on a mound surrounded by a dry moat. Urishay was a building of stone, partly rendered, gabled too, but its rear elevation had a distinct castle-air with virtually window-less walls rising sheer from the moat. Inside, there were at least 2 rooms with notable C17 panelling. One of them was in the possession of Roberson's, a London firm that dealt in rooms from country houses in 1920s; it has been rumoured that this room lies in packing cases in the basement of the Museum of Chicago. From the latter half of C19, Urishay was used as a farmhouse. The whole estate was put up for sale 1913 and the house was even offered, at a later date, to former tenants for £500. But the offer was refused and the house dismantled 1921, so it now stands as a gaunt shell. A simple oblong chapel, probably Norman, forms a companion ruin. Restored 1914, it was closed again 1923. *Pevsner*; *Robinson*; RCHM I.

*Under Down*

*Tyberton: bow meeting, Sept 1863*

*Urishay Castle*

*Vennwood*

*The Weir*

*Wellbrook: hall*

**Vennwood, Sutton St Nicholas.** The Caroline appearance of the house is due to a rebuilding after a fire 1909. The architects of the restoration were Groome and Bettington of Hereford. Before that date the house had a late-Georgian aspect, but it is possible that the building was an early-Georgian structure which was revamped in the early years of C19. The Unetts built the house, but in the mid-C19 it was purchased by the Jenner family. They held it until 1968 when it was bought by Mr J. G. Wordsworth (great-great-grandson of the poet) who has made extensive internal alterations. UNETT *of Freen's Court*/LG1863; JENNER *of Wenvoe*/LG1952.

**Weir (The), Swainshill.** Originally an C18 house, The Weir was further enlarged at the end of that century and in C20. It is a plain building of 7 bays and 3 storeys, but its position, high above a bend in the Wye, is outstanding. A superb garden was created this century on the steep banks of the river; it is essentially a spring garden and has been presented to the National Trust with the house. In C19, The Weir was owned by the Griffiths family, but it became the property of the Parrs after they sold Staunton Park (*qv*) 1924. PARR *of Mill House*/LG1972; *Robinson*.

*Wellbrook Manor*

**Wellbrook Manor, Peterchurch.** One of the most notable examples in the county of a C14 hall-house. The solar wing remains, but the buttery has disappeared. Although it appears as a wholly stone building outside, it is all wood within. All trusses of the hall are still visible upstairs, although the hall has been divided horizontally. Cusped wind braces in the solar wing. A large stone chimneypiece with curious corbels with small panels of tracery remains in the actual solar. And there is an original stone chimneyshaft. The house belongs to Mr M. L. Smith. *Pevsner*; RCHM I.

*Wessington Court*

**Wessington Court, Woolhope.** Vaguely Tudor style house of the 1890s. It possibly incorporates part of an earlier Victorian house

*Weston Hall*

*Wharton Court*

built for H. W. Booth. The long low entrance hall and a grand oak staircase behind a screen at one end are the notable features of the interior. The building enjoys a spectacular site with far-reaching views to the Forest of Dean. Between the wars Wessington was owned by A. W. Barlow and now it is a school. The earliest house on the estate was known as Hill House and it was the home of Sir William Gregory (1624–96), Speaker and eminent judge. *Robinson.*

**Weston Hall, Weston-under-Penyard.** One of the best Jacobean houses in the county. Of red sandstone and moderate size, Weston has a nearly symmetrical facade. The central gabled porch is flanked by gables with canted bays beneath them. There are mullioned windows and fine c18 style gates to the road. The Nourse family built the house and it descended with them until c19 when it was sold to a Mr Partridge. The Aldrich-Blake family bought the house 1881 and are still here a century later. ALDRICH-BLAKE/ LG1965; *Pevsner*; *Robinson*; RCHM.

**Wharton Court, Leominster.** An unusual house with an unusual plan and one of the finest staircases in the county. Wharton is a tall house, of 3 bays, and of stone, said to have been built for Richard Whitehall in 1604; but the porch, of 2 storeys, was added 1659. It has attached columns and pilasters below flanking the round-headed openings and pilasters above flanking the window. There are mullioned and transomed windows as well as the occasional sash. Apart from the outstanding staircase with its tall finials and pineapple pendants, the interior has original fireplaces across the outer corners of the 4 rooms below. These connect with the prominent later chimneys at the corners of the roof. The north-west room has an early c18 cupboard of semi-circular form with a semi-domed head and the south rooms have some c18 panelling. On the 1st floor, some c17 panelling survives. The Whitehalls were succeeded by the Hakluyts (of which family Rev Richard Hakluyt, the geographer, was a member), but it soon became part of the Hampton Court estate (*qv*) and is now used as a farmhouse. *Pevsner*; *Robinson*: RCHM III.

*Whitbourne Court*

**Whitbourne Court, Whitbourne.** Formerly a residence of the Bishops of Hereford, Whitbourne is a brick building adjoining the church. Since late c19 it has been the seat of the Harington Bts (of the family who gave us the water closet). Sold 1979. HARINGTON, Bt/PB.

**Whitbourne Hall, Whitbourne.** A remarkable example of high-Victorian taste. A great classical building in a deep valley surrounded by mature trees of a large park with a lake. Seen from a distance, the

*Whitbourne Hall*

enormous Ionic portico, derived from the Erectheum on the Acropolis, gives one little indication of the date of the building. For it was designed as late as 1860–62, by the architect E. W. Elmslie, for E. B. Evans whose fortune largely stemmed from vinegar and wine. Of beautifully cut stone, the 6 column portico (based on the client's ideas) is flanked by 1 bay each side. Round the corner, there is a large bow and the skeleton of a huge conservatory possibly designed by R. L. Roumieu. All rooms open from a central hall approximately 50′ × 40′. This is top-lit and has a dazzling array of geometrical tiles of surprising gaiety. Dining-room, drawing-room (with the bow) are huge rooms, but their decoration and contents survive remarkably intact. Smaller rooms include the library and morning-room. A grand staircase rises from the great hall which has pillars and columns carrying a gallery. Evans was determined to set his extraordinary house in a setting worthy of it. His arboretum, fashionable at the time, now shows the full glory of his selective planting. Sold to the Whitbourne Hall Community Ltd 1980. EVANS/LG 1972; *Pevsner*; *Robinson*; CL 20, 27 March 1975.

**Whitehouse, Vowchurch.** In remote and beautiful country, the house is "L"-shaped; one wing is late C16, gabled and rendered, with mullioned and transomed windows; the other, *ca* 1812, is stone with 3 widely spaced bays, parapet, pilaster strips and pointed windows. Inside, in the early C19 range, there is a wide pointed arch in the hall—leading through to a simple staircase. At the head of the stairs there

*Whitehouse: staircase*

*Whitehouse in 1812*

is an arcade of pointed arches. Whitehouse was originally a half-timbered house of 5 gables. Because it lay neglected for many years at the end of C18 and beginning of C19—while family litigation raged—part of the house became unsafe and was taken down. It was replaced by the 1812 wing. Whitehouse has passed by descent since it was first built. From the Vaughans it went to the Howorths; in the early C19 it passed to the Wood family. Mrs L. F. P. Bletchly (*née* Wood) inherited the house 1980. WOOD/LG1952; RCHM II; *Robinson.*

**Whitfield, Allensmore.** The architect Philip Tilden tells in his autobiography how he was summoned to Whitfield to unpick the Georgian pearl from within the Victorian Gothic oyster. Enormous additions of *ca* 1850

*Whitfield* ca *1863*

had enveloped the mid-Georgian house which is a plain, but substantial, brick building of *ca* 1755–60 (with alterations which gave it its present appearance *ca* 1775–80.) Both south and north sides boast pairs of generous bows. The attic storey and rustication, on the north

*Whitehouse*

front, are reminders of Victorian alteration which had extended the house either side of the Georgian block. Tilden tidied up matters by removing the incongruous c19 wings and he created a new staircase at the same time (*ca* 1950). The library ceiling was copied from one of c17 at Urishay Castle. A particularly fine chimneypiece of *ca* 1755 stands in the drawing-room and a substantial stable-block of about the same date, with an arcade of blank arches, straddles the approach. Clives have been here since late c18. The present squire (whose mother is Lady Mary Clive, one of the literary family Pakenham) has created a long water aligned on the south front. CLIVE/LG1965; Tilden, *True Remembrances* (1954); *Pevsner*; *Robinson*.

**Whitney Court, Whitney.** A large, strung-out neo-Tudor house built to the designs of T. H. & A. M. Watson 1898–1902, by J. L. A. Hope. Long and low entrance hall. Magnificent situation above Brecon road. Kilvert visited older house. HOPE, *sub* LINLITHGOW, M/PB; *Pevsner*; *Kilvert's Diary*.

**Whittern (The), Lyonshall.** Richard Green, formerly of Yorkshire, built a large stone house in limp Tudor style 1879. The architect was Redmayne. "L"-shaped, with pointed gables and the main entrance in the angle, the house survived until the mid-1930s when it was demolished and replaced by the present Bognor Regis style structure which enjoys the old terrace. This belongs to Richard Green's grandson. An attractive, late-Victorian, stable-range survives. An older Whittern was the property of the Brydges, Gott and McMurdo families. GREEN/LG1952; *Robinson*.

*Whitwick Manor*

**Whitwick Manor, Yarkhill.** When the Oram family came here in the late 1950s, they undertook an extensive restoration of a building which for many years had been a secondary house on the Cowarne Court estate (*qv*). The entrance, with its broken segmental pediment, was put up at this time. The c18 facade, however, masks a building which is said to date from 1680. There has been extensive internal alteration including a new staircase. A large terrace composed of lawns and balustrades admirably sets off the house which enjoys wide-reaching views of Herefordshire hills from its elevated site. Always a manor, the house belonged to the Jaunceys from c17 to c19. F. H. Thomas owned Whitwick in Victorian times and he sold it to Hon Percy Wyndham (later of Clouds, Wilts, and father of the politician George Wyndham), who owned Cowarne Court as well. He, in turn, sold it to the Bournes. WYNDHAM, *sub* EGREMONT AND LECONFIELD, B/PB; BOURNE/WCF; *Robinson*.

*Whitfield*

*Whitney Court*

*The Whittern*

*Wigmore Hall*

**Wigmore Hall, Wigmore.** A very picturesque house of C16 and later, Wigmore is
black and white and has a gabled 2-storey
porch in the middle. The house, at one time,
bore a semi-Georgian guise, but the C18
alterations were unpicked and it returned to
something of its original appearance in C20.
The Davies family built and kept the place
until *ca* 1920. The late C18 squire of
Wigmore, Rt Hon Somerset Davies, MP,
bought Croft Castle (*qv*); his daughter and
heiress, Anne, married Rev James Kevill and
their son took the surname of Kevill-Davies.
Major H. C. Akroyd is recorded as owner
1929. LACON (*formerly* KEVILL-DAVIES)/
LG1972; RCHM; *Pevsner*; *Robinson*.

**Winsley House, Hope-under-Dinmore.**
Old seat of the Beringtons from C16 until mid-
C19 when it was sold first to the Kinnersley
family and then, in 1857, to John Arkwright of
Hampton Court. Since that time it has been a
farmhouse. A late-C18 provincial front of 5
bays and 2 storeys surmounted by a pediment
fronts a building which stretches back to at
least C14. There is a roof of the latter period
with cusped wind-braces. The early C16 is
represented by a timber-framed porch, with
contemporary inscription, at the back of the
building. BERINGTON *of Little Malvern
Court*/LG1969; ARKWRIGHT *of Kinsham
Court*/LG1965; *Pevsner*; *Robinson*; RCHM III.

**Wormbridge House, Wormbridge.** Seat of
the Clives before they moved to Whitfield
(*qv*). It was a large C17 building with an
unusual array of shaped gables. The centre
was probably earlier than the 3 bay ends.

Wormbridge was demolished 1798. CLIVE *of
Whitfield*/LG1965; *Robinson*.

*Wormbridge House*

*Wormsley Grange*

**Wormsley Grange, Wormsley.** The house
is of considerable importance as the birthplace
of the connoisseur Richard Payne Knight and
the horticulturist Thomas Andrew Knight.
The views from the windows would surely
have inspired even lesser men. Architecturally, however, Wormsley, which is early
Georgian, presents a grim appearance. It is of 5
bays and $2^1/_2$ storeys and of a dark and lifeless
stone. Inside, there is nothing of note. The
Victorians added bays on the garden front and
there are remarkable stone oasthouses nearby.
Wormsley has been used as a farmhouse for a
long period and it forms part of the Foxley
estate (*qv*). The Knights were probably
responsible for the planting of the estate. The
Rouse-Boughton-Knights owned the house
into late C19 and they were followed by the
Davenports of Foxley (*qv*), who own it still.
ROUSE-BOUGHTON-KNIGHT/LG1937;
DAVENPORT *of Foxley*/LG1952; *Pevsner*;
*Robinson*.

**Wyastone Leys, Ganarew.** In a beautiful
position, at a bend of the Wye, Wyastone Leys
is basically a late C18 house, rebuilt by John
Bannerman to the designs of William Burn
1861–62. It has Jacobean shaped gables and
turrets with ogee caps. There are quoins, too,
and a porch with Tuscan columns. The
original house was built by S. O. Atlay; his
successors, Mr Meek and Richard Blakemore,
made alterations before the Bannerman
ownership which began 1861. Owners this
century have included the families of Levett
and Waller. BLAKEMORE/LG1850/3;
BANNERMAN/LG1921; LEVETT *of Milford
Hall*/LG1937; WALLER *of Pen Park*/LG1969;
*Colvin*; *Pevsner*; *Robinson*.

*Wyastone Leys*

*Wythall*

**Wythall, Walford-on-Wye.** Wythall is an exceedingly picturesque black and white house of early C16 to early C17. The front has a variety of gables of different sizes at different heights. The building has a 3 storey part which contains the entrance, then a lower roof, another gable, and a final 2 storey wing—with yet another gable—as far end of the composition. All is reflected in a wide pool in front of the house. The rear elevation has been partly rendered and has C17 cross-windows. Seat of the Collins (who descend from John Kyrle, Pope's "Man of Ross") family since mid-C19. COLLINS/LG1952; *Pevsner*; RCHM.

**Yatton Court, Aymestrey.** An unusual Georgian stone house, ashlar-built and tall, of 4 by 3 bays. The shorter sides, which have tripartite, Venetian and tripartite-lunette windows, form the facades. More of these windows appear on a lower wing. No mouldings appear on the facades. John Woodhouse erected the present house, which replaced an old timber structure; and from him it descended to his great-granddaughter, wife of Rev. Thomas Taylor Lewis (1801–58), who made the local quarries famous through his geological discoveries here. T. B. Ward owned the house 1929, but it was let at that

*Yatton Court*

time to Mrs Hugh L. Heber-Percy. Now owned by Mrs Gardner. HEBER-PERCY, *sub* NORTHUMBERLAND, D/PB; *Pevsner*; *Robinson*.

# SHROPSHIRE

SHROPSHIRE, with its rich and varied landscape and splendid border country, has always been handsomely endowed with country houses. They remain thick on the ground to this day and most of them are well-preserved as Shropshire remains fashionable and many owners appear to have adequate funds with which to maintain them.

Two fortified houses head the lists of outstanding seats—Acton Burnell and Stokesay. Both date from the 13th century and are of the greatest national importance. Grand half-timbered houses reached their zenith in the 16th century and outstanding examples are Park Hall (*ca* 1570 and now gone) and Pitchford Hall (*ante* 1578). Plaish, Upton Cressett and Whitton are fine brick houses of the later 16th century.

The 17th century ranged from Ludstone Hall with its beautiful shaped gables to Longnor Hall built in 1670. Others on the roll-call of the 17th century are the large and lost Shavington (1685) and Halston Hall of 1690. Baroque building is well-represented in Shropshire. Cound Hall, Acton Round Hall and Aldenham Park are but three of the earlier examples and the first-mentioned undoubtedly influenced a rash of outstanding houses by Francis Smith—Davenport, Kinlet, Buntingsdale, Mawley—not all documented but his impress is unmistakable. Hardwick Hall is a later Baroque house with tremendous punch.

The Palladians came to the county with Linley Hall in the 1740s, but it is a fairly isolated case and George Steuart's great fanfare of Attingham Hall in the 1780s gave the county its greatest neo-Classical building—notable within as well as without—apart from its spindly portico. Mylne was busy in Shropshire and his work ranged from notable interiors at Halston to the unusual Woodhouse of 1773–4. The recently rediscovered Thomas Farnolls Pritchard of Shrewsbury was undoubtedly responsible for much building and alteration in the County. Hatton Grange is a complete work of his and he is known to have worked at Bitterley, Benthall and other houses.

Bonomi put up a tough house for a nabob in 1794: Longford Hall. James Wyatt created beautiful interiors at Badger and a good exterior at Aston. Lewis Wyatt gave Shropshire a late-Georgian masterpiece at Willey Hall. Haycock of Shrewsbury had a wide practice—his vanished Onslow (1820) to his extant Millichope (1840) show the extraordinary versatility of that architect. Nash came to the county and left the earliest Italianate villa, Cronkhill, and Longner too—light and pretty with a picturesque plan.

Castellated houses ranged from Capability Brown's vanished Tong Castle to Smalman's Quatford, via Sundorne and Rowton. Victorian prosperity added more notable seats—Shaw's Adcote and Preen, Harris's Stokesay and Bedstone, Nesfield's Cloverley and Aston Webb's Yeaton Peverey—to name a few.

Losses in the 20th century have been serious but their impact has not been as great as in neighbouring Herefordshire and a seemingly inexhaustible feast remains. Shropshire, like Devon, is a county where a few really long-established families remain in their original fastnesses—the Gatacres of Gatacre and the Plowdens of Plowden are notable examples of families that have the proud distinction of being descended in the male line from a medieval ancestor who took his surname from lands which they still hold.

# Principal Bibliography

CL     *Country Life*

*Colvin*     Colvin, H. M.: *A Biographical Dictionary of British Architects 1600–1840* (1978)

DEP     *Burke's Dormant and Extinct Peerages* (1883)

EDB     *Burke's Extinct and Dormant Baronetcies* (1841)

IFR     *Burke's Irish Family Records* (1976)

*Leach*     Leach, Francis: *The County Seats of Shropshire* (1891)

LG     *Burke's Landed Gentry*, 18 edns (1833/37–1972)

PB     *Burke's Peerage and Baronetage*, 105 edns (1826–1970)

*Pevsner*     Pevsner, Nikolaus: *Shropshire* (1958)

VSA     Burke, Sir Bernard: *A Visitation of Seats and Arms of the Noblemen and Gentlemen of Great Britain and Ireland*, 2 vols (1852–53); 2nd series, 2 vols (1854–55)

WCF     *Walford's County Families*

*Acton Burnell Hall*

**Acton Burnell Hall, Acton Burnell.** Robust stone house of 7 bays and 2 storeys with a prominent portico of 4 Ionic columns. All this is said to date *post* 1811. Canted bays on the north end of the house and giant pilasters along the east front. There was a fire at Acton Burnell 1914 and the interior is neo-Georgian after that date. The house has a long service wing terminated by a chapel designed by Charles Hansom 1846. C18 grotto in grounds, as well as the celebrated ruins of Acton Burnell Castle which are in reality the remains of a C14 fortified and embattled house. Acton Burnell Hall was the seat of the Smythe Bts. SMYTHE, Bt, *of Eshe Hall*/PB1940; *Leach*; *Pevsner*

**Acton Hall, Acton Scott.** This has been the seat of the Actons since it was built in late C16. Of brick with many pointed gables and mullioned and transomed windows. The drawing-room shows original plaster ceiling, while panelling dating from the building of the house remains in the drawing and Justice rooms. ACTON/LG1972; *Pevsner*.

**Acton Reynald, Shawbury.** At first glance large and Victorian; but, in fact, a building incorporating remains of a C17 house. The 2 storeyed east side has a series of bay windows—3 said to date from 1601 and the 4th from 1625. The portico on the south side, composed of Tuscan columns and elliptical arches, is of 1625 too. There was a rebuilding programme 1800, but the general Victorian going-over was probably the work of G. H. Birch, who is known to have altered the interior. Formerly the seat of the Corbet Bts, Acton Reynald has been a school for many years. CORBET, Bt/PB;*Leach*; *Pevsner*.

*Acton Round Hall*

**Acton Round Hall, Acton Round.** Handsome Baroque house of 1714 built for Sir Whitmore Acton, 4th Bt, and attributed to the Smiths of Warwick. It used to serve as a dower

*Acton Hall*

*Acton Reynald*

house to Aldenham Park (*qv*). A long spell of neglect from 1717 to 1918 served to preserve the orginal interior, which has restrained panelled rooms and a staircase with 3 twisted balusters to a tread. The exterior is of brick and of 7 bays. Blocked pilaster strips enliven the facade. The pediment on the entrance front has gone, but that on the garden front remains intact. The present owner, Mr H. L. Kennedy, has added whimsical follies in the park. There

is a Moorish temple and an obelisk, which is in fact a finial from vanished Tettenhall in Staffs. ACTON, B/PB; CL 2, 9 March 1978; Lees-Milne, *Country Houses: Baroque* (1970); Pevsner.

**Adcote, Little Ness.** Imaginative stone house designed by Norman Shaw and built 1879 for Mrs Rebecca Darby. Tall entrance front with Elizabethan straight gables, but

spectacular south side with the huge hall bay-window under a steep gable and supported by a giant buttress. The best apartment within is the hall itself, with great stone arches carrying the roof. At one end a minstrels' gallery over a screens passage and over the fireplace there is a hood 15ft high. Now the property of Adcote School. CL Oct 1970; *Pevsner*; Saint, *Richard Norman Shaw* (1978); CL 25 Dec 1909; Girouard, *Victorian Country House* (1979).

*Adcote*

*Adderley Hall: the Georgian house*

*Albrighton Hall*

**Albrighton Hall, Albrighton.** A Jacobean house much altered in C19. Wide entrance front with some original windows and prominent chimneys linked by arches. The Jacobean staircase survives. Seat of the Sparrow family from early C19 onwards. W. M. Sparrow (*d* 1881), great-grandson of the Wolverhampton colliery owner William Sparrow (the first person in South Staffs to erect a steam-engine for the purpose of raising water from his coal mines), left Albrighton to his nephew W. A. Brown, who took the surname of Sparrow. SPARROW/LGI952; *Leach.*

*Adderley: the Devey house*

**Albright Hussey, Battlefield.** Fragment of a larger house. It is timber-framed and brick with recorded dates of 1524 and 1601. Some details of the timber-framed portion are obviously later additions; the brick part probably represents the beginning of a rebuilding programme intended to sweep away the entire timber house. Boldly moulded ceiling beams in one room. The house has served as a farmhouse. *Pevsner.*

**Adderley Hall, Adderley.** The vast and rambling house built 1877–81 for H. R. Corbet was demolished 1955. Its architect was George Devey and Adderley was very typical of him. Battlemented, pointed gables, bay windows, a tower and much diaper brickwork were the ingredients. On the entrance side there was more regularity with a central projecting porch. Lifeless interiors. The Devey house replaced a Georgian house of 11 bays with a giant portico which was destroyed by fire. CORBET, Bt/PB.

**Aldenham Park, Morville.** Long the seat of the Actons, but now of Mr Christopher Thompson, Aldenham is a Baroque house of early C18 with a long facade of 11 bays—the only relieving accent being the raised 3 bay centre with round-headed windows. But at the rear of the house there is evidence of the rebuilding of 1691. The courtyard in the centre was converted to a hall 1830. Lord Acton, the great historian, added a large library wing which has been removed. Fine late C17 staircase with twisted balusters and notable doorcases on the 1st floor. Splendid wrought-iron gates in grounds. ACTON, B/PB; *Colvin;* CL 23, 30/6 & 7/7/77; *Pevsner.*

*Aldenham Park*

*Apley Castle*

**Apley Castle, Wellington.** The portico of this house which has been re-erected as an eye-catcher at Hodnet Hall (*qv*) is all that remains after demolition 1955. Apley was composed of 2 distinctive parts: a garden front of 7 bays, built 1791–4 to the designs of Joseph Bromfield (J. H. Haycock's estimate was rejected); and an entrance side composed of English, French and Italian motifs and dated 1856. St John Charlton was the c18 client; the Meyrick family were among the last owners. TAPPS-GERVIS-MEYRICK, Bt/PB; *Colvin*; *Pevsner*.

**Apley Park, Stockton.** Castellated Gothic house of considerable size and variety built for Thomas Whitmore 1811. The architect was probably John Webb; he is referred to in the diaries of Hon Anne Rushout as being employed as architect at Apley. The entrance front has a large 1 storeyed, 3 bay porch, with turrets at the ends of the facade and a castellated pediment. To the right of this is a huge Gothic window suggesting a chapel, but in reality masking the corner of a pre-1811 Georgian house. The south front, enjoying a fine view, has turrets at its ends as well as in the middle. Square entrance hall preceding a great staircase with iron handrail and beneath a

glazed octagonal lantern on plaster fan-vaulting. Gothic ribbing in all principal rooms and Gothic bookcases in library. Apley was the seat of the Fosters; Col A. W. Foster was succeeded by his nephew, Major-Gen E. H. Goulburn. It is let to a school. FOSTER/LG1937; GOULBURN/LG1972; VSA; Colvin; *Pevsner*; CL 25 May 1907; *Morris*; *Neale* (1826).

**Ashford Hall, Ashford Bowdler.** Plain but substantial brick house of 2½ storeys with a pediment. Originally 5 bays wide, Ashford is said to have been extended to its present 7 bay

*Ashford Hall*

width soon after building in 1760s. Good staircase with turned balusters—three to a tread—and fittings brought in from the demolished portions of Shobdon Court and Wigmore Hall, both in Herefordshire (*qv*). Seat of Russell family in late c19 and owned in this century by J. S. Edwards-Heathcote (*d* 1943). EDWARDS-HEATHCOTE *formerly of Langton Hall*/LG1952; RUSSELL/WCF; *Pevsner*.

**Astley House, Astley.** Charles Eade lived here 1937. A Georgian house which has been dressed up so it appears Grecian. Coupled pilasters and a porch of Greek Doric columns. Pediments at either end. One wing survives and it has a pediment a Greek Doric column in antis.

**Aston Hall, Aston Munslow.** Major J. I. Benson lived here 1937. Aston is a handsome house of *ca* 1600. "E"-shaped with star-shaped chimneys and approached through prominent c17 gatepiers with tall vases. Staircase with flat balusters.

**Aston Hall, Aston-on-Clun.** Substantial rendered building of 3 storeys and 5 bays with a Greek Doric porch. Probably datable to the 1820s. *Pevsner*.

**Aston Hall, Oswestry.** By James Wyatt for Rev J. R. Lloyd 1789–93. Restrained front of 7 bays and 2 storeys with 1 storeyed porch flanked by Ionic columns and pilasters. At the angles arched niches and blank ovals with garlands hanging over them. More niches and ovals on the south side where there are 3 widely spaced bays—those on the ground floor being tripartite with a blank segmental arch. The staircase rises in one flight and returns in two. Restrained Grecian stucco friezes in rooms flanking the hall. Brick chapel of 1742 with stone dressings. Aston was altered in c19. The entrance gate has Greek Doric columns. Seat of the Lloyd family whose recent squires have included Lt-Gen Sir Francis Lloyd. LLOYD/LG1952; *Colvin*; *Pevsner*.

*Apley Park*

*Astley House*

*Aston Hall, Aston Munslow*

*Aston Hall, Aston-on-Clun*

**Attingham Park, nr Shrewsbury.** Built by Noel Hill, 1st Lord Berwick 1784 to the designs of George Steuart, it was given to the National Trust by the 8th Lord Berwick and remains as the architect's chief work. Ashlar, 11 bays and 2¹/₂ storeys and fronted by a portico which looks as though it has outgrown itself. 4 bay pavilions are swept behind the main building but linked by long colonnades of Ionic columns. Nash added a picture gallery and staircase 1805. The original internal decoration is particularly attractive in the style of Wyatt. The furniture and many of the pictures were collected by the 3rd Baron when Minister at Naples. Of Steuart's rooms, the circular boudoir can be regarded as the most original and charming. Attingham, in its splendid Repton landscape, proved to be a much sought-after centre for adult summer education in the fine arts. NOEL-HILL, BERWICK, B/PB1953; *Colvin*; CL 5, 12 Feb 1921; *Pevsner*; Stroud, *Humphry Repton*.

*Aston Hall, Oswestry*

*Attingham Park*

*Badger Hall*

*Badger Hall: staircase*

**Badger Hall, Badger.** The 7 bay, 2½ storey house of the 1730s was drastically remodelled by James Wyatt 1779–83 for Isaac Hawkins Brown. Originally it was of brick with rusticated pilaster strips and flanking pavilions. Wyatt gave the house a series of fine interiors—many with delicate plasterwork. The library and the staircase were among the more spectacular apartments. These interiors provided a worthy setting for the great art collection assembled by the Capel Cure family. Badger was demolished 1952, but

*Belswardyne Hall*

Wyatt's Classical pigeon house designed after the Tower of the Winds at Athens survives. CAPEL CURE *of Blake Hall*/LG1965; *Colvin.*

**Bedstone Court, Bedstone.** Yet another Victorian house occupied as a school. Designed by Thomas Harris and built 1884, Bedstone is large with countless gables and numerous chimneys all carried out in a C19 version of the local black and white style. Onetime seat of the Ripley Bts and still in their ownership RIPLEY, BT/PB; *Pevsner.*

**Bellaport Hall, Norton-in-Hales.** Red brick Tudor style house of C19. Formerly seat of the Coulsons and latterly of the Wakeman-

Colvilles. WAKEMAN-COLVILLE/LG1952; COULSON/WCF.

**Belswardyne Hall, Cressage.** Greatly enlarged in C19, Belswardyne is said to date from 1542. Two brick chimneybreasts with blue diaper brickwork flank the entrance and they are probably contemporary with the original building. C17 plaster ceiling in one room by the same hand which executed similar ceilings at Wilderhope Manor (*qv*) Built for Thomas Harnage, it remained the property of that family until Sir Henry Harnage, 3rd and last Bt, died 1888. Later owned by the Wood family. HARNAGE, Bt/PB1888; WOOD/LG1952; *Pevsner.*

*Benthall Hall*

**Benthall Hall, Benthall.** Delightful late c16 house said to be built by William Benthall (*d* 1572), with notable staircase of *ca* 1610. From the earlier period there are panelled rooms and a moulded plaster ceiling. The contribution of T. F. Pritchard in c18 added fine chimneypieces in the drawing and dining rooms. The house of ashlar stone and brick with mullioned windows nestles close to the tiny parish church. Benthall was garrisoned by Col Lawrence Benthall for Charles I 1642. His grandson Richard (*d* 1720) left the estate to his affianced cousin Elizabeth Browne. The will was disputed by his two sisters but the House of Lords finally decided in favour of

*Berrington Hall*

Elizabeth's brother John Browne 1746. After Browne's death the estate passed by will to the Harries family who sold it 1843 to 2nd Lord Forester. Benthall remained with the Weld-Foresters until 1934 when it was repurchased by the Benthalls. The Hall was given to the National Trust 1958 by Mrs J. F. Benthall; the Trust's tenant is Sir Paul Benthall, the industrialist. WELD-FORESTER, FORESTER, B/PB; BENTHALL/LG1972; CL 30 June 1917; *Pevsner*.

**Berrington Hall, Berrington.** Mid-Georgian house of brick with centre block of 5 bays and 2 storeys, flanked by 2 bay pavilions attached by straight links. H. Pritchard-Gordon lived here *ante* World War II.

**Berwick House, Berwick.** Another fine house of the Smith of Warwick school (Davenport, Buntingsdale, Kinlet, Mawley, etc). Built for Thomas Powys 1731, only the fine south-east front of brick with stone dressings survives unscathed from the restoration of 1878 which transformed much of the house inside and out into Italianate Victorian. This fine front is of 9 bays and 2½ storeys with the centre and the angles accentuated by giant Corinthian pilasters. The original entrance hall survives with finely carved overdoors and Corinthian pilasters. Robert Taylor made alterations and additions for Thomas Jelf Powys in 1780. These have been removed. In c19 Berwick became the seat of James Watson, MP, whose heiress married into the Phillipps family; the heiress's own heiress married a Neale. NEALE (*formerly* PHILLIPPS)/LG1952; *Pevsner*; *Colvin*; *Leach*.

*Berwick House*

*Brand Hall*

*Blodwell Hall: summerhouse*

**Bitterley Court, Bitterley.** The modest front of *ca* 1700 with its 1½ storeys surmounted by a pediment hides a Jacobean building behind. An even greater surprise is the number of C18 chimneypieces designed by T. F. Pritchard. Formerly seat of the Walcots and Wheelers. WALCOT/LG1937; WHEELER/LG1937; *Leach*; *Colvin*; *Pevsner*; Harris, *Pritchard Revividius.*

**Blodwell Hall, Llanyblodwel.** The present 7 bay Georgian house with the recessed centre is said to be the service quarters of a grand house built for the Bridgemans but demolished long ago. A glimpse of that vanished grandeur can still be seen in the fine stone-faced summer house which is dated 1718. This is rusticated and has an arched entrance with pilasters. The tympanum of the pediment above has a rich display of shield and garlands. Lonely gatepiers mark the original entrance to the forecourt of the house. BRIDGEMAN, BRADFORD, E/PB.

**Boreatton Park, Boreatton.** Huge, Tudor-style house of the 1850s. Monotonous and somewhat bleak as little or nothing is provided to relieve the great stretches of brick, pointed gables and mullioned and transomed windows. Built for the Hunts who bought the estate 1664 and now live at Boreatton Old Hall. Used as a school in recent years and owned by the Shropshire County Council. HUNT/LG1969.

**Bourton Manor, Bourton.** Norman Shaw is said to have rebuilt an older house 1874. Irregular and picturesque it has 1 half-timbered gable while the remainder of the 1st floor is tile hung. There is an early C19 staircase inside. J. H. A. Whitley lived here in 1930s.

**Bragginton Hall, Wollaston.** Red brick C17 house with red sandstone dressings. Three storeys with gables. Recessed 5 bay centre with projecting wings. Robust columns flank the doorway which has the date 1675 above. This date coincides with the fashion for oval windows, samples of which are found at the back of the building.

**Brand Hall, Norton-in-Hales.** Handsome 7

bay, 2 storey brick house with pediment supported by giant pilasters. Splendid display of Styche family arms in the tympanum. Brand is, however, a building of *ca* 1700 whilst the arms were granted nearly 40 years later. Quoins and pronounced window surrounds. The arches which flank the entrance are possibly remnants of an old forecourt arrangement. Good staircase of turned balusters approached through segmental arches at the end of the entrance hall. Owned in C19 by Sir John Soane's friend Purney Sillitoe, and by the Griffin family, Brand was purchased in this century by Capt John Radford-Norcop. SILLITOE *formerly of Fordhall*/LG1969; RADFORD-NORCOP *formerly of Betton Hall*/LG1952; GRIFFIN/WCF; *Pevsner.*

*Boreatton Park*

*Braggington Hall*

*Broadward Hall*

**Broadward Hall, Clungunford.** Castellated house of moderate size; possibly C18, with a wave of Victorian Romanticism responsible for the battlements on the main house and on the outbuildings as well. Sometime seat of the Crichton (late C19) and Meredith (mid-C20) families. CRICHTON/LG1894; MEREDITH/LG1952; *Pevsner.*

*Brogyntyn*

entrance front with hood moulds and pointed gables and a garden front enlivened by a canted bay on the ground storey and a circular battlemented tower on the service wing to the right. High quality but lifeless interior rich in oak joinery. The best thing about the property, apart from the commanding site, is the high quality stable-range left over from the earlier house. This is *ca* 1730; of brick with quoins at the angles and a pediment over the 3 centre bays which break slightly forward. A cartouche with swags adorns the tympanum. Pretty cupola. The owners included the Moseley and Crichton-Browne families. Buildwas has been unconvincingly suggested as a possible model for "Blandings Castle", based more on geography than anything architectural. MOSELEY/LG1952.

**Brogyntyn, Selattyn.** Francis Smith designed this house 1735–36 for William Owen and in 1814–5 Benjamin Gummow designed the portico and other alterations for Mary Jane Ormsby and her husband William Gore. They were the ancestors of the Lords Harlech who owned Brogyntyn (previously known as Porkington) until 1950s. The original 9 bay, 2 storey house was refaced and given a balustrade as well as a portico. The C18 staircase with 3 slim balusters of different shape to each tread survives. In the hall there is a carved chimneypiece dated 1617 from an earlier house. An arch flanked by lower 1 bay lodges is at the entrance to the estate. ORMSBY-GORE, HARLECH, P/B; *Colvin*; *Pevsner*.

**Broncroft Castle, Diddlebury.** Described by Leland, *ca* 1540, as a "goodly place like a castle". Most of what one sees today is mid-C19. Castellated and asymmetrical, Broncroft offers a number of towers of varying shapes and sizes and windows plainly copied from Stokesay Castle (*qv*). But incorporated in this C19 frolic there is a genuine C14 tower—the lower one of the 2 prinicipal towers. Kelly refers to restoration, but this might refer to the C19 additions. F. W. Pember lived here *ante* World War II; it is now owned by Mr C. T. C. Brinton. BRINTON *formerly of Drayton House*/LG1972; *Pevsner*.

**Buildwas Park, Buildwas.** A Gothic house (demolished 1957) of 1820s of 5 bays on the

*Broncroft Castle*

*Buildwas Park*

**Buntingsdale, Sutton-upon-Tern.** On the straps securing the rainwater heads appear the initials "B.M." and the date 1721. The initials refer to Bulkeley Mackworth for whom the house was almost certainly designed and built by Francis Smith of Warwick. It is without question one of Smith's most original designs. Entrance and garden fronts are almost identical. Tall, of 9 bays with basement, 2 principal and an attic storey. The whole enlivened by giant pilasters with beautifully carved capitals, a top balustrade and pediments. To the right is an addition of 1857 built in keeping to the design of an architect named Smith from Shrewsbury. It was carried out with remarkable sensitivity. Fine 2 storey entrance hall with a wooden gallery in front of a handsome doorcase with open pediment. A staircase of turned balusters leads to the 1st floor which has a series of wide arched openings. Other rooms show corner fireplaces and in the grounds there is a large lake. *Ca* mid C18 the house was purchased by the Tayleurs, cousins of the Mackworths, and they retained it until well into C20. Shortly *ante* World War II, Buntingsdale had become officers' headquarters of the RAF No. 10 Flying Training School. MACKWORTH, Bt/PB; TAYLEUR/LG1937; CL 3 Nov 1917; *Pevsner*.

**Burford House, Burford.** On the site of the Castle of the Cornwalls and for William Bowles, proprietor of Vauxhall glass works, this plain brick house of 5 bays and 2½ storeys was erected 1728. At a later date 2 bay, 2 storey wings were added, but these were demolished 1950s. The entrance hall of 1728 survives. It is

*Buntingsdale*

*Burford House*

panelled and has two arches. From the Bowles family the house passed to the Rushouts; *poste* and *ante* World War II it was owned by one of the oldest of the great English brewing families, the Whitbreads. The horticulturist Mr John Treasure, the present owner, has created a fine garden bordering the Teme here. In the garden is an C18 garden house with 4 Tuscan columns. RUSHOUT, NORTHWICK, B/PB1887; WHITBREAD *of Southill*/LG1965; CL 26 Dec 1947; *Pevsner*.

**Burwarton House, Burwarton.** What was once a vast sprawling mansion in the Italianate style was drastically reduced and reconditioned in late 1950s. Much of the house was designed by the eminent Victorian architect Anthony Salvin and built in 1876–77. The huge library by him in the classical style was suffered to remain at the time of the partial demolition. Fine planting in the grounds. Seat of the Viscounts Boyne. HAMILTON-RUSSELL, BOYNE, V/PB; CL 17 March 1960; *Leach*; *Pevsner*.

**Caynham Court, Caynham.** Late-Georgian house of 3 storeys with canted bays rising the full height at either end. The building is rendered and stands in a park with lush vegetation. Formerly seat of Sir Peter Curtis, 6th Bt (*d* 1976). CURTIS, Bt/PB.

**Chatwall Hall, Cardington.** Of mid-C17, with mullioned windows and 2 gables. There is panelling inside dated 1659 and the entrance is through a Queen Anne door in a recent porch. Seat of the Corfields since C16; the present squire is Rt Hon Sir Frederick Corfield, QC, a former Minister for Aerospace. CORFIELD/ LG1972; *Pevsner*.

**Cheswardine Hall, Cheswardine.** Ambitious neo-Elizabethan house of 1875. On the entrance front there is a 4 storey tower amid an array of steep gables and mullioned and transomed windows. Prominent porch. The estate was bought by Thomas Hudson, MP, 1835; he was succeeded by his grand-nephew, Charles Donaldson, who took the additional surname of Hudson. The late squire's first wife was Jane Carr, the actress; his widow is well-known as the campaigner for the cleaning-up of Soho. DONALDSON-HUDSON/LG1952; *Pevsner*.

**Chetwynd Park, Chetwynd Rural.** Large and many gabled mansion of C17; contributions were also made in C18 and C19. Plasterwork with vine trails survives from the earliest period of building and the dining-room has a screen of marbled columns dateable to C18. C19 alterations included the rendering of the entire building. The Pigott family sold Chetwynd to the Boroughs late C18. PIGOTT, *sub* CORBET of *Sundorne*/LG1937; BOROUGH/ LG1952.

**Cloverley Hall, Calverhall.** Eden Nesfield designed an ambitious house here 1864. In the Elizabethan style, it was red brick with mullioned and transomed windows and straight gables. The principal part of the house was demolished 1950s; all that remains are the connecting ranges between house and outbuildings. The tower of this group with steep hipped roof is another surviving feature. Built for the Heywood-Lonsdales of Shavington (*qv*), Cloverley was the home of Christopher Nicholls *ante* World War II. HEYWOOD-LONSDALE *of Shavington*/LG1965; Colvin & Harris (ed), *The Country Seat* (1970).

*Clungunford Hall*

**Clungunford Hall, Clungunford.** Severe early C19 house of 4 bays—the centre being recessed and containing porch with Doric columns. Pronounced eaves.

*Burwarton House*

*Caynham Court*

*Cheswardine Hall*

*Chetwynd Park*

*Chetwynd: dining room*

*Cloverley*

*Condover Hall: entrance front*

**Condover Hall, Condover.** Grand Elizabethan house built for Thomas Owen at the very end of c16. "E" plan entrance with canted bays on the wings and gables. Projecting wings on garden front as well—connected by 9 bay arcade which might be an alteration by Robert Mylne as he is known to have made designs for Condover 1766. All Georgian interiors have been swept away. 2 square towers rise from the centres of the north and south sides. Latterly the seat of the Cholmondeleys, Condover now belongs to the Royal National Institute for the Blind. CHOLMONDELEY/LG1952; *Colvin; CL; Pevsner.*

**Coton Hall, Alveley.** The ruins of a chapel—oblong, with pediments at its ends and a Venetian Gothick window which represent alterations of ca1765 and which are attributed to T. F. Pritchard—stand on the lawn in front of the restrained early c19 house. This is of 7 bays and 2 storeys and is rendered. It has a prominent porch, and an Italianate tower, forming part of an early Victorian wing, provides a vertical accent to the right of the main building. An earlier house on the site belonged to the Lee family, ancestors of the famous Virginian family who built Stratford on the Potomac. The Gatacres had the place in c19; Capt H. D. Wakeman-Coleville owned it *ante* World War II; and the Howard Thompson family are more recent owners. GATACRES *of Gatacre*/LG 1972; WAKEMAN-COLVILLE *formerly of Bellaport*/LG1952; HOWARD THOMPSON/LG1952; *Pevsner.*

**Coton Hall, Edstaston.** Rambling and irregular Victorian house in the Tudor style much beloved by Devey. Much diaper brickwork. Lately the seat of the Viscounts Hill, descended from the great Peninsular general. CLEGG-HILL, HILL, V/PB.

**Cound Hall, Cound.** One is struck by the extraordinary tallness of this house which was designed by John Prince and built 1704 for Edward Cressett. It is 9 bays by 5 of red brick

*Condover Hall: garden front*

*Cound Hall*

*Cound Hall: staircase*

in the grounds. Formerly the seat of the Hills and lately the home of Lt-Col E. A. Fielden. FIELDEN *of Grimston Park*/LG1965; HILL/WCF; CL 18 Oct 1946; *Pevsner*.

**Coynton Hall, Ryton.** White Regency house with a central bow around which is a one storey colonnade of Tuscan columns. The service wings stretch at right angles to the main block. *Pevsner*.

**Cronkhill, Atcham.** Designed by John Nash and built 1802 for the agent to Lord Berwick's Attingham estate (*qv*). Notable, above all else, as the earliest Italianate villa ever built in the British Isles. There are a round tower, square tower and colonnade all tied together in a charming and quite informal design. Very simple interiors which faintly disappoint after the interest of the exterior. Now the property of the National Trust, but let. NOEL-HILL, BERWICK, B/PB1953; Davis, *Architecture of John Nash*; Summerson, *John Nash*; *Pevsner*.

**Cruckton Hall, Cruckton.** C18 revamping of an older house. Formerly owned by the Jenkins family. Mrs J. H. Cock lived here *ante* World War II; it is now a school. JENKINS/WCF.

**Davenport House, Worfield.** Henry Davenport, a nabob, commissioned Francis Smith to design and build this generous brick house 1726. 9 bays wide with 2 storeys and an attic storey above the main cornice. Large vases on top. Four spacious service wings are

*Cruckton Hall*

with stone dressings. Both east and west facades are almost identical with giant pilasters which have great impact. Doors have broken segmental pediments. Spectacular staircase of the late C18 within. It has a light metal handrail and rises through 2 storeys quite independently of the back wall so that it appears to fly. Two fluted columns support this staircase. Earlier this century Cound belonged to the McCorquodales, but now it belongs to the Morris family and has been turned into flats. MCCORQUODALE/LG1952; Lees-Milne, *English Country Houses*; *Baroque* (1970); *Colvin*; *Pevsner*; CL 25 May 1918.

**Court of Hill, Burford.** Much visited by the diarist Mrs Lybbe Powys on account of her relations there, Court of Hill stands high with a glorious view from its sound 7 bay, 2 storey front. Of brick with quoins and trim of stone. Staircase with square open well and heavy balusters. Jacobean panelling and overmantel in former entrance hall—obviously brought in from elsewhere. Another room shows a very good early C19 ceiling with honeysuckle and friezes of oak and vine. Octagonal dovecote and Georgian pavilion with Tuscan columns

*Cronkhill*

*Davenport House*

*Decker Hill*

*Delbury Hall*

connected to each corner of the house by curved brick walls making a fairly grand layout. The entrance side of the house has a later C18 porch with fluted Ionic columns. Unusual entrance hall with walls wood panelled and having smooth ashlar rustication in imitation of exterior walls. The doorways have Gibbs surrounds and there are niches facing the entrance door. Rustication continues on the walls of the staircase hall. The staircase itself is of wood and has three finely carved balusters to each tread. It rises to a 1st-floor landing with three round-headed doorways. The wood panelled saloon on the ground floor contains fine inlay work in the floor, on the doors and in the marquetry panel above the chimneypiece and in the flanking pilasters. The room is reminiscent of the magnificent inlay in the little drawing-room at Mawley Hall (*qv*). The White Drawing-Room has a fine chimneypiece and overmantel. Battlemented dovecote in grounds. Davenport descended in the family of the same name until C20 when a daughter of the house married a Leicester-Warren and carried it to that family. LEICESTER-WARREN (*formerly* DAVENPORT)/LG1952; *Colvin*; CL 27 June & 4, 11 July 1952; *Pevsner*; *Leach*.

**Decker Hill, Shifnal.** Late-Georgian house of *ca* 1810. Rendered with bows and a memorable entrance composed of 2 giant unfluted Ionic columns in antis. Seat of the Botfields from whom it passed to Rev William Garnett of Haughton Hall, Cheshire, who took the additional surname of Botfield 1863. In this century Hon F. H. C. Weld-Forester (*d* 1952) lived here; it now serves as Shifnal Golf Club. WELD-FORESTER, *sub* FORESTER, B/PB; *Pevsner*.

**Delbury Hall, Diddlebury.** Plain and sizeable brick house of the 1750s. Of 7 bays and 2½ storeys with lower 2 bay, 2 storey wings, Evidence of the earlier house is found on the garden front where there are panelled rooms.

Seat of the Dawsons in late C19; V. S. Wrigley lived here *ante* World War II. *Leach*; *Pevsner*.

**Dinthill Hall, Bicton.** Handsome house of red brick and 2 storeys dated 1734. Entrance with segmental pediment; quoins at the angles and parapet. Twisted balusters on the staircase and some earlier panelling. *Pevsner*.

**Downton Hall,** Stanton Lacy. C18 seat of the Rouse-Boughtons, with fine plasterwork of mid-C18 in the saloon and elsewhere. But much alteration was done in 1830s, including the Tuscan porch and circular entrance hall with Ionic columns. Top balustrade with heavy lettering. Gothick entrance lodge of *ca* 1760. ROUSE-BOUGHTON, Bt/PB1963; CL 21 July 1917; *Pevsner*.

**Dudmaston Hall, Quatt.** An early C18 house built for the Wolrich family. Dudmaston was much rebuilt *ca* 1730. From the earliest period the hall and one or two minor rooms retain their original panelling. The early C19 alterations altered the roofline of the house and the pediments at either end of building date from that time. The most notable C19 alteration within was the addition of the staircase with its unusual wrought-iron balustrade. A similar one is found at Whatcroft

*Dinthill Hall*

*Downton Hall*

*Dudmaston Hall*

*Dudmaston: staircase*

*Dudmaston: hall*

Hall, Cheshire. Sir John Wolrich, 4th and last Bt, was drowned when crossing the River Severn 1723; his mother succeeded him in the estate and from her it passed to her brother, Lt-Col Thomas Weld, and thence to William Whitmore 1774. The late G. C. Wolryche-Whitmore left Dudmaston to his niece Rachel (*née* Hamilton-Russell), the wife of Sir George Labouchere, former Ambassador to Spain, and the Laboucheres gave it to the National Trust 1978. WOLRICH, Bt/EDB; WOLRYCHE-WHITMORE/LG1952; CL 8, 15, 22/3/79; *Pevsner*.

**Earlsdale Hall, Pontesbury.** Late-Georgian remodelling of an earlier house. Rendered, with slightly lower 2 storey porch. Pretty pointed windows with hood-moulds. Formerly seat of the Caton-Jones family; now owned by Major Lindsay Wallace. CATON-JONES/LG1937.

**Eaton Mascott Hall, Berrington.** Brick house of 1734 with a recessed centre between projecting wings. Over this centre is a broken pediment on scrolls with a tripartite window in it and below it. Venetian windows flank the entrance. A small late C17 building with blank arcading appears at the rear of the house. Eaton Mascott is the seat of the Holcroft Bts. HOLCROFT, Bt/PB; *Pevsner*.

**Elsich (or Elsych) Manor, Diddlebury.** Irregular stone house with timber-topped turret and 2 broad gabled projections. The chimneystacks are placed diagonally. Probably Elizabethan, Elsich might have been originally 2 houses. C. E. Edwards, an auctioneer, made over the property to his son 1948. EDWARDS/LG1952; *Pevsner*.

*Earlsdale Hall*

*Eaton Mascott Hall*

*Elsich Manor*

*Gatacre Park*

*Great Lyth*

**Great Lyth, Stapleton.** Monumental shaped gables are the main features of this brick house which has a recessed 3 bay centre between the 2 bay wings. Semi-circular pediment over the door and cross windows. Recently restored after much neglect. *Pevsner*.

**Habberley Hall, Habberley.** Dated 1593. Timber framed with vertical studs and diagonal braces. T. C. V. Satherthwaite lived here *ante* World War II.

**Halston Hall, Whittington.** Famous as the home of the legendary sportsman Squire Mytton. 2 storey brick front of 9 bays and 2 storeys flanked by semi-circular walls of 1850. Pediment and parapet and prominent chimneys at the ends above blank arches. The garden front has recessed 3 bay centre between 2 bay wings. The best room inside is the saloon which Robert Mylne designed for John Mytton 1766–68. This is in the Adam style and has apses at both ends. The staircase was brought in from a house in Herefordshire. Capt Joseph Eccles owned Halston *ante* World War II. ECCLES/LG1937; *Colvin*; *Leach*; *Pevsner*.

**Hampton Hall, Worthen.** Red brick house mainly of 1686. This probably represents the centre with hipped roof, broader windows and circular windows. But alteration has taken place whereas the wings remain untouched. There is a porch of 1749 and the staircase is probably contemporary with it. The house enjoys far-reaching views from its elevated position. A. F. V. McConnell lived here 1937. *Pevsner*.

**Hardwick Hall, Ellesmere.** Lt-Col J. R. Kynaston is the present owner of this handsome house which was probably erected *ca* 1720 for his family. Hardwick is similar to houses in the same county by Francis Smith, such as Buntingsdale, Mawley and Kinlet. The principal front (now the garden front) is tall on account of its striking 3 bay ashlar centre, which is surmounted by a huge

**Ferney Hall, Clungunford.** Designed by S. Pountney Smith in a ham-fisted neo-Jacobean style; built 1875. Symmetrical with shaped gables, but on the east front an open-storeyed tower with an ogee cap. After the Sitwells left, Frank Cushny owned Ferney *ante* World War II. SITWELL/LG1937; *Pevsner*; *Leach*.

**Gatacre Hall, Claverley.** The old recusant family of Gatacre have lived here for many centuries. Their large C18 house survives in a beautiful park. The Gatacres of Gatacre are one of a dozen or so families—particularly well represented in this county—which have the proud distinction of being descended in the male line from a medieval ancestor who took his surname from lands which they still hold. GATACRE/LG1972.

**Gatacre Park, nr Bridgnorth.** The Actons built this Classical house of brick in 1850 to replace a late C16 house which was pulled down in the preceding year. Now home of Sir Edward Thompson, the engineer and industrialist, whose father bought it 1923. THOMPSON/LG1952; VSA.

*Habberley Hall*

elliptical tympanum containing a shield and garlands. The remainder of the building is brick with stone dressings. Semi-circular walls connect the house to large pavilions, each of which has a central stack, hipped roof and dormers—very much in the style of *ca* 1700. The staircase is the main survivor of fairly drastic internal alterations in C19. It is in a square well and has 3 twisted balusters to each tread with carved tread-ends. On the old entrance front, which enjoys a fine view over lawns, a terrace was built in C19. This eliminated an outer staircase leading to the principal door and hides the basement windows. In the grounds to the west there are some very fine gates with gatepiers which have Corinthian pilasters and carry splendid eagles. KYNASTON/LG1952; CL 15 June 1918; *Pevsner*.

**Hardwicke Grange, Hadnall.** Thomas Harrison of Chester designed this large Gothic house for the Peninsular general 1st Viscount Hill. It had a 3 bay centre recessed between one bay wings. An arcade on the ground floor connected the wings. Latterly owned by the Bibbys, it was demolished 1931. Lord Hill built the Waterloo Windmill in the grounds to commemorate his military exploits. This still stands. CLEGG-HILL, HILL, V/PB; BIBBY, Bt/PB; *Neale*.

**Hatton Grange, Shifnal.** Built 1764–68 for the ancestors of the present owners, the Kenyon-Slaneys, to the designs of T. F. Pritchard. Originally the house was of 7 bays and 2½ storeys. The tightly knit 3 bay centre projects slightly and is crowned by a small

*Halston Hall*

*Hampton Hall*

*Hardwick Hall*

*Hatton Grange* ca *1890*

*Hawkstone Hall*

*Hawkstone: The Citadel*

pediment. Since *ca* 1900 the main front has gained 2 storeyed canted bays on either side of the central projection. Pavilions with Venetian windows lie back on either side of the building. Charming plasterwork of mid-c18 survives in various rooms inside and there is a staircase with slim twisted balusters. Attractive grounds with lake. The heiress of R. A. Slaney of Hatton married the grandson of the great judge Lord Kenyon, who took the additional surname of Slaney 1862. Their son, William, was a PC and a noted all-round gamesplayer. KENYON-SLANEY, *sub* KENYON, B/PB; *Colvin*; CL 29 Feb 1968; *Leach*.

**Hawkstone Hall, Hawkstone.** Large house of 1720 built for Sir Richard Hill with wings of *ca* 1750 added by his nephew Sir Rowland Hill, 1st Bt. Main block 9 bays and 2½ storeys. Attached columns and pediment. Semi-circular corridors link the house to 5 bay wings of 2 storeys. Notable rooms include saloon, staircase, ballroom and chapel. Magnificent park with a number of garden buildings.

Thomas Harrison, of Chester, designed a
dower house in the park known as The Citadel
1824–25. Lord Marchamley owned the house
earlier this century. CLEGG-HILL, HILL, V/PB;
WHITELEY, MARCHAMLEY, B/PB; *Colvin*;
*Pevsner*; CL 27/3, 3/4, 3/7 & 10/7/58.

**Henley Hall, Bitterley.** Long facade of red
brick. The centre 7 bays represent a
rebuilding of *ca* 1725. Then, in 1772, 3 bay
wings were added to the left and right; at the
same time the notable staircase with 3
balusters to a tread was built. Even more
alterations took place 1875 and 1907. But
Elizabethan or Jacobean work is said to be
incorporated in the structure and a star-
shaped chimneystack and a panelled room
with elaborate plaster ceiling (which is
possibly Victorian) tell of it. Stables with
archway and cupola; a large square summer
house and sumptuous Early Georgian gates
and screen from vanished Wirksworth Hall,
Derbyshire. Seat of the Woods. WOOD/
LG1952; CL 16 & 23 Aug 1946; *Pevsner*.

**Hodnet Hall, Hodnet.** The original house
was low and rambling of brick and half-
timber; this was the onetime seat of the
Vernons and the property was later acquired
by the Hebers. In 1870 Anthony Salvin
designed the large neo-Elizabethan house
which stands, minus its top storey, today. It is
"E"-plan and obviously inspired by Condover
Hall (*qv*). Good staircase hall with arcades and
some C18 chimneypieces. The daughter of the
celebrated Anglican divine and hymn-writer
Reginald Heber married Algernon Percy,
a great-nephew of the 5th Duke of Northumberland, 1839; the couple took the
surname of Heber-Percy when she succeeded
her uncle at Hodnet eight years later. The
family has created a magnificent 60 acre garden
here, now maintained by the present owner Mr
A. E. H. Heber-Percy and his wife, who is a
daughter of the present Viscount Leverhulme.
HEBER/LG1882; HEBER-PERCY/LG1937 and *sub*
NORTHUMBERLAND, D/PB; *Pevsner*.

**Isle (The), Bicton.** Large red brick house said
to date from late C17. It is built on land
surrounded by a loop of the Severn. Early
Georgian staircase. Older black and white
house and late C17 summer house nearby. Seat
of the Sandfords who removed here in C16.
SANDFORD *of the Isle of Rossall*/LG1972;
*Pevsner*.

*Henley Hall*

*Hodnet Hall: the old house*

*Hodnet: the new house*

*The Isle*

**Kinlet Hall, Kinlet.** 7 bay block of red brick
with stone dressings, 2½ storeys high. The
central 3 bays on the garden front are slightly
recessed. On the entrance front the house is
prolonged by walls, behind which are the
offices, linking the main block to 4 bay wings.
The urns which decorated the parapet of the
main building and the arches in the screen
walls have been removed. Inside, there is a
screen of Roman Doric columns in the
entrance hall; a wide staircase with 3 twisted
balusters to a tread; and a panelled room of
high quality in the centre of the garden front.
Dark-blue marble columns divide another
room into 3 parts. This was the library and is
said to date from 1827. Francis Smith of
Warwick designed the house 1727–29 for
William Lacon Childe, MP. The estate had
originally belonged to the Cornewalls and
Bramptons from whom it passed to Sir George

*Kinlet Hall*

Blount and thence to the Lacons, who intermarried with the Childe family 1640. William Lacon Childe's heiress married Charles Baldwyn, MP, whose son, a celebrated sportsman and agriculturalist of his day, took the surname of Childe. He was allegedly known throughout England as "The Flying Childe" on account of his daring horsemanship. Kinlet remains in the ownership of the Childes, though it is now let to a school. CHILDE/LG1952; *Colvin*; *Leach*; *Pevsner*.

**Langley Hall, Langley.** Only the timber-framed and stone gatehouse remains. Above

*Larden Hall*

*Langley Hall*

the double-chamfered archway there are two gables on the stone side of the building whilst the other timber-framed front shows much diagonal strutting. Mullioned windows. The house, long vanished, was the seat of the Lee family. *Pevsner.*

**Larden Hall, Shipton.** Highly picturesque house of the Leche family. Demolished 1967, Larden is said to have been transported to the USA and rebuilt there. The ingredients were timber-framing for one part and stone for the other. Tall with lower wing and all irregular. The restored stone parts of the house were dated 1607, but the timber-framed part supposed to be earlier was probably close to the early C17 in date with lozenges within lozenges. J. C. R. Russell-Parsons lived there *ante* World War II. *Pevsner.*

*Lea Hall*

**Lea Hall, Preston Gubbals.** Elizabethan brick house of 1584 with 2 gables and projecting wings on east side. Spectacular contemporary fireplace with fluted Ionic pilasters. *Pevsner*.

**Leaton Knolls, Leaton.** Edward Haycock designed this severe but interesting Grecian house for J. A. Lloyd; it was built *ca* 1835. Ashlar, with a 5 bay entrance front of 2 storeys and a Doric colonnade its entire length. Round the corner a bow with shallow dome and semicircular colonnade. Mr Lloyd (who captained the Harrow XI in which Byron played) was presumably interested in architecture as there is a reference to the house being "erected on his own plan for he is his own *Vitruvius*". Demolished 1955. LLOYD *of Fosseway House formerly of Leaton Knolls*/LG1952; *Colvin*.

**Leighton Hall, Leighton.** Alterations during the past 100 years have radically altered the appearance of the building which is basically a brick house with stone dressings, dated 1778. Contemporary stables with arch and lantern over. Seat of the Kynnersley-Browne family, to whom the property passed from the Leightons early in C18. KYNNERSLEY-BROWNE/LG1952; *Pevsner*; *Leach*.

**Lilleshall Hall, Lilleshall.** For the 1st Duke of Sutherland, Sir Jeffry Wyatville designed this irregular Tudor style house which was built 1829. Of stone with mullioned and transomed windows and straight gables. The porch tower of 4 storeys is very similar to Wyatville's Golden Grove, Carmarthenshire, built for 1st Earl Cawdor. Magnificent grounds surround Lilleshall which was later owned by the Walkers and is now a college. LEVESON-GOWER, SUTHERLAND, D/PB; WALKER/WCF; Linstrum, *Sir Jeffry Wyatville*; *Colvin*; *Pevsner*.

*Leaton Knolls*

*Leighton Hall* ante *1888*

*Lilleshall Hall*

*Linley Hall*

**Linley Hall, More.** Unusual Palladian house designed by Henry Joynes and built for Robert More, FRS, MP, the traveller and botanist (who introduced the larch to these shores) 1742. 5 bays wide, the centre 3 recessed between the outer ones which carry small pediments. Ionic porch with pulvinated frieze and pediment. The actual entrance is at basement level on the east side and the principal rooms are reached by a fine C18 wrought-iron staircase. Above this lower entrance is a great Venetian window. Fine C18 decoration in the saloon and attractive C19 wallpaper in the main room with the bay to the west. The ground floor rooms are vaulted. Grand 2 storeyed stables with central pediment and cupola. Like the entrance to the house, the door here has a Gibbs surround. Now the property of Sir Jasper More, the politician and writer. MORE/LG1952; *Leach*; *Colvin*; CL 7 & 14 Sept 1961.

**Llanforda, Oswestry.** On the site of an early C18 house of the Smith school, a plain and low building was erected 1780. This, in turn, was demolished 1949. But the stables with central arch and raised angle bays with pyramid roofs remain. Llanforda was one of the properties belonging to the vast Welsh landowning dynasty the Williams-Wynns. WILLIAMS-WYNN, Bt/PB; *Pevsner*.

**Lodge (The), Richard's Castle.** C18 of the Salweys; of 5 bays and 2 storeys. The 3 middle bays rise into an attic projection and there is a porch. Canted bays on the ground floor on the side elevations. Lower service wing to one side. SALWEY/LG1952; *Leach*.

**Longden Manor, Longden.** Large stone house of 1866 in a free Tudor style, but somewhat lifeless and dull. This former seat of

*The Lodge*

*Longden Manor*

the Swires was demolished 1954; the property is owned by Mrs A. N. Fielden (*née* Swire). SWIRE *of Hubbards Hall formerly of Hillingdon House*/LG1965.

**Longford Hall, Longford.** A nabob's house. Ralph Leeke went to India *ca* 1770 and on his return in 1780s commissioned Joseph Bonomi to design a new house. It is a monumental 7 by 4 bays with continuous giant pilasters and an enormous porte-cochère of giant Tuscan columns. The tripartite entrance gives way to a small entrance hall, of considerable charm with its Grecian frieze, and pedimented entrance with columns to the staircase which has a bronze railing and an oval lantern springing from fluted spandrels. *Post* World War II the house was bought by Mrs John Hall whose son, Mr Patrick Hall, owns it today. LEEKE/LG1937; CL 16 Aug 1962; *Colvin*; *Pevsner*.

**Longner Hall, Atcham.** Seat of the Burtons, which was designed by John Nash 1803 to replace an older house. Free grouping of elements in Tudor style. The main fronts face south and west and they are connected by a glazed colonnade of pointed windows. Tall porch on the entrance side and high clock turret on the stables. The best interior is the staircase hall with large fan vaults and a semi-circular balcony above a large pendant. More Gothicry in other rooms, notably the drawing-room with more prominent vaults. Humphry Repton landscaped the grounds in 1803–04. According to Browne Willis, the Burtons "were a family of great antiquity, being possessors of Longner in the time of Edward IV..." Edward Burton, a Protestant who narrowly escaped persecution in the reign of Mary I, is said to have died through joy on hearing the news of her death.

*Longford Hall*

*Longner Hall, Atcham*

*Longner Hall, Atcham: staircase*

BURTON/LG1972; Stroud, *Humphry Repton*; Davis, *Nash*; Summerson, *Nash*; Colvin; Pevsner; Leach.

**Longnor Hall, Longnor.** Fine Caroline house built 1670 for Sir Richard Corbet, 2nd Bt. 7 bays, 2 storeys of red brick with stone dressings. Big shaped gable in the centre of the entrance side. This is probably a C19 alteration. Good entrance doorways with segmental pediments on both fronts. High quality interior with sumptuous staircase with moulded balusters and elaborate inlay work. Drawing-room and entrance hall show doorcases richly carved and typical of the date of the house. On the extinction of the Baronetcy 1774, the estate eventually passed to Ven Joseph Plymley who assumed the surname of Corbett 1804. CORBETT/LG1969; CL 17 Feb 1917, 13 & 20 Feb 1964; Comforth & Hill *English Country Houses: Caroline.*

*Longnor Hall, Longnor*

*Loton Park: entrance front*

*Loton*

*Ludford House*

**Loton Park, Alberbury.** Large brick house composed of 2 distinct parts: one Queen Anne and the other Jacobean-looking. There was further work in 1870s. The principal north front of the early C18 is 11 bays and 2½ storeys, with part balustrade in the parapet. Central door with segmental pediment. The Jacobean-looking entrance side needs unravelling. Some of the gables, etc, have been added since 1792 (date of some illustrations of the house). It is known that gables and porch were added 1838. These were to the designs of Thomas Jones. In 1773-74 Robert Mylne made alterations for Sir Charlton Leighton, Bt; in 1819 Edward Haycock was responsible for more alterations. The saloon has panelling with pilasters. Loton still belongs to the Leightons, the present owner being Sir Michael Leighton, 11th Bt. LEIGHTON, Bt/PB; *Colvin*; *Pevsner*.

**Ludford House, Ludford.** 4 great chimneystacks rise sheer from the road and the

*Ludstone Hall*

*Lutwyche Hall*

*Lydham Manor*

spacious courtyard is entered through an archway in between. Late Elizabethan or Jacobean timber work on the north and east sides. T. F. Pritchard remodelled the east front for Sir Francis Charlton, 4th Bt, 1761. The staircase dates from the same period. Ludford is now the property of the Whitaker family. CHARLTON, Bt/EDB; *Colvin*; CL; *Pevsner*.

**Ludstone Hall, Claverley.** Moated Jacobean house lately the home of the Rollasons who did so much to preserve it. Built of brick for John Whitmore. Shaped gables, mullioned and transomed windows. The overmantel in the hall is probably original but other features (*e.g.* ceiling and screen) are not. Panelling in drawing-room with decorated pilasters. Staircase with flat balusters. ROLLASON *formerly of Hampton Manor*/LG1952; *Pevsner*; CL.

**Lutwyche Hall, Easthope.** Victorian Jacobean revamping transformed an "E"-shaped house of 1587. The architect was S. Pountney Smith for the C19 work, but even before his time the Georgians had filled in the space between the original wings with a hall containing unusual and fine plasterwork. There is an agreeable C18 staircase with 3 balusters to a tread. The Lutwyche estate was purchased in late C18 by Moses Benson, a rich West Indian merchant. The racing journalist and backgammon champion Charles Benson ("The Scout" of the *Daily Express*) is a cadet member of this family. After the Bensons sold up 1946, Lutwyche became Wenlock Edge School; but it has since reverted to being a private house. BENSON/LG1969; *Pevsner*; *Leach*.

**Lydham Manor, Lydham.** Formerly known as Oakeley Park and was the seat of the family of that name. In C20 it became Lydham Manor and, although the old house has gone, the C18 stables have taken the place of the principal house and assumed the name. It was John Haycock who designed the unusual building in early C19 for the Oakeleys. It stood high, was rendered and had a porch. Straight links connected the 5 bay, 3 storey main block to octagonal pavilions which had balustrades. These pavilions and links were demolished 1930s followed by the main building 1960s. The new Lydham Manor belongs to the Sykes family who bought the property from the Oakeleys. OAKELEY/LG1898; SYKES *of Norrington*/LG1972; *Colvin*; *Leach*.

*Lythwood Hall*

**Lythwood Hall, Baystonhill.** Rather feeble house designed by George Steuart and built 1782; it was demolished in 1950s. A tall front of 3 storeys and 7 bays with a pediment. Delicate 1 storey portico with attenuated columns. An elegant staircase rose in a slow curve at the end of the entrance hall. Steuart drew up unexecuted designs for Onslow (*qv*) which were very similar to Lythwood. The late Capt H. D. M. Hulton-Harrop was the last of the family to be seated there. HULTON-HARROP *of Gatten formerly of Bardsley/*LG1965; *Pevsner*.

**Madeley Court, Madeley.** Under restoration at time of writing, and a fragment of its former self. Probably mid-C16 and approached by a notable gatehouse with polygonal towers. The original interior has virtually disappeared. Built by the Brookes, Madeley was later lived in by Abraham Darby. Curious astronomical toy in grounds. CL17 July 1917.

*Madeley Court*

**Marrington Hall, Chirbury.** Restoration work in C19 and C20 has largely obscured the original house of 1595. Many gabled and timber-framed it was until recently the seat of the Price-Davies family. PRICE-DAVIES *of Marrington Hall/*LG1952; *Pevsner*.

**Mawley Hall, Cleobury Mortimer.** Attributed convincingly to Francis Smith, Mawley was built 1730 for Sir Edward Blount, 4th Bt. 9 by 7 bays and 2½ storeys high with giant Tuscan pilasters and 3 bay pediment. Large vases on parapet. The exterior is relatively restrained but the interior is rich and splendid with craftsmanship of the highest quality. There is a magnificent overmantel

*Marrington Hall*

*Mawley Hall*

*Mawley: hall*

*Mawley: detail of staircase*

*Mawley: chapel (now demolished)*

with military emblems, etc, in the hall which has a fine plaster ceiling and leads through three rusticated arches to the staircase. This is surrounded by lavish plasterwork on the walls and ceiling. The handrail represents a snake and undulates up and down all the way. On the string there are finely carved emblems of fishing, shooting, architecture, music, etc. Another ground-floor room shows magnificent inlay work on the walls, floor, etc. Later c18 dining-room. A late-Georgian chapel attached to a corner of the house has been demolished. c18 stables. Mawley left the Blount family in 1950s and for a time the building was in the gravest danger of demolition. But it was bought and superbly restored by Mr and Mrs Anthony Galliers-Pratt who have recently added a painted ceiling by Graham Rust. BLOUNT, Bt/PB; GALLIERS-PRATT, *sub* CAYZER, Bt, *of Gartmore*/PB; CL 2 July 1910; *Colvin; Pevsner.*

*Millichope Park*

**Meeson Hall, Bolas Magna.** A red sandstone house of 1640 with 3 straight gables. Good chimneypiece contemporary with the house in the dining-room. O. D. Murphy lived here 1937. *Pevsner.*

**Millichope Park, Millichope.** The drive to the house plunges through a rocky gorge and gives one no clue as to what to expect. At the end is this remarkable Greek Revival house, designed by Edward Haycock, and set in a Picturesque landscape. The site is older and the present house built 1835–40 for Rev R. N. Pemberton replaced one of half-timber. All that remains of the earlier Millichope is an Ionic temple dated 1770 by George Steuart as a memorial to the Mores who owned the estate. The lake and landscape around it probably date from the 1830s or early 1840s. The house stands on a terrace high above the lake and until the late 1960s the entrance was by way of an opening flanked by stubby Tuscan columns below the portico of fluted Ionic columns. This led through to a ramped staircase which in turn led up to the main 2 storey hall with its tiers of wooden Ionic columns. Practical considerations in the late 1960s led to the filling in of the lower entrance and a number of other alterations brought the house completely in tune with living in the last quarter of the C20. Rev R. N. Pemberton was succeeded by a distant connexion C. O. Childe, of the Kinlet (*qv*) family. In 1891 it was sold to H. J. Beckwith, great-grandfather of the present owner Mr Lindsay Bury. BALDWYN-CHILDE *of Kyre*/LG 1921; *Colvin*; CL 10 & 17 Feb 1977; *Pevsner.*

*Minsterley Hall*

**Minsterley Hall, Minsterley.** Timber-framed house of considerable size but much restored. Some gables show original concave lozenges and lozenges within lozenges. The Thynne arms appear on an overmantel inside where there is panelling in two rooms. H. S. Barratt owned the house *ante* World War II. *Pevsner.*

**Moor Park, Richard's Castle.** Queen Anne-style mansion which rambles. 11 bays on its main front with giant pilasters and shaped gables. Formerly seat of the Fosters, Moor was owned by the Lords Inchiquin before it became a school *ca* 1950. O'BRIEN, INCHIQUIN, B/PB; FOSTER/WCF; *Pevsner.*

**Moreton Hall, Weston Rhyn.** 7 bay, 2 storey brick house of C17. Crossed windows, hipped roof. Inside, a staircase which looks Jacobean. Used as a school in recent years; previously owned by the Wood family. WOOD/WCF; *Pevsner.*

*Morville Hall:* C18 *view*

*Morville*

**Morville Hall, Morville.** An C18 view of this house which was identified 1971 shows how the Elizabethan Morville had been altered *ca* 1748. But the house retained its basic Tudor shape with towers in the angles. It was probably William Baker who Georgianized the building and who added the giant Tuscan columns attached to the fronts of the wings, etc. And he must have been responsible for the long links and pretty 3 bay pavilions. But in 1770 another storey was added to the house and this destroyed some of the features attributable to Baker. A plaster ceiling in the

kitchen survives from the Elizabethan era. In C19 the Hanbury-Tracys owned the house, but it was the Bythell family who presented the house to the National Trust in C20. The house with its outstretched wings makes a handsome group with the parish church of St Gregory. HANBURY-TRACY, SUDELEY, B/PB; CL 15, 22 Aug 1952; *Colvin*; *Pevsner*.

**Nash Court, Nash.** Comfortable brick house of *ca* 1760; 5 bays, 2¹/₂ storeys. A pediment over the central window on the 1st floor provides a slight relieving accent and there is a

porch of attached columns. Contemporary stables with cupola. After the Pardoes pulled out, Brig-Gen Sir Dalrymple Arbuthnot, 5th Bt, owned the house *ante* World War II. PARDOE/LG1937; ARBUTHNOT, Bt/PB; *Pevsner*.

**Ness Strange Hall, Great Ness.** C18 house of brick with irregular facade of 3 storeys with a lower 2 storey wing. 2 canted bays of 3 storeys breaks the long facade. Formerly seat of the Edwards family, Ness Strange became an hotel between the wars. EDWARDS/LG1906.

**Netley Hall, Stapelton.** A late Classical house of 5 bays and 2¹/₂ storeys with a top balustrade. Edward Haycock was its author and its date 1854–58. The restrained exterior hides a spectacular 2 storey hall with Tuscan pilasters and a screen of Tuscan columns, behind which rises a very grand staircase starting in one flight and returning in two. Former seat of the Hope-Edwardes family. HOPE-EDWARDS/LG1937; *Pevsner*; *Leach*.

**Oakly Park, Bromfield.** An early C18 house which was the subject of alterations by William Baker (1748–58) and John Haycock (*ca* 1784–90)—with a final remodelling by C. R. Cockerell 1819–36. The last attempt was the most successful. Cockerell added a 1 storeyed screen on the entrance side flanked by symmetrical porches with Tuscan columns in

*Ness Strange Hall*

*Netley Hall*

*Oakly Park: showing Cockerell's remodelling of the entrance front and (below) conservatory and parterre.*

*Onslow*

*Onslow: drawing room*

*Orleton Hall*

antis. On the south front Cockerell added an attached portico with pilasters and a balcony above. His conservatory was taken down early 1930s. Oakly contains a charming oval entrance hall which leads through to the dramatic staircase hall with a slow curving staircase of wrought iron and on the upper floor a screen of Egypto-Grecian columns with a piece of the frieze of Bassae over it. There is an entrance lodge by Cockerell as well. Oakly is the seat of the Earls of Plymouth. WINDSOR-CLIVE, PLYMOUTH, E/PB; *Colvin;* CL 1 & 8 March 1956; Hussey, *English Country Houses; Late Georgian* (1958); Pevsner; Watkin, *C. R. Cockerell.*

**Onslow, Bicton.** Robert Mylne made additions to an older house for Richard Morhall 1774. Six years later George Steuart drew up designs very similar to Lythwood Hall (*qv*) for rebuilding the house for Rowland Wingfield. These remained unexecuted and it was left finally to Edward Haycock to remodel the house thoroughly in Grecian style *ca* 1815–20—the client then being John Wingfield. Haycock gave the house a monumental portico, with giant Doric columns; and an entrance hall, with a fine staircase in one flight and returning in two. Onslow was demolished 1955 and replaced by a modern house which includes the large chimneypiece from the drawing-room in the old house. Greek Doric lodges. The property is now owned by Mr. C. J. Wingfield. WINGFIELD/LG1952; *Colvin; Pevsner.*

**Orleton Hall, Wrockwardine.** The 9 bay, 2¹/₂ storey entrance is a refronting *ca* 1830 by Edward Haycock for Edward Cludde, whose family had owned the estate since early C18. Orleton is now owned by a descendant of the Cluddes, Mr V. M. E. Holt, to whom it was made over by his uncle, 5th Earl of Powis. Half-timbering is said to survive at the rear of the building; indeed on that side the house is approached by a timber-framed gatehouse of 1588. This has been tricked up at various dates and has a Gothick dormer and Georgian lantern. Gazebo with low ogee roof on garden wall. HOLT/LG1969; *Leach; Pevsner; Colvin.*

**Oteley, Ellesmere.** Large stone mansion in the Elizabethan style built for C. K. Mainwaring 1826–30, replacing an older house nearby. Strong display of straight gables, battlemented and to the north a tower containing an archway which formed the entrance. Bastions guarded the approach and the situation overlooking Oteley Mere was a fine one. Demolished 1959. The Mainwarings inherited the property from the Kinaston family which had intermarried with the Oteleys of Oteley in the reign of Henry VIII. Sir Francis Kinaston, Esquire of the Body to Charles I, translated Chaucer's *Troilus and Creseide* into Latin verse. MAINWARING/LG1969; *Leach; Pevsner.*

**Park Hall, nr Oswestry.** Outstanding half-timbered house of *ca* 1600 which was destroyed by fire 1918 when in the possession of A. W. Corrie. Wide, many gabled front with receding centre in the middle of which the three storey porch projected slightly. Rich display of timber patterns between continuous rows of glass windows. Built by Thomas

Oteley

Park Hall

*Pell Wall*

Powell, it remained in the possession of his descendants until C18. Sir Francis Charlton, 2nd Bt bought the property 1717 and from his family it eventually passed to the Kinchants. In 1870 it was sold to Mrs Wynne Corrie. Much of the interior appeared to be of 1640 and the dining-room contained a magnificent fireplace with paired columns above and below. Fine oak staircase with prominent finials. CHARLTON, Bt/EDB; KINCHANT/LG1914; CL 4 March 1905.

**Pell Wall, nr Market Drayton.** The house used to be in Staffordshire, but was included in a section of that county transferred to

Shropshire. It was designed by Sir John Soane 1822 and built for his friend Purney Sillitoe, also of Brand Hall (*qv*). The wide entrance front of 3 bays is divided by pilaster strips with incised lines typical of Soane. The porch incorporates Ionic columns used in the original entrance. A generous bow relieves the side elevation and Victorian additions cling to the left-hand side of the building. In spite of extensive alterations within, chimneypieces by Soane survive in the hall and small drawing-room and the latter apartment retains its original, shallow vaulted ceiling. The extraordinary triangular lodge on the north drive represents an attempt by Soane to unite

Gothic and classical motifs. In late C19 Pell Wall was the seat of the Griffins; it has recently been occupied by St Joseph's School. SILLITOE *formerly of Fordhall*/LG1969; GRIFFIN/WCF; Pevsner (*Staffordshire*); Stroud, *Sir John Soane* (1961).

**Peplow Hall, Peplow.** Originally a 7 by 6 bay block of brick with a big parapet, built 1725. The house was considerably enlarged 1887 and alterations such as removal of the original staircase (3 slim balusters to a tread) to a new position were made at that time. Fine C18 wrought-iron gates by Jones of Wrexham. Major Sir Robert Lynch-Blosse, 12th Bt,

*Pitchford Hall* ca *1870*

*Plaish Hall*

Milne pour a solution of Ponds Extract over her bare leg "out of a heavy leady Marie Antoinette watering can". Her son C. R. A. Grant of Cotes bequeathed Pitchford to his stepdaughter, Mrs Oliver Colthurst 1972. GRANT *of Cotes*/LG1965; COLTHURST, Bt/PB; *Pevsner*; Lees-Milne, *Ancestral Voices* and *Prophesying Peace*; CL 7, 14 April 1917.

**Plaish Hall, Cardington.** An "H"-shaped house probably of the 1540s, but incorporating fragments of a C15 structure. Red brick with stone chimneybreasts. The best room is one with miniature ceiling pendants. The hall was divided horizontally within living memory. G. S. M. Warlow owned Plaish *ante* World War II. CL; *Pevsner*.

**Plas Yolyn, Dudleston.** A rather grand Regency house of brick. It is of 5 widely-spaced bays—the centre 3, which form a $2^1/_2$ storey projection, are accentuated by quoins at the angles and there is a bold pedimented porch on Roman Doric columns. The end bays are of 2 storeys only. Seat of the Morrall family. MORRALL/LG1952; *Pevsner*.

owned Peplow *ante* World War II; it now belongs to Hon R. V. Wynn. LYNCH-BLOSSE, Bt/PB; WYNN, *sub* NEWBOROUGH, B/PB; *Pevsner*.

**Petton Park, Petton.** Neo-Elizabethan house of 1892 with straight gables and an asymmetrically placed square turret. Former seat of the Sparling and Cunliffe families. CUNLIFFE/LG1937; SPARLING/WCF.

**Pitchford Hall, Pitchford.** Spectacular black and white house built for Adam Otley, a wool merchant, in 1570s. "E"-planned house with far-projecting wings. Star-shaped chimneystacks. C17 and C18 alterations inside. In the grounds there is a Gothick summerhouse in a tree. Until recently the seat of the Grants of Cotes (of which family Elspeth Huxley, the writer, is a member). Let in 1920s by Gen Sir Charles Grant to his friend Field-Marshal Sir Archibald Montgomery-Massingberd of Gunby Hall, Lincs. Sir Charles's eccentric wife, Lady Sybil, holed up in the orangery and once made Mr James Lees-

*Plas Yolyn*

*Plowden Hall*

**Plowden Hall, Lydbury North.** The venerable recusant family of Plowden has lived on this land for centuries; the present timber-framed building is mostly Elizabethan in keeping with the fact that the family's standing was raised in this period by the eminent lawyer Edmund Plowden. His descendants in the male line stayed out of public affairs more or less until *post* World War II when Sir Edwin Plowden (now a life peer) held several high government appointments, notably the Chairmanship of the Atomic Energy Authority. His wife, Lady Plowden, is equally well-known for her work in education and broadcasting. A junior Protestant branch of Plowden of Plowden became one of the great dynasties of British India. The building's irregular outline makes it all the more lovable. Notable Jacobean overmantel in the drawing-room and everywhere much panelling. C17 and C18 staircases and a small chapel. PLOWDEN *of Plowden*/LG1972; CL 6 Feb 1975; *Pevsner*; *Leach*.

*Pool Hall*

*Preen Manor*

**Pool Hall, Alveley.** The early C18 front of 5 bays and 3 storeys masks an older building—gables of which survive at the rear. But the 2 storeyed porch is probably C17 tricked up at the time of the general refacing. The site is partly moated. The Grove family is known to have been here in C16 and C17; but latterly it has served as a farmhouse. *Pevsner.*

**Pradoe, Eardiston.** Charming brick house of late C18. 3 storeys and generally plain, but relieved by a canted bay towards the garden. Lower wings. It is situated in an extensive and attractive park. The Kenyons have owned the property since early C19 and they built the Chapel at Eardiston for private use. This was erected 1860 to the designs of Rhode Hawkins. TYRELL-KENYON, KENYON, B/PB; *Pevsner*; Katharine Kenyon, *A House that was Loved* (1940).

**Preen Manor, Church Preen.** A short-lived and dramatic house designed by Norman Shaw, Preen commanded a magnificent view and was a tall building of stone and half-timber in an "L"-shape. Many gabled with mullioned and transomed windows. Built 1872, it had disappeared by 1921 apart from the ground floor with its great Gothic entrance porch. Preen by Shaw was said to have incorporated an older house. After demolition the remaining fragment was added to and a much lower house emerged. The church of St John Baptist adjoins at right angles. Shaw's client was Arthur Sparrow, whose grandson and namesake sold the estate 1918. The newer house belonged to C. F. Hill *ante* World War II. HANBURY-SPARROW *formerly of Rushbury and Eaton-under-Heywood*/LG1952; Saint, *Richard Norman Shaw* (1978); *Pevsner*; *Building News* XXI.

**Prees Hall, Prees.** Unusual brick house with the middle 3 bays on the ground and 1st floors recessed behind the pediment of the same width which continues as part of the parapet on either side above the remaining bays. Pyramid roofs surmount 1 bay wings which are connected with the main block by small links of 1 bay each. Prees is the birthplace of General 1st Viscount Hill (1772), the Peninsular commander, and in this century became the country house of the descendants of Adam & Charles Black, publishers of *Who's Who*, etc. CLEGG-HILL, HILL, V/PB; BLACK/LG1952; *Pevsner.*

*Priorslee Hall*

**Preston Montford Hall, Montford.** Brick house of early C18 of 5 bays and 2 storeys. Quoins, hipped roof and late C18 entrance with pediment over tripartite doorway.

**Priorslee Hall, Priorslee.** Good quality early C18 house of brick with stone quoins. The usual 7 bays with recessed 3 bay centre. Bold segmental pediment on brackets over the entrance. C19 dormers are too pronounced and detract from what is otherwise a very pretty facade. T. E. Freeston lived here 1937. *Pevsner.*

**Quatford Castle, Quatford.** Far-reaching views are enjoyed from this mock C19 castle. It is dated 1830 and was erected by a builder, John Smalman, for himself. Irregular with a plentiful display of battlements, machicolations and rambling outbuildings. Seat of the Bevans. BEVAN/LG1952; *Colvin.*

**Reaside Manor, nr Cleobury Mortimer.** Early C17 house, now a farm. It was probably larger. The gabled porch probably formed the centre. Star shaped chimney stacks. Good square staircase with open well.

*Reaside Manor*

*Rorrington Hall*

*Rossall*

**Rorrington Hall, Rorrington.** Highly picturesque timber-framed house probably late c16 and the heightened in mid-c17. The rear elevation received a brick refacing much later. Now a farmhouse.

**Rossall, Bicton.** Built 1677 for Edward Gosnell, a London merchant who became Mayor of Shrewsbury. 5 bays and 2 storeys with later 5 sided porch. Original staircase with heavy balusters and some other internal c18 alteration. 5 bay flanking service wings of high quality. They have central pediments and doorcases with rusticated surrounds. Sir Robert Giles lived here between the wars.

**Rowton Castle, Alberbury.** In spite of its appearance as a large castellated building of the Romantic revival, it is in fact basically a house of the age of Anne. It was of red brick and rectangular; panelling of this date survives inside. The early c19 additions, which include the entrance screen and big round tower, were made first in 1809–12 to the designs of George Wyatt, and then 1824 on the marriage of Col Henry Lyster and Lady Charlotte Ashley-Cooper, dau of 6th Earl of Shaftesbury. Lady Charlotte's nephew, Sir Montagu Lowry-Corry, eventually inherited the castle. He served as Disraeli's private secretary and was ennobled as Lord Rowton 1880. Shortly *ante* World War II it belonged to Major A. E. Lees; in recent years Rowton has served as an institution, with various subsidiary buildings added in the vicinity. LYSTER/LG1863; LOWRY-CORRY, ROWTON, B/PB1903 and *sub* BELMORE, E/PB; *Colvin*; *Pevsner*.

**Ruckley Grange, Tong.** In place of a many gabled dull Victorian house Sir Ernest George & Yates designed and built the present house 1904. The client was Capt C. G. R. Walker. A neo-Elizabethan stone house with mullioned and transomed windows; the entrance front is "E"-shaped, but not strictly symmetrical. An

*Rowton Castle*

*Rudge Hall*

*Sandford Hall*

arcade appears on the ground floor of a 2 bay projection to one side. Lately the home of Mr Harry Attwood. *Leach*; *Pevsner*.

**Rudge Hall, Rudge.** Neo-Georgian house of 1930 with recessed 3 bay centre between wings with Venetian windows on the ground floor. The estate originally belonged to the Boycott family whose heiress married into the Wights of Ormiston, East Lothian. The Wight-Boycotts sold Rudge 1921 and W. R. Wilson lived here 1937; it now belongs to Mr Alan Henn.

**Sandford Hall, Fauls.** A modest but charming early C18 house of red brick and stone quoins; of 5 bays and 2 storeys, the centre bay breaking slightly forward and rising to a dormer with a segmental head. There is a 1 bay addition to the right. The Sandfords owned the lands here from medieval times, finally selling their ancient seat *ca* 1935. SANDFORD *of The Isle of Rossall*/LG1972; *Leach*; *Pevsner*.

**Sansaw, Clive.** C19 house in a style resembling a building of Queen Anne's day.

Formerly a seat of the Tippinges and the Bibbys, it has now passed to the Thompson family. THOMPSON (*formerly* BIBBY)/LG1952 Supp; TIPPINGE/WCF.

**Shavington, Moreton Say.** When Shavington was demolished 1959 Shropshire lost the grandest house of its date in the county. Built for 6th Viscount Kilmorey 1685 the facades of brick were long and plain. The 17 bays of the garden front were lifted from monotony by the higher attic storeys in the middle and at the ends. But on the entrance

*Shavington: entrance front*

*Shavington: garden front (formerly entrance front)*

*Shavington: staircase*

side the centre was recessed between far-projecting wings. Norman Shaw added the porch and the circular windows in the corner projections 1885 and further alterations were made by Sir Ernest Newton 1903. Very grand staircase with broad handrail and strong twisted balusters. One mid-C18 ceiling survived through this very thorough refurbishment by Shaw and Newton. Shavington later became the seat of the Heywood-Lonsdales. NEEDHAM, KILMOREY, E/PB; HEYWOOD-LONSDALE *of Shavington*/LG1965; *Pevsner;* CL 3 & 10 Aug 1918.

**Shipton Hall, Shipton.** House and stables present a memorable picture to the traveller on the road. It is an Elizabethan building of 1587 built for Richard Lutwyche. "H"-shaped, the usual symmetry is broken by the 4 storeyed tower which contains the porch. Mullioned and transomed windows apart from the rear elevation where all is Gothick. The redecoration of the hall, the building of the staircase with Gothick arches and the fine library on the 1st floor, are the work of T. F. Pritchard *ca* 1750. He probably designed the 9 bay stables which complement the house and which are situated at right angles to it. Myttons owned Shipton until late C19 when it was bought by the Bishops. J. N. R. N. Bishop owns it today. MYTTON/LG1875; *Colvin;* CL19 March 1910; *Pevsner.*

**Sibdon Castle, Sibdon Carwood.** Early C17 house considerably rebuilt in early C18 when the fine staircase was put in. Gothicized *ca* 1800, the main front faces the church and garden. It is 7 bays and 2 storeys with higher accent in the middle which contains a lunette window. All windows are segment-headed. The entrance side faces an attractive courtyard of outbuildings. Built for the Freemans, the house was bought in C20 by the Holdens formerly of Nuthall Temple, Nottinghamshire. HOLDEN *of Hawton and Sibdon*/LG1969; CL 1 & 8 June 1967.

**Soulton Hall, Wem.** Good Caroline house of 1668. It had gables when built but alterations in C18 left it as it is now. 3 storeys, 3 bays with stone dressings on the red brick. Mullioned

*Shipton Hall*

*Sibdon Castle*

date 1588 inside the hall. 2 gables on the main front—that on the right over a wide projection, that on left over a narrower one. The gable to the left is shaped. Ashlar faced porch. Mullioned and transomed windows apart from that of the hall which is mullioned only. Plaster frieze with scrolls and shields in the hall. *Pevsner*.

**Steventon Manor, nr Ludlow.** Stone Jacobean house with "E"-shaped front with 3 gables. Sashed windows and porch with round-headed entrance. Star-shaped stacks and hall with original fireplace and panelling. *Pevsner*.

**Stoke, Greete.** The west front with its two handsome shaped gables is dated 1702. At the same time a new south front was added to the building which is basically older as is evident on the east side. Capt J. W. D. Evans owned the house 1937, but it was lately the home of Lt-Col Sir Richard Verdin (*d* 1978). VERDIN *of Stoke Hall and Garnstone*/LG1969; *Pevsner*.

and transomed windows; entrance with Roman Doric columns. Fine gatepiers in the walled garden. Built for the Hills, it later became a seat of the Deakins and W. R. Lea lived here *ante* World War II. *Pevsner*.

**Stanley Hall, Astley Abbots.** John Smalman added an extraordinary main block in Jacobethan style *ca* 1816 for Sir Thomas Tyrwhitt Jones. A medley of unusual towers and pedimented windows with a recessed centre and many battlements—all composed

an odd confection whose loss in *ca* 1923 must be regretted. What is left is the original and sizeable house of red sandstone and part brick said to date from 1642. Porch with patterned bargeboarding on the entrance side and stables with c18 detail. Now the seat of the Thompson family. *Neale*; *Pevsner*; *Colvin*.

**Stanwardine Hall, Stanwardine-in-the-Wood.** Said to have been built by Robert Corbet, brother of Sir Andrew, of Moreton Corbet. Elizabethan house of brick with the

*Stoke*

*Stanley Hall*

*Stokesay Castle*

**Stokesay Castle, Stokesay.** The best preserved and oldest surviving fortified manor house in England. Lawrence of Ludlow, a great wool merchant, bought Stokesay 1280 and his descendants remained there for 300 years. In 1620 the Cravens bought the property, but they parted with it 1869 to J. D. Allcroft, a notable glove manufacturer. The present owner, Lady Magnus-Allcroft (the wife of Sir Philip Magnus-Allcroft, 2nd Bt, otherwise Philip Magnus, the historian), is his granddaughter. Stokesay's great hall was built 1270–80 and its tall windows show no fear of a hostile outer world. The timber roof of the hall belongs to the late middle ages and the time of the building of the hall. The curiously-shaped south tower dates from 1291. The solar belongs to the same date and has Elizabethan panelling and a sumptuous fireplace. MAGNUS-ALLCROFT, Bt/PB; *Pevsner*; CL 23 April 1910.

*Stokesay Court: C18 house*

*Stokesay Court: C19 house*

*Styche Hall*

**Stokesay Court, Stokesay.** Ambitious if rather uninspired house of 1889 by Thomas Harris. It replaced an early C18 house. Far-projecting wings on the entrance side and canted bays flanking semi-circular one on the garden front. Mullions and shaped gables. Large hall with grand carved staircase at one end of it. Seat of the Allcroft family. ALLCROFT/LGI952; *Pevsner*; Girouard, *Victorian Country House* (1979).

**Styche Hall, nr Market Drayton.** Sir William Chambers rebuilt Styche in early 1760s for the Clives. It has a 7 bay front of 2½ storeys and canted bays rise the full height on either side of the central bay. Staircase below oval dome and a few doorcases and chimneypieces from Chambers's day. Contemporary stables. The real importance of the house lies in the fact that it was the birthplace of Clive of India. Styche descended to the Earls of Powis who have now sold it.

*Sundorne Castle*

HERBERT, POWIS, E/PB; Harris, *Sir William Chambers* (1970); *Colvin*; *Pevsner*; Bence-Jones, *Clive of India* (1974).

**Sundorne Castle, Uffington.** A house of *ca* 1740 was built for the Corbets, but early in C19 it was enlarged out of all recognition and made picturesque by an unknown architect. The only regular front was the entrance side with its two tall towers flanking the way in. The staircase of *ca* 1740 with its 3 twisted balusters to a tread survived, but other rooms were supposedly redecorated by Mylne *ca* 1774. There were interiors of early C19 as well. Mostly demolished 1955. CORBET/LG1937; *Pevsner*.

**Sweeney Hall, Oswestry.** No-nonsense house of 1805. 5 bays and 2 storeys with giant Tuscan pillars at the angles. The builder was T. N. Parker and it passed by descent to the Leightons. LEIGHTON/LG1952; *Leach*; *Pevsner*.

**Tong Castle, Tong.** The Moorish Gothick house designed by Capability Brown for George Durant. It was built 1765 and replaced an older house of the Vernons. Long castellated fronts with battlements and pointed windows and Moorish domes on top. A fragment of plasterwork discovered when the house was a ruin suggests the possibility of T. F. Pritchard having a hand in the interior decoration. Tong became Bridgeman property later in its life, but it was destroyed by fire and dismantled 1913. The shell was taken down 1954. BRIDGEMAN, BRADFORD, E/PB; CL.

**Totterton Hall, Lydbury North.** Onetime seat of the Earls of Powis, but now the property of the Whitaker family. 5 bays and 2 storeys. Of brick with giant pilaster strips. Stout porch with 2 pairs of Tuscan columns. Good park. HERBERT, POWIS, E/PB; WHITAKER/LG1965; *Pevsner*.

*Sweeney Hall*

*Totterton Hall*

*Tong Castle*

*Tunstall Hall*

**Tunstall Hall, Norton-in-Hales.** In recent years a school for girls was established here, but previous to that it was the seat of the Broughton-Adderleys. It was built 1732 and has a brave front of brick of 9 bays and 2¹/₂ storeys. Relieving this expanse are the pediments of all the ground-floor windows and the entry showing a segmental one. On the garden front the central door has a Gibbs surround and triangular pediment. Segments and straight pieces make up the bow to the right-hand side of the building. Inside this bow is semicircular. Plasterwork with vine trails is found in the dining-room and in the entrance hall there is a decorated metope frieze. BROUGHTON-ADDERLEY/LG1972; *Pevsner*.

**Tyn-Y-Rhos Hall, Weston Rhyn.** The Victorian appearance of this house hides a much older building. Oak staircase and fireplaces with early Delf tiles. The home of Mr & Mrs Walter Thompson. THOMPSON, *sub* LLOYD (*co Tipperary*)/IFR.

*Upton Cressett Hall*

*Upton Cressett: gatehouse*

*Walcot Hall*

*Wenlock Abbey*

**Upton Cressett Hall, Upton Cressett.**
Tudor house of 1540 and 1580. Mullioned and
transomed windows; twisted and star-shaped
chimneystacks. The detached gatehouse has
gabled and polygonal turrets. Upton Cressett
was the seat of the Thursby-Pelhams.
Recently restored, it is now the property of Mr
William Cash. THURSBY-PELHAM (*now*
CHAPMAN) *of Upton Cressett*/LG1965; *Pevsner*.

**Walcot Hall, Lydbury North.** Large and
plain house of brick designed by Chambers for
Clive of India (ancestor of the Earls of Powis).
2 storeys, 11 by 8 bays. Balustrade on top and
entrance porch of one storey with 4 Tuscan
columns. Two ceilings by Chambers survive
the drastic internal alterations of 1933. In the
late 1930s the Stevens family lived here.
Monumental stables with central arch and
lantern and splendid grounds with large lake.
HERBERT, POWIS, E/PB; Harris, *Chambers*
(1970) *Pevsner*; *Colvin*; Bence-Jones, *Clive of
India* (1974); CL 14 Oct 1939.

**Wenlock Abbey, Much Wenlock.** Since
1857 the property of the Milnes-Gaskells and
now of their present representative Mr Lewis
Motley. The Norman infirmary of the Cluniac
priory and the range added to it in the late C15
form the present house which is surrounded by
the dramatic ruins of the former great Abbey.
MILNES-GASKELL/LG1965; CL 1 & 8 Dec 1960.

**Westhope Manor, Westhope.** Neo-Tudor
house of 1901 designed by Sir Guy Dawber.
Many gabled and handsome. Seat of the
Dyers. DYER/LG1937; *Pevsner*.

**Whitton Court, Whitton.** Eminently
attractive house of C14, C15 and C16. All in pink
brick. The Tudor period is represented best.
The house encloses a small courtyard and
there is gabled black and white work. Big C16
panelled screen in hall; C17 panelling and
fresco painting of C17 and C18 elsewhere.
Lately the home of Lord Runcorn. VOSPER,
RUNCORN, B/PB1967 and *sub* VOSPER/LG1969;
CL 30 May, 6 June 1968; *Pevsner*.

*Whitton Court*

*Whitton Hall*

*Wilderhope Manor*

*Willey Hall*

**Whitton Hall, Westbury.** Handsome early Georgian rebuilding of an older house. Brick, with the centre 3 bays recessed. Older service wings. Inside, a very pretty staircase and outside, in the grounds, a dovecote and derelict folly. Former seat of the Topp family; owned by Sir Hill Child, Bt, in more recent times. CHILD, Bt/PB1956; *Pevsner.*

**Wilderhope Manor, Wilderhope.** Tudor house built 1586. Of limestone. Many gabled with mullioned and transomed windows. C17 plaster ceilings within. Property of the National Trust who let it to the Youth Hostels Association.

**Willey Hall, Willey.** Seat of the Lords Forester. Designed by Lewis Wyatt and built *ante* 1825. Monumental entrance front of 9 bays and 2 storeys and round the corner a big bow with columns around it. Large and grand hall with columns carrying a gallery. Shallow oval dome over staircase. Apsed library and indeed a succession of rooms of amazing originality and still containing much of the original fittings, *e.g.* draperies and wall hangings. Finely placed in a large park. WELD-FORESTER, FORESTER B/PB; Robinson, *The Wyatts* (1980); *Pevsner*; CL 19 Feb 1921.

**Woodcote Hall, Woodcote.** F. P. Cockerell's Jacobean style house with its odd Gibbs surrounds thrown in replaces an early C19 building which was destroyed by fire *ca* 1875. But that earlier house incorporated parts of a building of C16 and those parts remain

*Woodcote Hall: after the fire 1875*

*Woodcote: F. P. Cockerell's building*

*Woodlands Hall*

The centre is composed of 2 sets of Ionic columns—one in front of the other and rising the whole height of the building. More Ionic columns embrace the bow window on the south side of the house; while inside there is an impressive entrance hall with a screen of Ionic columns, behind which the staircase rises in one flight to return in two. Seat of the Mostyn-Owen family who descend from Robert Owen of Woodhouse (High Sheriff of Shropshire 1618). The present squire is Mr William Mostyn-Owen, director of Christies and Berenson's former secretary who is married to Gaia Servadio, the writer. MOSTYN-OWEN/LG1969; *Colvin*; *Pevsner*.

**Woodlands Hall, Glazeley.** Late Georgian stone house with pointed windows on all facades. These are linked by continuous hood-moulds in the form of bands around the building. 4 by 5 bays with a porch. The house was reduced to its original size *ca* 1950 when later additions which obscured the original design were removed. A small brick 1 storey extension was added 1971. The stables are also Gothic with a wide pointed arch in the centre. Plain staircase with some pointed arches within. Wylde-Brownes owned the property before it was bought 1911 by E. T. Crook whose daughter, Mrs Pitt, owned the house until her death 1979. CROOK/LG1952.

embedded in the present house. Cockerell's best interior is the 2 storey hall with arcades on the upper floor. Early C18 stables. Long the seat of the Cotes family, Woodcote was bought by the Fosters after the fire. COTES/WCF.

**Woodhouse, West Felton.** An unusual house designed by Robert Mylne and built 1773-74. It is brick and the entrance front boasts an uncommon centrepiece framed by Ionic pilasters which occur at the angles too.

*Woolstaston Hall*

**Woolstaston Hall, Woolstaston.** The remaining wing of a large "H"-shaped house of the late C17. 7 bays and 2 storeys. The doorway has pilasters on which garlands hang down. *Pevsner*.

**Wrockwardine Hall, Wrockwardine.** A building composed of two parts: the first is dated 1628; and the second 7 bay front of 2 storeys and hipped roof is Georgian. Staircases of both periods inside. Thomas Balfour lived here 1937. *Pevsner*.

**Yeaton Peverey, Baschurch.** By Aston Webb for Sir Offley Wakeman, 3rd Bt, 1891. Low powerful silhouette of red sandstone but uninspired at the same time. Set off by a forecourt with domed summer houses at the corners it is in Jacobean style and is irregular with an entrance tower, asymmetrically placed turret and a lively mixture of mullioned windows. More variety and attractiveness on the garden front mainly on account of the half-timbering on the first floor. Lifeless interiors. WAKEMAN, Bt/PB; *Pevsner*.

*Yeaton Peverey*

# WARWICKSHIRE

A VARIETY of well-wooded landscape ranging from the Cotswolds to the red sandstone of the burgeoning areas of Birmingham makes Warwickshire amongst the more attractive counties in England.

Medieval architecture in Warwickshire gave the county a handful of buildings of national importance. Warwick Castle towers above all—its origins being discernible as 13th-century and even earlier. It is a monumental building in a splendid setting—both natural and man-made. To the 14th century belongs Maxstoke Castle with its tall gatehouse, a somewhat simpler version of Harlech in Wales. Late medieval building in Warwickshire has displays of notable timber-framing such as is found at Mancetter Manor. But in the 15th century we are confronted with houses of importance composed of stone and brick. Baddesley Clinton is stone yet Pooley Hall is of brick. Then there is the combination of brick and stone as exemplified in such houses as Compton Wynyates and Coughton Court. The major Elizabethan house in the county is Charlecote, which, in spite of being altered, still retains its original porch and gatehouse.

The Elizabethan style in Warwickshire, however, continued well into the 17th century: the grand Aston Hall was only started in 1618, whereas in other counties it would have been considered as distinctly old-fashioned. But Aston's centrally placed hall does away with the medieval and Tudor fashion of a hall with the entrance and screens passage at one end.

The vanished Chesterton was a house of artisan mannerist style shown in a number of smaller buildings in the county; Packington Old Hall and the stables at Packwood are examples of this.

Warwickshire's Baroque houses travel by way of the porch at Castle Bromwich, Winde's now sadly altered wing at Combe Abbey and Umberslade, to Stoneleigh Abbey. Honington can be regarded as the most perfect Wren-type house in the county and it forms a group with Farnborough, Wootton and Upton of plain early Classical houses.

Stoneleigh's great west range by Francis Smith was begun in 1714 and is a major building of the English Baroque—one of the noblest in the land. Almost contemporary with it is Newbold Revel. Sanderson Miller, the architect/squire of Radway, was responsible for a spate of Gothick building in the county. Beginning at Radway with various park buildings in addition to the house itself, the feast of Gothickry built up through Alscot Park to Arbury Hall—the finest Early Gothic Revival house in England—and the result of many hands.

The Georgians, first in the person of James Gibbs who gave Ragley its splendid hall and then in Robert Adam who altered Compton Verney, gave way to much 18th-century building in Warwickshire. Curiously most of the more important interiors of that period were a result of alterations to older houses. Both Ragley and Compton Verney were earlier and they were followed by the magnificent interiors to Honington, again a late 17th-century house. Packington Hall, another c18 rebuilding, contains the most complete Pompeian Room in England. It was designed by Bonomi and was completed by about 1800.

Into the 19th century we are confronted by a number of stupendous houses. Blore's vanished Weston; his extant Merevale Hall; Bilton Grange by Pugin in the 1840s; and Scott's limp Walton Hall of about 1860. High Victorian mansions reached their zenith with Ettington Hall rebuilt by Prichard about 1860—a powerful building with attractive grouping and a dramatic contrast to the feeble Wroxall and Caldecote. Paving the way to the c20 and Lutyens is Ashorne Hill House.

Losses have been serious—Four Oaks, Newnham Paddox, Stivichall, Warwick Priory, Nesfield's wing at Combe Abbey and the ruinous Guy's Cliffe all represent a range of building periods and styles and notable architects whose disappearance can only be bitterly regretted. Long-established families still *in situ* include the Dugdales, Leighs, Shirleys, Lucys, Seymours, Shuckburghs, Holbechs and Throckmortons.

# Principal Bibliography

CL     *Country Life*

Colvin     Colvin, H. M.: *A Biographical Dictionary of British Architects 1600–1840* (1978)

DEP     *Burke's Dormant and Extinct Peerages* (1883)

EDB     *Burke's Extinct and Dormant Baronetcies* (1841)

IFR     *Burke's Irish Family Records* (1976)

LG     *Burke's Landed Gentry*, 18 edns (1883/37–1972)

PB     *Burke's Peerage and Baronetage*, 105 edns (1826–1970)

Pevsner     Pevsner, Nikolaus: *Warwickshire* (1974)

VCH     *The Victoria History of the County of Warwick*, 6 vols (1904–51)

VSA     Burke, Sir Bernard: *A Visitation of Seats and Arms of the Noblemen and Gentlemen of Great Britain and Ireland*, 2 vols (1852–53); 2nd series, 2 vols (1854–55)

WCF     *Walford's County Families*

*Admington Hall*

room with rich fan-vault pattern on the ceiling. The dining-room and the principal staircase are Victorian, but ogee-headed doors give way to the library and study. The secondary staircase would have surely sent Walpole into ecstasies. It has a wrought-iron handrail and Gothick and Rococo stucco under a skylight and runs through 3 storeys, giving way to the final room which is octagonal. Good park with Gothick hothouse of 1753; the rotunda and obelisk of 1757 have gone. Richard Hulls probably designed the entrance lodges. ALSTON-ROBERTS-WEST *of Alscot Park*/LG 1972; *Colvin; Pevsner;* CL 15, 22 & 29 May 1958; *Neale* III(1820); Gunnis, *Dictionary of British Sculptors.*

**Admington Hall, Admington.** This house was situated in the County of Gloucestershire until 1935. The irregular and somewhat formal entrance front is C18, the only relieving accents being the tripartite windows on the 1st and 2nd floors and the projecting porch below them. But all this hides the earlier C17 house which shows at the back with an array of gables and mullioned windows. Dovecote in grounds. Formerly the seat of the Holland Corbett family, Admington was owned in 1931 by Lt-Col William Gibbs and is now the property of Mr and Mrs J. P. Wilkerson. HOLLAND CORBETT/LG 1886; *Pevsner.*

**Allesley Park, Allesley.** Grand 3 storey house of late C17. Very much in the style of its contemporary Wrottesley Hall, Staffordshire, which was reduced after a fire 1897. Allesley was demolished 1907. For much of its life it had belonged to the Bree family; in 1897 it was bought by Messrs W. C. D. and E. Turrall. The grounds boasted a fine avenue of elms half-a-mile in length. MAPLETON-BREE/ LG 1952; VSA.

**Alscot Park, Preston on Stour.** Seat of the Alston-Roberts-West family descended from James West, Joint Secretary of the Treasury, who bought the estate 1749. An earlier house was there and part of it was retained, but precisely what is not clear. Mullioned windows show here and there. Edward and Thomas Woodward appear to have been busy at the house between 1750 and 1764 and the canted bays must be theirs. After West retired he built a higher ashlar wing making a "T" with the older part and on this "T" Thomas Hopper added a porch *ante* 1820. A feast of Gothickry within. Starting with the entrance hall which has giant panels of thin shafts and ogee arches, one proceeds to the drawing-

*Alscot Park*

*Alscot Park*

*Alveston House*

**Alveston House, Alveston.** Delightfully situated in meadows behind the Avon, Alveston is a good standard house built for Thomas Peers 1689. 7 bays with central 3 recessed with pediment. Hipped roof and quoins. Roman Doric porch of *ca* 1750 on south side of the house. A noble avenue of limes is aligned on this front and links the old church with the house. Gazebo with ogee roof on main road. By the river bank there is the site of a vanished grotto. The male line of the Peers family became extinct with the death of Newnham Peers 1803 and the house was sold to Henry Roberts of Stratford 1810. Samuel Saunders lived here 1904. Latterly the seat of Lt-Col R. H. R. Brocklebank. BROCKLEBANK *formerly of Childwall Hall*/LG1965; CL 25 May 1945; *Pevsner*; VCH III.

**Amington Hall, Amington.** Early C19 house of stone. 3 bay entrance front with doorcase of Ionic columns supporting a pediment. Round the corner a longer 7 bay front punctuated by a central bow surmounted by a shallow dome. Built for the Repington family near the site of an older house and eventually inherited by the A'Court family who became A'Court-Repingtons. Lieut Charles A'Court-Repington's *Diaries* were a notable feature of the literature of World War I. The house was sold in C20 to the Fishers but was finally demolished. REPINGTON/LG1833/7; HOLMES A'COURT, *sub* HEYTESBURY, B/PB; VCH IV.

**Ansley Hall, Ansley.** Onetime seat of the Ludfords for whom Sir William Chambers designed a Chinese Temple 1767 (now de-

*Amington Hall*

stroyed). A curious house with its stables on the road. The dominant periods are Tudor and early Georgian. Of the former is the south range with its later Gothick windows and orangery. North and east ranges are C18. The whole ranges round a courtyard. Much of the original interior has gone. Ansley has belonged to the National Coal Board for many years and is used as a recreation centre. *Pevsner*; Harris, *Sir William Chambers* (1970).

**Ansty Hall, Ansty.** In spite of its Georgian appearance, the building is mainly of C17. It is a tall 7 bay block of brick with lower additions

*Ansty Hall*

*Arbury Hall*

to one side. The date 1678 on a doorcase must represent the 2 lower storeys as the top floor was added 1800. The entrance doorcase has a broken pediment on brackets. The principal front is in a rhythm of 2-3-2 with a pediment crowning the 3 bays in the middle, but the rear of the house shows 1-5-1. The Taylor family lived here prior to the marriage of their heiress to Clarke Adams 1744. It has since descended in the latter family, the present owner being Mr D. J. Stopford Adams who bought it from his cousin Mr P. E. Woollcombe-Adams 1956. ADAMS/LG1965; *Pevsner*; VSA.

**Arbury Hall, Arbury.** Possibly the finest early Gothic Revival house in England. The present house is basically one of 1580, but its extravagant display of C18 Gothickry all but drums out any earlier features. But from an earlier age the stables survive and they can be dated *ca* 1670. Of brick with central projecting archway and pavilions. Wren was consulted over the portal, but his drawings remained unused. Sir William Wilson of Warwick was paid for drawings too—perhaps he designed the entire stable-block. In the north-east corner of the house is the chapel and it contains decoration of the Carolean age. A ceiling of great richness showing wreaths, flowers, fruit, etc, was executed by Edward Martin 1678. The walls, less spectacular, are divided into panels separated by swags of fruit falling from winged cherubs' heads. The Newdegate family came into Arbury in 1586 and they remain here still. It is to Sir Roger Newdegate, 5th Bt, the founder of the Newdegate prize for poetry at Oxford, that we owe the overwhelming Gothick taste which prevails today. Sanderson Miller was his adviser but it seems William Hiorn put plans into the actual building. He began with bows and the library *ca* 1750. Then Henry Keene became supervisor, overseeing the creation of the drawing-room and dining-room 1771–79. After Keene came a local man, Couchman, and under him the saloon was finished. It is very likely that much was designed by Sir Roger Newdegate himself as drawings for miscellaneous detail do exist. The principal rooms display the

light-hearted and pretty Gothickry we associated with Walpole's Strawberry Hill, Twickenham. In size the dining-room comes first. It was formerly the entrance hall and shows great vaults, tall canopied niches and a huge chimneypiece. The drawing-room has a tunnel vault running to a bow window with fan-vaulting. The chimneypiece is based on the monument to Aymer de Vallance in Westminster Abbey. In the library are ogee-headed bookcases and segmental ceiling with classical painting by William Wise. Arbury was immortalized by George Eliot as "Cheverel Manor" for her father was agent to the estate and she was born here. The heiress of Sir Francis Newdegate, Gov of W. Australia, married the younger son of Viscountess Daventry, widow of Capt Rt Hon Edward FitzRoy, Speaker of the House of Commons 1928–43; their son, Cmdr J. M. FitzRoy

Newdegate, assumed that surname by Royal Licence. FITZROY NEWDEGATE, *sub* DAVENTRY, B/PB and LG1952; CL 13 April 1907, 13 Sept 1913 & 8, 15, 29 Oct 1953; *Pevsner*; VCH; *Connoisseur* Sept 1968.

**Arlescote Manor, nr Radway.** Elizabethan house remodelled late C17. 7 bays with a hipped roof in a walled enclosure with lofty gatepiers and gazebos with ogee roofs which are reminders of an elaborate garden layout which once existed here. A canal which formed part of the original plan still survives. The centre 3 bays are recessed and have mullioned and transformed windows whereas the wings have sash windows. William and Mary panelling in parlour. The Cooper and Goodwin families preceded the Lovedays to whom the property passed in C18. LOVEDAY/LG1972; CL 5 Sept 1947; *Pevsner*; VCH V.

*Arlescote Manor*

*Armscote House*

*Armscote Manor*

*Ashfurlong Hall*

*Ashfurlong: garden temple*

**Armscote House, Armscote.** Similar to Armscote Manor (*qv*). Early C17 again of the Cotswold type with gabled wings and mullioned windows. But a lower and broader silhouette to its companion. Pretty wrought-iron gate.

**Armscote Manor, Ettington.** Small and charming early C17 house of the Cotswold type in local stone which has weathered to a soft grey patina. Mullioned windows with projecting bays with pointed gables. Probably built for the Halford family, Armscote was in a depressed condition when Capt Yorke bought it 1914. He commissioned Guy Dawber to restore the house and make a modest addition in keeping. George Fox, founder of the Society of Friends, was arrested here 1673. Mr J. F. Docker is the present owner. CL 13 Jan 1923; *Pevsner*.

**Ashfurlong Hall, Sutton Coldfield.** 7 bay ashlar house of C17 and C18 with 3 bay pediment above pilasters. One passes a temple on the drive with portico of 2 pairs of unfluted Ionic columns. Sometime seat of the Colmore family. Now the property of Mr E. H. Moore. COLMORE/WCF.

**Ashorne Hill House, Newbold Pacey.** Grand, Tudor style house designed by E. Goldie and built 1895–97. Of stone and blue brick, the entrance side with its 2 bays is almost

symmetrical while the garden front is plainly asymmetrical with hall bay window, staircase tower, 2nd bay and a lower wing tailing off to the right. Sumptuous neo-Jacobean interiors of high quality. At the beginning of this century it was the seat of A. M. Tree, son of the US Minister to Russia, who married the Chicago store heiress Ethel Field (later wife of Adm of the Fleet 1st Earl Beatty). Their son, Ronald Tree, MP, bought Ditchley Park,

Oxon. Now the management college of the British Steel industry. TREE/LG 1969; *Pevsner*; *The Builder* 1898.

**Astley Castle, Astley.** At one time Astley must have been an establishment of considerable size. What remains of the main house now is a long rectangular building all castellated and appearing Elizabethan on account of its features. There is a Jacobean chimneypiece

*Ashorne Hill House*

inside. Licence to crenellate was issued 1266 and it is possible that parts of the gatehouse and curtain wall are as early as this. Former seat of the Greys, Dukes of Suffolk, of whom various monuments are found in St Mary's, Astley. It was on the Duke of Suffolk's attainder and execution 1554 that the castle, originally moated, was dismantled—to be rebuilt later in C16. In C20 the castle belonged to the Newdegates of Arbury (*qv*). FITZROY NEWDEGATE *of Arbury and Harefield*/LG1952; GREY, SUFFOLK, D/DEP; VSA; *Pevsner*; VCH VI.

**Aston Hall, Aston, Birmingham.** A monumental Jacobean house begun 1618 but not completed until 1635. It is of brick and the main front faces east with projecting wings enclosing a forecourt. The skyline is punctuated by shaped gables and 3 dominant towers—a curious sight in the middle of suburban Birmingham. It is possible the architect was John Thorpe; the client was Sir Thomas Holte, 1st Bt. There are staircases either side of the hall and the north wing is entirely devoted to offices. The principal rooms are on the 1st floor. But the entrance hall, approached from the middle, was certainly designed for display. 3 archways of stone and a great marble fireplace. Pilasters featured on the north and south walls frame grisaille paintings, but the plaster ceiling of some sumptuousness is probably early C19. Richly carved balustrades and elaborate newels are a feature of the great staircase which climbs to the second floor and is in a square well. The chapel, drawing-room, King's Bedroom and Long Gallery contain elaborate plasterwork and great chimneypieces. In the grounds, which are a public park, are small square lodges. C18 stables and C18 Gothick gateway. Aston Hall is maintained as a public museum by the City of Birmingham. The Holte baronetcy died out 1782 and early in C19 the house was owned by James Watt the younger. HOLTE, Bt/EDB; GIBSON-WATT/LG1969; *Pevsner*; CL 2 Sept 1905 & 20, 27 Aug, 3 Sept 1953; VCH.

**Atherstone Hall, Atherstone.** The core of the house was probably early C18 and was built for Abraham Bracebridge. It was of 6 bays and 3 storeys. At a later period—probably early C19—lower additions were built either side of the original building and the whole structure was rendered. Library with apsed ends and screens of marbled columns. Late C18 ballroom. In 1872 it was bought by Rev Beardmore Compton whose son took the additional surname of Bracebridge. Atherstone was demolished 1963. COMPTON-BRACEBRIDGE/ LG1952; VSA.

**Avon Carrow, Avon Dassett.** Castellated, Tudor style house of late C19. In the centre a square tower with octagonal towers at its corners. This flanked by 2 storey wings each with a gable and with mullioned windows. On the entrance side, wings embrace a long narrow courtyard at the head of which is a squat 2 storey tower backing on to the larger tower. Oriel window over entrance. Built for a Capt Boyle, it subsequently became the property of the Barons Profumo and was the childhood house of John Profumo, former Secretary of State for War. Latterly owned by the Worrall family. Now converted into flats. PROFUMO/LG1952.

*Aston Hall*

*Atherstone Hall*

*Atherstone: drawing room chimneypiece*

*Avon Carrow*

*Baddesley Clinton*

**Baddesley Clinton Hall, Baddesley Clinton.** One of the best moated houses in England. Of brick and stone, mullioned windows and tall chimneys, it sums up the romantic ideal. Dating from C15 it was begun by John and Nicholas Brome and passed to the Ferrers family 1517. Descendants still live there today. The north range is basically C15, but its battlements are Victorian—the great window above the entrance is an Elizabethan alteration. Henry Ferrers, the antiquarian, was responsible for much of the work undertaken in late C16 and early C17. The west side of the house has gone and the south side was altered by the Victorians to make communication easier, but it was successfully carried out with a porch and a timber-framed gable. The east range which contains the hall and principal apartments presents a Queen Anne face to the moat that adds to the happy mixture of periods. The romance of the exterior is amply rewarded within. The hall has moulded C15 beams and an ornate Elizabethan stone chimneypiece. More chimneypieces of C16 and C17 in other rooms and fine heraldic stained glass dating back to 1560. On an upper floor is the chapel created 1634. Outside there are stables of C17. The house stands close to the church of St Michael and is approached through a well-timbered park. It is said that the place would have been sacked by the Cromwellians if only they had been able to find it. Presented to the Government 1980 by Mr T. W. Ferrers-Walker and transferred to the National Trust. FERRERS/LG1952; CL 30 Dec 1905, 9, 16 April 1932 & 22, 29 June 1978; *Pevsner*; VCH.

**Baginton Hall, Baginton.** By Francis Smith of Warwick for William Bromley, Speaker of the House of Commons, it was built *ca* 1710 on the site of an older house which was destroyed by fire that year. Funds voted by the House defrayed the cost of rebuilding. On an eminence and of stone it was of 3 storeys and 7 bays with a top balustrade. Over the entrance

*Baraset*

*Barford House*

*Barrells*

door cut into the stone was the inscription "Dii Patrii Servate Domum, 1714". But another fire destroyed this new house on 7 Oct 1889. Bromleys married into the Davenports of Capesthorne, Cheshire; once united the surname became Bromley-Davenport and so it remains to this day. BROMLEY-DAVENPORT *of Capesthorne*/LG1965; VSA; *Colvin*; VCH VI.

**Baraset, Alveston.** Built for a nabob, William Harding, who gave it an Indian name, Baraset was an early C19 house composed of a tall 5 by 5 bay block of 3 storeys attached to a lower service wing. Top balustrade. Cannon used at the Battle of Copenhagen decorated the lawn in front of the entrance. This seat of the Hardings was demolished 1920s. HARDING/LG1921; VSA.

**Barford House, Barford.** A Regency building with an impressive entrance front. 4 attached unfluted Ionic columns with giant angle pilasters give this white house importance and dignity. It is of 9 bays with the more decorated end bays slightly lower. Brooke Robinson, MP, lived here 1904. *Pevsner*.

**Barrells, Henley-in-Arden.** A house of 3 builds. First, a plain 7 bay C18 block to which Bonomi made additions thus giving the house its real architectural importance. Then, in C19, an octagonal tower was built and additions were made outside as well as inside. The hall had a screen of marbled columns supporting round-headed arches. The house was destroyed by fire 1933. In C18 Barrells was the seat of the Earl of Catherlough. In 1904 it was the property of T. H. G. Newton. KNIGHT, CATHERLOUGH, E/DEP; NEWTON/WCF; *Colvin*.

**Barton House, Barton-on-the-Heath.** An interesting and probably late-Tudor house of "H"-shaped plan and resembling houses in the Cotswolds. A spectacular giant arch connects the 2 porch towers in the angles, but one questions whether the arch is in fact original work. Under the arch a big Victorian window lights the hall. The left wing contains the Oak Room with unusual panelling and the staircase with square balusters. A stucco ceiling is in the right-hand wing. Overburys were here in early years, but by the C20 it belonged to Col Stanley Arnold. Dr I. A. Bewley Cathie, the pathologist, is the present owner. CATHIE/LG1965; *Pevsner*; VCH V.

*Barrells: hall*

*Barton House*

**Billesley Manor, Billesley.** Basically a building of *ca* 1610–20 erected for Sir Robert Lee. The main front of the house faces south and it is composed of four dormer gables above an array of six-light mullioned and transomed windows. Detmar Blow was responsible for alteration and restoration in early C20, for the Hanbury-Tracy family. He added an extension 1 bay wide and 1 bay deep behind the principal range and he put back the left gable and window to its right to make the front symmetrical once more. Blow was busy inside as well, giving the hall a gallery which was not there before and another room was filled with C18 panelling. Jacobean chimneypieces and a priest-hole are to be found on the 1st floor. The house is built of Lias stone. Owners this century have included H. C. F. Somerset, H. G. Bois and E. M. Gliksten. HANBURY-TRACY, *sub* SUDELEY, B/PB; SOMERSET *sub* BEAUFORT, D/PB; CROWDY/WCF; *Pevsner*; VCH III; CL 9 July 1927.

*Billesley Manor*

*Bilton Grange: entrance tower*

*Bilton Hall*

*Bilton Grange*

**Bilton Grange, nr Dunchurch.** Pugin's Tudor Gothic house of 1841–46 received various additions after it became a school at the end of C19. Both the chapel of 1889 and the left wing of 1891 left the original house in the middle. It was built for Capt J. H. W. Hibbert. A grand entrance tower with steep roof singles out the Pugin building and there is a great hall and a wing containing a gallery 100 feet long. This wing has canted bays and even gables. Good work by Pugin inside including several chimneypieces, heraldic floor and balustrade with openwork black-letter. HIBBERT *formerly of Ashby St Ledgers*/LG1965; VSA; *Pevsner*; Girouard, *Victorian Country House* (1979).

*Bilton Hall*

**Bilton Hall, Bilton.** Thomas Addison, the essayist, bought the house 1711 from William Boughton and he spent his remaining years here. It was built for a Boughton early in C17. Of brick with mullioned and transomed windows, the porch dated 1623 runs the whole height. A longer garden front is composed of the original house and an early C18 extension. There is an early C18 staircase with 2 balusters to a tread and with carved tread-ends. The house used to be approached through a wide avenue of elms. On the death of Addison's daughter in 1798 Bilton was left to the Bridgeman-Simpson family. Early in C19 it was leased to the celebrated sporting writer C. J. Apperley ("Nimrod"). By the beginning of C20 it was the home of Walter Barnett, but it has changed hands at least twice since. BRIDGEMAN-SIMPSON, *sub* BRADFORD, E/PB; *Pevsner*; VCH VI; D. C. Kingsbury, *Bilton Hall* (1957).

**Birdingbury Hall, Birdingbury.** The symmetrical front looks neo-Jacobean and probably results from a late C19 rebuilding—perhaps in 1873 when the neighbouring Georgian church received radical "improving" treatment. But there is a staircase of *ca* 1630 inside the house as well as a Georgian one said to have come from Kenilworth Castle. The Wheler family owned the estate and the widow of Sir Charles Wheler left it to the Biddulphs 1687. They held it until C20. Now a conventions centre. BIDDULPH, Bt/PB; *Pevsner*; VCH VI.

**Blakesley Hall, Yardley, Birmingham.** Timber-framed and plaster house of considerable size dating from C16. "L"-shaped plan with projecting porch wing at south east end. The upper storey is jettied on brackets and the framing has a herringbone effect. In early C17 a brick addition in the form of a kitchen was added to the north side. The house has been altered inside, but partitions remain in situ on the 1st floor. Now a museum. *Pevsner*.

**Blyth Hall, Shustoke.** Here the antiquary Sir William Dugdale wrote his famous *History of Warwickshire* in C17 and it was here he died 1685. The house still belongs to the Dugdales. It is Sir William's building we see, but it was altered by his grandson so it assumed its present early C18 appearance with 11 bays and 2 storeys. The front projects slightly at either end and there is a hipped roof with pedimented dormers. The entrance boasts a segmental pediment and this is answered by the segmental pediment of the dormer in the centre. To match the exterior there is one early C18 staircase inside, but a mightier one is C17 and more C17 work is found in the outbuildings with their shaped gables. Further additions in C19. DUGDALE, Bt, *of Merevale*/PB; *Pevsner*; VCH IV.

**Botts Green House, Nether Whitacre.** Possibly medieval in origin, but it looks late C16 and the date 1593, although lately placed, seems right for the house. Long, low silhouette. It is a large wholly timber-framed building with exposed timbers in wide variety—herringbone strutting, concave-sided lozenges and cusped concave sided lozenges. Sandstone porch with concave-sided lozenge of stone. *Pevsner*; VCH IV.

*Birdingbury Hall*

*Blakesley Hall*

*Blyth Hall*

*Botts Green House*

*Bourton Hall*

*Bourton: staircase*

**Bourton Hall, Bourton-on-Dunsmore.**
Something of a mystery as it is not certain just
what is Georgian and what is Victorian in
keeping. It is of ashlar and its main front boasts
2 symmetrical canted bay windows which
appear late-Georgian. The east side has
alternating pediments on the principal
windows and the west side shows a 3 bay
pediment. Attached to the west entrance side is
a 2 storeyed gallery connecting house and
chapel. The latter has a Quattrocento facade.
The stairwell of the principal staircase is
reminiscent of that in Ashburnham House,
London with an opening of oval shape on the
second floor with Ionic columns supporting
the ceiling. SHUCKBURGH/LG1914; DARLING-
TON/ WCF; *Pevsner*; VCH VI.

**Bramcote Hall, Polesworth.** Unusual and
attractive house with a curious Baroque flair.
Of brick, 9 bays wide with a much tighter 5 bay
depth. What gives the house its undoubted
zest is the high attic storey with 4 bays flanked
by concave sides rising from the cornice.
*Pevsner.*

**Caldecote Hall, Caldecote.** Bold brick
mansion in a free Jacobean style. Symmetrical
fronts apart from a substantial projecting
wing. An uninspired building and the same
can be said of the large stables. R. J. and J.
Goddard were the architects; the date
1879–80. It replaced an earlier house which
was the scene of a memorable defence by
George Abbott on 28 Aug 1642. Abbott, with a
small band of supporters, defended the building against a "furious and fierce assault" by the
Royalists. The property of Capt H. L.
Townshend *ante* World War I; now Mr C. E.
Colbourn lives there. VSA; FENTON/WCF; VCH
IV; *Pevsner.*

**Castle Bromwich Hall, Castle Bromwich.**
The courtyard has been filled in, but this was
originally a courtyard house of the Jacobean
period built for the Devereux family. The
Bridgemans bought the place 1657 and their
alterations at that time gave the house its
present character. Sir John Bridgeman added
the 3rd storey and gave the house its truly
memorable feature on the outside. That is the 2
storey porch of rusticated stone with coupled
columns on the ground floor which support an
open segmental pediment. The barley-sugar
columns on the inside of the pairs and niches
above with allegorical figures give it unique-
ness and character. In spite of the mid-C17
style of the porch it is of a possibly later date as
Sir W. Wilson is known to have provided the
figures 1697 and Capt William Winde was
working at the Hall in late C17. The 2nd Earl of
Bradford, direct descendant of the Bridgemans, called in Thomas Rickman to make
alterations 1825 and 1840. It was Rickman
who added a new kitchen with accompanying
tower to the north-east and at the same time he
remodelled the entrance hall and gave the long
gallery a new ceiling. The highlight of the
interior is the sumptuous plasterwork by
Gouge. The staircase ceiling has flowers,
leaves and fruit in magnificent abundance and
more rooms demonstrate Gouge's skill. The
dining-room and the boudoir pave the way to
the saloon up the late C17 staircase and at the
south-west corner of the house. Paintings by
Laguerre. Stables of early C17 and early C18.
DEVEREUX, HEREFORD, V/PB; BRIDGEMAN,
BRADFORD, E/PB; *Pevsner*; CL 4 Aug 1900, 17
Aug 1912 & 9 May 1952; VCH IV; *Colvin.*

*Caldecote Hall*

*Chadwick Manor*

**Chadwick Manor, Temple Balsall.** Large Jacobean style house of 1875. Prominent shaped gables. Now an hotel. *Pevsner*.

*Bramcote Hall*

*Castle Bromwich Hall*

*Charlecote Park*

**Charlecote Park, Charlecote.** At first glance Charlecote looks wholly Elizabethan and its attractive gatehouse with polygonal angle turrets is very much so. But the house itself is largely C19 and contains outstanding decoration of this later period which is now being appreciated. It is entered through a porch which is likely to be a reminder of the basic date of the building—1558. Fluted Ionic pilasters flank the arch below and paired Corinthian columns are attached above. A C17 balustrade tops the porch. The house has long projecting wings with gables, canted bay

windows and outer stair turrets. It shape is reminiscent of other great Elizabethan houses such as Melford Hall in Suffolk. But the earliest work inside is the principal staircase of *ca* 1700 with twisted balusters. Of the C18 is the chimneypiece of Adam type found in an end room. A second stair of *ca* 1700 has a ceiling painted in the Verrio-Laguerre style. There are two stages of C19 work at Charlecote. The first *ca* 1829 and the second *ca* 1847–67. Thomas Willement supervised the first phase and to this time belongs the remodelling of the hall with its wood-looking plaster ceiling and

Elizabethan-type chimneypiece. Two good rooms survive with original decoration of these years behind the hall. They are the dining-room and the library and they boast stucco ceilings with pendants and fine flock wallpapers. The garden front facing a bend in the river is a Victorian composition designed by John Gibson. Gables, big bay windows, chimneys and turrets are all combined to give an asymmetrical composition. Stables and brewhouse are Elizabethan, orangery and south-west lodge are by Gibson, the grounds were laid out by Capability Brown. Lucys owned the estate from the C13 until 1946 when it was presented to the National Trust. Shakespeare is said to have been caught poaching here; in return he lampooned the Lucy of the day as "Mr Justice Shallow". The place features in Sir Brian Fairfax-Lucy's disturbing tale, *The Children of the House.* CAMERON-RAMSAY-FAIRFAX-LUCY, Bt/PB; CL 24 Jan 1914 & 11, 18 April, 2 May 1952; VCH; *Pevsner*; Fairfax-Lucy, *Charlecote and the Lucys*; Stroud, *Capability Brown.*

**Chesterton House, Chesterton.** A noble house of stone built *ante* 1658 for Sir Edward Peyto. Of 3 tall storeys with giant pilasters its author was John Stone of the famous Oxfordshire family of stonemasons. Peytos had been here since Edward I, but the marriage of their eventual heiress into the Verney family brought an end to the building. John Peyto Verney, 14th Lord Willoughby de Broke (who married Lord North's sister), demolished the house 1802, preferring his principal seat, Compton Verney (*qv*). A solitary reminder of the vanished house lies in the unusual Chesterton Mill. Said to have been

*Charlecote: entrance front*

*Charlecote: hall*

designed by one of the Peytos, it stands high on arches and has a circular room and dome. The tawny stone of the region adds to its enchantment. VERNEY, WILLOUGHBY DE BROKE, B/PB; *Colvin*; *Pevsner*; Colvin, *Architectural Review* (Aug 1955).

**Clifford Manor, Clifford Chambers.** A low front of *ca* 1700 conceals pre-Reformation work. Sir Edwin Lutyens rebuilt most of the house and even tacked on a large half-timbered piece moved from elsewhere. This was demolished in 1950s. Good later c18 chimneypieces. Sometime property of the Rees-Moggs, Clifford now belongs to Mr D. Prophet. REES-MOGG/LG1969; CL 4,11 Aug 1928.

*Clifford Chambers: entrance front*

*Clifford Chambers: showing half-timbered wing (now demolished)*

*Clopton House*

*Coleshill Hall*

*Combe Abbey: entrance with Nesfield range to right*

**Clopton House, Stratford on Avon.** The symmetrical late C17 front to the west hides a house of some complexity. For it is partly *ca* 1600, with more of the late C17, and was much pulled about 1830. On the entrance side there is a stone ground floor and timber-framed upper storey. The hall is across a courtyard in the range which looks west and was refaced in late C17. Staircase and principal rooms of late C17. Coarse plasterwork in some upper rooms. Formerly the seat of the Hodgsons, Clopton was owned in the 1960s by the Beecham family, famous for its powders and pills and the great conductor, Sir Thomas. HODGSON/ LG1921; BEECHAM, Bt/PB; VSA; *Pevsner*; VCH; *Neale* IV.

**Coleshill Hall, Coleshill.** Replacing a C17 house, the stables of which now serve as a farm. A large but gaunt Gothic house of 1873 built for the Wingfield-Digby family. Porte-cochère tower. The house, built of red and blue brick with Bath stone dressings, stands on an eminence and is now the centre of a large hospital. WINGFIELD-DIGBY *of Sherborne Castle and Coleshill*/LG1965; *Pevsner*.

**Combe Abbey, Coventry.** In spite of much of the building having been demolished, this former seat of the Earls of Craven still presents a sizeable house in the landscape. Evidences of the Cistercian Abbey remain—the entry courtyard represents the cloisters and the entry to the chapter house is in the standard position. It is the extraordinary east range by Eden Nesfield which has gone—it was high and projected into the moat. In 1680–91 William Winde added a new west front, but even this has been truncated. But the pedimented centre with an ornamental carving by Pearce remains. Grand north saloon with a splendid plaster ceiling by E. Gouge, but much of its former grandeur was stripped away when the house was sold and reduced in size in 1920s. Grounds by Brown. The house is now owned by the City of Coventry. CRAVEN, CRAVEN, E/PB; CL 4, 11 Dec 1909; VCH; *Colvin*; *Pevsner*; Stroud, *Capability Brown*.

**Compton Scorpion Manor, Ilmington.** Two distinct fronts. The 1st is late C16 or early C17 with mullioned windows, and on the other side all is C18 and sashed with a parapet. The home of Sir Adrian Beecham, 3rd Bt, son of the conductor. BEECHAM, Bt/PB; *Pevsner*.

**Compton Verney, Kineton.** Built for George Verney, 12th Lord Willoughby de Broke, it remained in the possession of the Verneys until 1921 when it was sold to 1st Lord Manton who altered it. It has belonged to Mr H. Elland in more recent years. Lord Willoughby erected a house that is Vanbrugh's in style, but not in authorship. The west range is of stone and 2 storeys in a 3-5-3 rhythm of fenestration. The centre is raised with a balustrade. From this range stretched 2 wings to the east; both were 4 bays long. But Robert Adam was called in 1760 and he extended the wings in the original style and then he tied the wings together with a delicate portico of giant unfluted Corinthian columns. Inside the portico is a coffered ceiling and a rich frieze, but the latter belongs to John Gibson's work of C19. The hall was originally 2 storeys with a cove by Gibson and framed panels by Antonio

*Combe Abbey: with Winde additions on left*

*Compton Scorpion Manor*

Zucchi which were executed 1766. These depicted ruin fantasies. But this great hall was truncated and a main early Georgian type staircase erected in it after the Mantons bought the house. Many of the other interiors which were by Gibson were swept away at the same time and a featureless neo-Georgian interior introduced. Windows gained glazing bars again, replacing the plate glass of the Victorians, but sills were lowered. Gibbs was responsible for the 9 bay stables with pediment and turret and Capability Brown designed the chapel 1772. This is a plain rectangle with Adamish decoration inside. The very beautiful park with its great lake and many sweeping cedars is almost certainly by Brown as well. The 3 arch bridge might well be his too. VERNEY, WILLOUGHBY DE BROKE, B/PB; WATSON, MANTON, B/PB; CL; *Pevsner*; VCH; Croft-Murray, *English Decorative Painting*.

*Compton Scorpion Manor*

*Compton Verney*

*Compton Wynyates: entrance front*

*Compton Wynyates* ante *1867*

**Compton Wynyates, Compton Wynyates.**
For many the epitome of a romantic English
country house, Compton Wynyates lies in a
hollow and dazzles one with the pinkness of its
brick. It is a courtyard house and once stood
surrounded by a moat,—but that was drained
in the Civil War. The entrance faces west and is
long and low with 2 half-timbered gables
perched on projecting bays. Battlements, tall
brick chimneys in a variety of patterns, taller
tower looming to the right. The fronts ebb
back and forth and are mostly of the early c16.
On the south side, facing a great topiary garden
of 1895, is the chapel window with windows
symmetrically arranged on either side of it.
The east front was remodelled in early c18, but
restored again by Sir Matthew Digby Wyatt
1867. The main staircase lies behind Wyatt's
Gothic bay. In the courtyard is a big bay
window of c1520. It is said to have come from
Fulbrooke Castle near Warwick. Inside the
hall retains its screens passage with linenfold
panelling, but the hall roof is said to have come
from Fulbrooke. Ceilings in wide variety in the
dining-room, drawing-room, council room
and chapel drawing-room. The Comptons'
London property, Canonbury House, provided the wooden chimneypiece in the
drawing-room. Good original ceiling in
Henry VIII's bedroom. Comptons were here
as early as Edward I. Slowly they stepped up
the ladder of the peerage until they received a
marquessate 1812. The present owner is 7th
Marquess of Northampton. COMPTON,
NORTHAMPTON, M/PB; VSA; CL 3 Aug 1901 & 30
Oct, 6 Nov 1915; VCH; *Pevsner*; Robinson, *The
Wyatts* (1980).

**Corley Hall, Corley.** Medieval timber-
framed and cross-gabled house, but much
altered. Inside, an elaborate overmantel with
pilasters and arches and some Early
Renaissance panels with heads. George Eliot
had Corley in mind for the central setting in
*Adam Bede*. Now owned by Dr K. Miller.
*Pevsner*; VCH IV.

**Coton House, Churchover.** Ashlar-faced
and datable to *ca* 1785. It is convincingly
attributed to Samuel Wyatt—the client being
Abraham Grimes. A wide bow on the main
front is answered within by a circular room.
Either side of this bow there is a tripartite

*Corley Hall*

*Corley: detail of overmantel*

window on the ground floor. Plain entrance
front of 5 bays. Spectacular staircase rising in
one flight and returning in two. Iron balustrade. Coton belonged to Mr Francis
Arkwright early in c20, but it now serves as a
company training centre. ARKWRIGHT *formerly
of Sutton Scarsdale*/LG 1965; *Colvin*; *Pevsner*;
Robinson, *The Wyatts* (1980); VCH.

*Coton House*

*Coton House*

*Coughton Court*

*Coughton Court*

*Diddington Hall*

*Eathorpe Hall*

**Coughton Court, Coughton.** Seat of the Throckmortons from the early C15 until transferred to the National Trust 1946. Originally this was a courtyard house with a moat around it. But in 1668 the east range containing the hall was destroyed and the moat filled in. The most spectacular part of the existing building is unquestionably the gatehouse which provides a strong vertical accent on the main west range. It dates from 1510–20 and its principal feature is a 2 storey oriel to the west and the east—this is flanked by angle turrets, then one more bay 2 storeys in height. Lower ranges to the left and right with Gothick ogee-headed windows pointing to the remodelling of this range in 1780. Further extensions of 1835. Once through the gatehouse by way of the fan-vaulted entrance one is in the courtyard where the ranges either side stretching to the east are brick-based with timber-framing above. Alterations to these ranges were made *ca* 1600, mid-C17 and *ca* 1690 when the north range received an addition which is rendered, with quoins and noticeably late mullioned and transomed windows. Inside are a staircase and wooden chimneypiece from Harvington Hall, Worcs (*qv*), a study containing fine late C17 panelling, a dining-room on the first floor with a frieze of *ca* 1530 and 2 priest-holes in the gatehouse. Stable-block of C18. The Throckmortons, whose baronetcy dates from 1642, are everyone's idea of an ancient Catholic family. It was in the Tudor gatehouse at Coughton that the wives of the Gunpowder conspirators waited to hear the outcome. The Throckmortons themselves were not directly implicated in the Plot; when asked if they had been, a present-day Throckmorton replied laconically, "No, we had a plot of our own". THROCKMORTON, Bt/PB; *Pevsner*; CL 30 March 1918; VCH; *Neale*; *Morris*; *Leland*.

**Diddington Hall, Hampton-in-Arden.** Brick and Elizabethan with 3 equal projections crowned with gables and Victorian bargeboarding. Inside a late C17 staircase with twisted balusters. The seat of Lord Ludlow in early C20. Now owned by the Earl of Aylesford who leases it to Mr Leigh Harrison. LOPES, LUDLOW, B/PB1922 and *sub* ROBOROUGH, B/PB; FINCH-KNIGHTLEY, AYLESFORD, E/PB; *Pevsner*.

**Dunton Hall, Cudworth.** The home of Cornelius and Anne Ford, maternal grandparents of Dr Samuel Johnson. Built *ca* 1680 by 2nd Lord Leigh, it is brick, plain and of 5 bays and 2¹/₂ storeys. The staircase has twisted balusters. LEIGH, LEIGH, B/PB; *Pevsner*.

**Eathorpe Hall, Eathorpe.** On an older site which was the seat of the Vyners who also built the present house. It is late C18 with a core of 5 bays and 2 storeys. Later additions on either side have prolonged the facade so the building appears sizeable but plainish. Mr R. T. Vyner sold the property 1858 to 6th Earl of Clonmell and he and his successors, the 7th and the 8th and last Earl, remained here until 1930s. Subsequent owners have been Mr H. G. Twist and the present occupier Mr M. A. Hammon. SCOTT, CLONMELL, E/PB1935.

**Edgbaston Hall, Edgbaston Park, Birmingham.** The principal part of the building dates from 1717. It was built on an earlier site.

Red brick with stone quoins, it is of 2½ storeys with tall narrow windows on the ground and 1st floors. Projecting porch with Tuscan columns. Later additions and alterations including some by Sir Charles Barry 1852. Early C18 staircase and some panelling inside. Now Edgbaston Golf Club. *Pevsner.*

**Edstone Hall, Wootton Wawen.** Plain Greek ashlar mansion built *ante* 1829 for John Phillips. 7 bay front with slightly projecting 3 bay centre crowned by a pediment. Pediment on rear elevation too. Bold 1 storey portico of Tuscan columns. Grecian entrance lodges with paired Doric columns are the sole reminders of this house which was demolished in 1920s—later owners being Frederick Griffiths and W. J. Fieldhouse. The Birmingham architect, F. W. B. Yorke designed a replacement in 1930s. It is a free Tudor style house of totally irregular design. VCH.

*Edgbaston Hall*

*Edstone Hall*

*Elmdon Hall*

*Elmdon: hall*

**Elmdon Hall, Elmdon.** Severe stone house of 1785 built for the Spooner family. The usual 7 bays and 3 storeys with a pediment. Pilasters, a narrow porch of Ionic columns and a bow to the side do their best to enliven the facades. Stark within as well. A screen of marbled columns at one end of the hall. In 1797 Abraham Spooner married the Lillingston heiress, taking her surname; but in 1834 he was killed by a falling tree. Shortly afterwards the family sold out to W. C. Alston and in due course it was inherited by the Alston-Roberts-Wests of Alscot Park (*qv*). Elmdon, which replaced a Tudor house, was demolished 1948. It has left the church of St Nicholas stranded and defenceless against the din of the neighbouring airport. ALSTON-ROBERTS-WEST *of Alscot Park*/LG 1972; VCH.

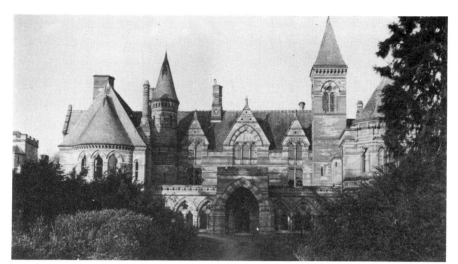

*Ettington Park*

*Ettington Park*

**Ettington Park, Ettington.** For the Shirley family, who have lived here since at least C14, John Prichard and J. P. Seddon remodelled an older and much altered house, turning it into the most important High Victorian house in the county. The years 1858–62 saw this transformation. The exterior is the feast, for the interior is disappointing. Eastlake waxed lyrical of the "genuine and unstrained architectural effect". A porte-cochère is at the centre of the entrance front flanked by pierced screen walls. Symmetrical gables but in the angles a square turret to the right and a round one to the left. Rounded and canted bay windows on all sides. Yellow and grey stone in bands is the material used and the plentiful supply of sculpture carved by Edward Clarke to designs by H. H. Armstead provides many reliefs representing events in the long history of the family. The entrance hall has a sumptuous chimneypiece; there is a Gothic library of 1820 with a chimneypiece said to have been copied from one at Windsor. Narrow staircase hall. The dining-room makes use of an C18 chimneypiece and a late C15 or C16 doorway. In the grounds there is a loggia of C17 brought from Coleshill Hall (*qv*). Ettington has been used as an hotel for some years. SHIRLEY *of Ettington and Lough Fea*/LG1952 and *sub* FERRERS, E/PB; VSA; *Colvin*; *Pevsner*; VCH; Girouard, *The Victorian Country House* (1979); E. P. Shirley, *Lower Eatington: Its Manor House and Church* (1880); *Neale* IV (1821).

**Farnborough Hall, Farnborough.** Now vested in the National Trust but the former seat of the Holbech family. The west front of 7 bays and 2 storeys with the raised pedimented dormer probably dates from 1684 when Ambrose Holbech bought the estate. All is brown stone with grey stone dressings. A more spacious entrance front to the north is of *ca* 1750 with 9 generous bays with slightly projecting 2 bay wings. The facade is enlivened by architraves above the windows and blank arched niches. Delicious entrance hall with busts of Roman emperors in front of oval

*Farnborough Hall*

*Farnborough: hall*

*Farnborough: drawing room (formerly dining room)*

*Farnborough: pavilion*

*Four Oaks Hall*

recesses and a sumptuous chimneypiece. Plasterwork of *ca* 1695 and mid-c18 on staircase which has fluted balusters. The drawing-room (formerly the dining-room) has mid-c18 stucco panels which formerly framed paintings by Canaletto and Pannini. Further delights are to be found in the grounds where there are a temple, an oval pavilion with Rococo plasterwork in an upper room and an obelisk at the end of the long terrace walk. A deer larder is closer to the house. Henry Hakewill designed the stables 1813–16. Spectacular views of Warwickshire countryside from the walk. HOLBECH/LG1965; *Colvin*; *Pevsner*; VCH; CL 11, 18 Feb 1954.

**Fillongley Hall, Fillongley.** Dobson built similar houses in Northumberland. The grand and severe front of 1824-25 is of 5 bays and 2 storeys. Its only relief is the loggia in antis of 2 unfluted Ionic columns. The entrance door shows a pediment on brackets. The noble entrance hall has a giant red column in each corner and a circular skylight with surrounding stucco-work. Seat of the Lords Norton. ADDERLEY, NORTON, B/PB; *Pevsner*; VCH.

*Four Oaks: hall*

*Fillongley Hall*

**Four Oaks Hall, Sutton Coldfield.** Extensive remodelling of late c17 house *ca* 1740 transformed a house with carved and scrolled gables into a monumental one with a pavilion attic storey at each corner. Sir William Wilson is said to have designed the original house 1696 for 3rd Lord Folliott. The c18 alterations have been attributed to William Hiorn. On the entrance side attached columns supported a pediment and the facade had a rather cramped appearance. It was of 9 bays whereas other facades were of 7. Entrance hall with screen of Ionic columns, swags of Rococo plasterwork and busts on pedestals. Seat of the Hartopps, Four Oaks was bought from the family 1880 with the intention of development as a racecourse, but the house was demolished *ca* 1900. FOLLIOTT, B/DEP; CRADOCK-HARTOPP, Bt/PB; *Colvin*; VCH; *Neale* IV (1821).

**Foxcote, Ilmington.** Long the seat of the Canning family, but now the property of Mr C. B. Holman, grandson of 1st & last Lord Trent

*Foxcote*

*Freasley Hall*

who, as Jesse Boot, founded the famous chain of chemist shops. A grand house of early c18 with later c18 2 bay extensions at either end. The facades are rich with detail—giant angle pilasters, attached angle columns, a pediment and an array of urns on the parapets—and all in golden stone. A former Roman Catholic chapel of 4 round-headed bays projects to one side of the garden front. Garlands decorate the panelling in the entrance hall and a late c18 staircase with wrought-iron balustrade is found at one end of the building. Mr John

Harris has attributed the house to Edward Woodward. HOLMAN *formerly of Dunley Manor*/LG1972; VCH; *Neale* IV (1821).

**Freasley Hall, Dordon.** Tall brick house of late c17. 5 by 3 bays with quoins and a hipped roof. A hint of Baroque is found on the chimneys each of which has an arched panel. Now a farmhouse. HEATH/WCF; *Pevsner*.

**Grendon Hall, Grendon.** This large house

of the Chetwynd Bts had a Jacobethan appearance when it was demolished 1933. But the shaped gables and mullioned windows were mostly of late Georgian date—in fact *ca* 1825 when the house was rebuilt for Sir George Chetwynd, Bt, to the designs of Joseph Potter. Earlier work on the house had been executed by Richard Trubshaw 1725. The client at that time was Walter Chetwynd. One of the features of the interior was a 2-storey picture gallery with coved ceiling. CHETWYND, Bt/PB; *Colvin*; VCH.

*Grendon Hall*

*Grendon: picture gallery*

*Grimshaw Hall*

**Grimshaw Hall, Knowle.** A perfect picture of a many gabled, timber-framed c16 house. The clustered chimney-shafts are prominent. The central porch projects with gables in 3 directions and there is a notable array of lozenge, herringbone and concave-sided lozenge patterns on the upper floor. Some of the oriel windows are on brackets and are genuine while others date from the restoration of 1886. Stout staircase and some panelling and fireplaces still survive from the original date of the house which is said to be *ca* 1650. J. H. Gillott owned the house 1904; a later owner was G. W. Murray. VCH; *Pevsner*.

**Grove Park, Hampton-on-the-Hill.** On an older site, C. S. Smith built this house for 11th Lord Dormer 1834. Large, Tudor-style and uninspired it had an irregular facade to the entrance front. Its importance one might say lay inside for here were 4 important chimneypieces of c17. 3 came from the almost totally vanished Eythorpe, Buckinghamshire and a 4th came from the famous source of Kenilworth Castle. These chimneypieces were grand. One, dated 1615, was of stone and another had paired decorated columns above and below. Demolished 1976, a new house immediately took its place. Long and low, its main accents are pyramid roofs at either end. The estate is still owned by the Dormers. DORMER, DORMER, B/PB; *Pevsner*; VCH; *Colvin*.

**Guy's Cliffe, Warwick.** Now in ruins and providing a romantic and moving picture perched on its rock. Began in 1751 in Palladian style, and attributed to William Hiorn, this front is 7 bays with pediments over the end ones. It is of stone with a rusticated basement. The entrance front to the west is supposed to be an addition of 1818, but its details make it look later and John Gibson is known to have worked there 1871. A later addition between the earlier parts is dated 1898. Inside the c18

*Grove Park*

*Guy's Cliffe*

*Guy's Cliffe: mid-C18 front*

*Guy's Cliffe: hall*

building there is a hall with handsome Rococo plasterwork. Niches flank the door at the back of the hall which has a broken pediment. The chapel of 1422 survives to the right of the Palladian front, but its front is late C18. The chapel is partly hewn into the rock. This extraordinary house was built for Bertie Greatheed. Through his daughter it passed to the Percys and it was Lord Charles Bertie Percy who commissioned John Gibson to make C19 additions. PERCY, *sub* NORTH-UMBERLAND, D/PB; *Pevsner*; VCH; *Neale*.

**Hall End Hall, Dordon.** Built early C17 as a rectangular block with staircase at rear, Hall End was a stone house of 2 storeys and attic, incorporating a small timber-framed building of *ca* 1500. Partial demolition in C18 left

patches of brick. Jacobean porch and fireplaces inside. Long used as a farmhouse, but pulled down in 1960s.

**Hams Hall, Lea Marston.** 13 giant cooling towers of Hams Hall Power Station mark the site of the house which was demolished 1920. Built for the Adderleys *ca* 1760, probably by

Joseph Pickford, it replaced an older house, evidence of which was marked by an avenue of trees planted in the reign of Charles I. The C18 house was of stone and of 7 bays and 2½ storeys. A centrepiece composed of attached columns on the 1st and 2nd floors was crowned by a pediment. Plain parapet with dentilled cornice. Small screen walls were attached to

*Hall End Hall*

*Hams Hall*

the entrance front and these boasted a pedimented door and niches. The interior was largely rebuilt later c18 and there were friezes by Thorwaldsen. But this interior was gutted by fire on 22 April 1890 to be rebuilt soon after. After demolition 1920, the upper facade of the entrance front was re-erected at Coates Manor (now Bledisloe Lodge), Gloucestershire. ADDERLEY, NORTON, B/PB; *Colvin*; VCH; *Neale* IV (1821).

**Hillfield Hall, Solihull.** Samuel Boddington occupied this unusual house 1904. Dated 1576 it is high and compact. Of plum brick it has 2 tower-like bays flanking the centre which has a stepped gable. Either side of the battlemented towers are more transomed windows. *Pevsner*.

**Honiley Hall, Honiley.** The present building is long and large and c20. It can perhaps be described as free Tudor. A notable vertical accent is demonstrated by the 4 storey tower at one end. But this modern house replaces a late c17 structure of which 2 service wings forming a forecourt to the church remain. These wings are of brick with archways and wooden mullion and transom crosses in the windows. And there are gables with oval windows over the end bays. The swagger gatepiers to the church with coats-of-arms and niches add to the air of a vanished great house. The Burgoyne and Carington families owned the old house. *Pevsner*; VCH.

**Honington Hall, Honington.** A very perfect late c17 house without that contains an extraordinary display of early Georgian plasterwork within. Built 1682 for the Parker family, the house is brick with stone dressings and the entrance front is composed of a recessed 3 bay centre and 2 bay wings which project slightly. Soberness is rescued from

*Hillfield Hall*

*Honiley Hall*

*Honington Hall*

*Honington: staircase vestibule*

*Honington: saloon*

*Honington: hall*

dryness by the rich entry door which has an open segmental pediment with garlands and a coat-of-arms. Even more daring are the busts of Roman emperors in round-headed niches above the ground-floor windows. The brick quadrant wall to the right of the building was built with its left counterpart (which has now disappeared) *post* 1731. Richly carved doorway with apsed hood around the corner and on the garden front the great canted bay in the middle which represents part of the Georgian alteration within. Notable rooms inside are the entrance hall with stucco panels and stucco ceiling attributed to Charles Stanley—panels on the west wall have been removed long ago so one can see through to the scrolly wrought-iron balustrade of the staircase—and the octagonal saloon which has a great coffered dome with a ceiling painting probably by Bellucci, Rococo garlands on the wall and Kentian doorways. On the 1st floor there is a room of C17 with stucco of *ca* 1682 and Chinese wallpaper. A temple with Tuscan columns now sits close to the garden front, but it was moved from elsewhere. The grounds offer a 5 arch bridge with ball finials, C17 stables and an

*Idlicote House*

*Ladbroke Hall*

octagonal dovecote. A large service wing was added to the north-west in late C19 but this was demolished 1979. It was surmounted by a large cupola and was built in keeping with the house. Honington is approached from the village green by way of 2 monumental gatepiers of 1740–50. Sir Henry Parker and his son are commemorated by a splendid monument in the church. Parkers were succeeded by Townsends who remained here until C20. The Wiggins bought the house in 1920s and it is now the home of Sir John Wiggin, 4th Bt. TOWNSEND/LG1906; WIGGIN, Bt/PB; CL 21, 28 Sept, 12 Oct 1978; VCH; *Pevsner*; Hussey, *English Country Houses: Early Georgian.*

**Hurley Hall, Hurley.** 5 bay, 3 storey house which can be assigned to the early Georgians. Segment-headed windows those above with alternating rustication. Italian and English painted panels within as well as a staircase with twisted balusters. *Pevsner.*

**Idlicote House, Idlicote.** Two thorough C19 restorations have somewhat obliterated the origins of the building. But in its appearance it looks early C19 with projecting canted bays the full height on either side. The centre is of the usual 7 bays and 3 storeys. A seat of the Lords Southampton for much of C20. FITZROY, SOUTHAMPTON, B/PB; *Pevsner*; VCH.

**Ilmington Manor, Ilmington.** Rambling, low house of the usual Cotswold type with mullioned windows and straight gables. Restored in C20 after neglect and habitation by families of villagers. The Flowers purchased the property 1918 and laid out the spectacular garden. The present owner is Mr D. L. Flower, the brewer. FLOWER *of The Hill*/LG1965; CL 15 March 1930; *Pevsner.*

**Ladbroke Hall, Ladbroke.** Good standard late C17 house of Hornton stone, probably incorporating an older structure. 7 bays and 2 storeys—the centre 3 bays recessed. Hipped roof. The entrance door provides the one notable accent with a large and brave open segmental pediment. The best thing inside is

*Ladbroke: staircase*

the staircase. Finely carved, it has 3 balusters to a tread, one fluted and the others of different twistings. The Ladbroke estate was bought by the Palmers in mid-C17 and remained in the family until mid-C20 when it was sold by their descendant R. C. A. Palmer-Morewood. Ladbroke is now divided into flats. PALMER-MOREWOOD *of Alfreton*/LG 1952; *Pevsner*; VCH; S. H. A. Hervey, *Ladbroke and Its Owners* (1914).

*Lifford Hall*

**Lifford Hall, King's Norton, Birmingham.** Rectangular house with gables on both sides and mullioned windows. Partly stuccoed and painted it is of red brick with stone dressings and can be assigned to early C17. C18 romantics had their fling with a brick wall and a stone watch-tower both sporting battlements. John E. Sturge Ltd are the present owners. *Pevsner*.

**Little Compton Manor, Little Compton.** Stone of a ripe apricot, but much of the house is a rebuilding after a fire in 1928. Before that time there were sashes instead of mullions. Complex building history ranging from the pre-Reformation east side to the south front which was remodelled (with other parts of the building) by Archbishop Juxon, later Chaplain to Charles I, 1620. Prominent pointed gables loom on the south front. But the doorcase this side has an C18 pediment. Part of the Georgian alteration swept away by the fire. Moulded ceiling beams in oldest part and a room of 1620 with panelling showing pilasters

and frieze. Most of the interior is new. Steep gables on dovecote which might be Jacobean. L. L. Yelf owned the house 1904. CL 22, 29 July 1939; *Pevsner*; VCH.

**Little Wolford Manor, Little Wolford.** "L"-shaped with a north wing of stone and early Tudor in date. But the wing projecting from it is stone below and timber-framed above and probably a little later. Some of the windows contain heraldic glass. The restoration of the house in recent years has given the great hall a new roof and extended one of the wings. A canted bay is of *ca* 1670. CL 10 April 1920; *Pevsner*.

**Longbridge Manor, Longbridge.** At right angles to each other—an early C18 brick range with hipped roof and recessed centre and a C16 half-timbered range now rendered, with a projection containing the staircase.

**Loxley Hall, Loxley.** Possibly Georgian, but the face it presents now is of a C19 Gothic

*Little Compton Manor*

*Little Wolford Manor*

*Little Wolford: chimneypiece in hall*

building following rebuilding 1850 and additions of 1868 by T. T. Allen. The sole flight of fancy seems to be the porch which is spiky, but in no definite style. Seat of the Gregory-Hoods in place of vanished Stivichall Hall (*qv*), but at the beginning of this century it belonged to the Cove Jones family. GREGORY-HOOD/LG1952; JONES/WCF; *Pevsner*.

**Malvern Hall, Solihull.** Constable's famous picture of Malvern Hall in the National Gallery has preserved for all time the now vanished landscape which once surrounded the house. All is concrete now and the building serves a utilitarian purpose as a school. Basically early C18 of 7 bays with a pedimented 3 bay centre, its real interest lies in the fact that it is one of the first houses to feel the hand of Sir John Soane. This was 1783–86 and it was he who added the lower 2 bay wings, the curved porch with Ionic columns, the stucco decoration of the entrance hall and the fine staircase starting in one flight and returning in two. The client was Henry Greswold Lewis.

*Longbridge Manor*

*Loxley Hall*

*Malvern Hall*

*Mancetter Manor*

*The Manor House, Barcheston*

*The Manor House, Haseley*

The stone balustrades of the forecourt have late C17 decoration, but were brought from elsewhere and stout wrought-iron gates herald the approach. Seat of the Williams family in late C19; David Troman lived here 1904. WILLIAMS/WCF; *Colvin*; *Pevsner*; VCH; Stroud, *Sir John Soane*.

**Mancetter Manor, Mancetter.** Timber-framed house of *ca* 1330. There is a 40 foot hall in the centre. A screens passage is at the north end and a projecting service wing. The corresponding south wing is about 1580. The forecourt has C18 gatepiers and a gazebo of the same period. Mancetter was the home of Robert Glover, the martyr. *Pevsner*.

**Manor House (The), Barcheston.** A mid-C17 house with a symmetrical front of trans-omed windows incorporating parts William Sheldon's house where he began his tapestry weaving. Formerly owned by the Wheelers, it now belongs to Sir Adrian Beecham, Bt, who leases it to Mr A. W. Morris. WHEELER/WCF; BEECHAM, Bt/PB; *Pevsner*.

*The Manor House, Barton*

**Manor House (The), Barton, Bidford-on-Avon.** with mullioned windows it is of lias and is dated 1663. BIRD/WCF; *Pevsner*.

**Manor House (The), Haseley.** Built 1875 for Alfred Hewlett by William Young. A large house ranging from Gothic to Elizabethan. Dominant is the tower with higher stair turret. The porte-cochère has an upper storey with oriel. Nothing special inside apart from the wide variety of tiles in the fireplaces. The Hewletts were here until World War II; since 1954 it has been the property of BMC. HEWLETT/WCF; *Pevsner*.

**Manor House (The), Meriden.** Imposing early C18 house of brick. 7 bays and 2 storeys with quoins at the angles and a brave segmental pediment above the front door. *Pevsner*.

**Manor House (The), Preston-on-Stour.** Pretty late C16 timber-framed house with attractive decoration in the gables while the ground floor has vertical studding. Close to the road it has a number of giant yews in its garden. *Pevsner*.

**Manor House (The), Studley.** Handsome gatepiers flanking splendid gates stand in front of this handsome brick house of *ca* 1700. 5 bays and 2 storeys with Ionic angle pilasters and a balustrade. Inside a staircase with 3 turned balusters to a tread.

The Manor House, Meriden

The Manor House, Preston-on-Stour

The Manor House, Studley

The Manor House, Wormleighton

The Manor House, Wormleighton

**Manor House (The), Wormleighton.** Once a mighty seat of the Spencers—possibly the size of Compton Wynyates (*qv*)—but the Civil Wars reduced the house by fire to the fragment that it is now. Just one range of brick, early c16, battlemented with large transomed windows on the ground and first floors. Moulded beams inside and a canted window not in its original position. Althorp, Northamptonshire, seat of the Earls Spencer, contains panelling from the 1st floor of the house here. A great stone gatehouse heralds the approach. It is dated 1613. Mullioned windows, round-arched entrance and the 2 storey main building of the gatehouse ends up with a triumphant 5 storey tower. Still owned by the Spencers who bought the estate 1506, the Manor House has been used as a farmhouse for many years. SPENCER, SPENCER, E/PB; *Pevsner*; VCH.

*Maxstoke Castle*

**Maxstoke Castle, Maxstoke.** Seat of the Fetherston-Dilke family. Dugdale states that licence to crenellate was made 1346. It is a strictly symmetrical building of the type found at Bodiam, Sussex, and Bolton, Yorkshire. It is a rectangle with a tower at each corner and a great gatehouse in the middle of one of its sides. The moat and surrounding parkland set off the building to perfection. The builder was William de Clinton, Earl of Huntingdon, and it was later remodelled by 1st Duke of Buckingham *post* 1440. Sir Thomas Dilke came into possession in 1589 and it has since remained in the hands of his descendants. Inside the courtyard there are ranges of buildings the oldest of which are c16. Most notable from the outside is the very large traceried window facing west on the west side. This probably lit the chapel and it lies north of where the great hall must have been. Successive alterations have obscured the original plan and one is left with a number of questions over the present apparent complexity of the whole. A block of rooms built in 1820 obscures evidence of the earlier arrangements and confuses the picture. On the north side of the courtyard is a pretty half-timbered range of c16. It contains a magnificent Elizabethan overmantel from Kenilworth Castle. There are c15 doors in the gatehouse. FETHERSTON-DILKE/LG1952; *Pevsner*; VCH; CL 11,18/4/74.

**Merevale Hall, Merevale.** Monumental Victorian house high on a spur of hills and situated in a grand oak-studded park. Built *ante* 1840 and designed by Henry Clutton and Edward Blore, the clients were the Dugdales, descendants of the famous antiquary and Warwickshire historian Sir William Dugdale. The show front is to the east. It is symmetrical and has an oriel window, shaped gables, mullioned and transomed windows—in short, a predominantly Jacobean style. A high tower soars at the north-west corner and is answered by a turret at the south-west corner. Stable-court, inner courts, extra service wing all adding up to a grand establishment so beloved by the confident Victorian squirearchy. The c19 stands still inside. Long gallery and staircase hall with staircase balustrade in the mid-c17 style. It replaced an earlier house of the later c17. This was of 7 bays with a hipped roof. The Stratford family lived in the older house until it was inherited by the Dugdales. Sir William Dugdale, 2nd Bt, is the present owner. DUGDALE, Bt/PB; *Colvin*; *Pevsner*; VCH; CL 13, 20 March 1969; *Neale* v (2nd series, 1829); *Morris* III.

**Meriden Hall, Meriden.** Remodelled by Francis Smith for Martin Baldwin *ca* 1720. 7 bays and 2½ storeys the centre 3 crowned by a pediment. Stone, moulded window surrounds and rusticated pilasters. But the early c18 carcass hides later c18 rooms within, including a large east room with screens of columns at either end and a pretty ceiling. The seat of C. W. Digby at the beginning of c20. DIGBY/WCF; VCH; *Colvin*; *Pevsner*.

**Middleton Hall, Middleton.** From this place the Willoughby family take the title of their barony. Their former seat is an interesting and complex structure with a building history ranging from *ca* 1100 to *ca* 1730. Of the latter date is the west front of 8 bays divided by fluted giant pilasters; more giant pilasters to the north. Also to the north is an irregular range opening into a courtyard. Then, to the left of that, a timber-framed c17 fragment with

*Merevale Hall*

*Meriden Hall*

an overhang on giant scrolls. This part of the building contains parts of a roof of *ca* 1400. The oldest part is represented by a Norman window on the ground floor in a rendered range. Middleton can claim to be the oldest domestic building in the county still in use.

The house was still owned by the Willoughbys into C20. WILLOUGHBY, MIDDLETON, B/PB; *Pevsner*; VCH.

*Middleton Hall*

*Moor Hall*

*Moreton Hall: drawing room*

*Moreton Paddox: chapel*

**Moor Hall, Sutton Coldfield.** Big house in dull red brick replacing an older structure which belonged to Bishop Vesey in C16. It was designed by Henman & Cooper and erected 1908. LLOYD *of Sutton Coldfield*/LG1886.

**Moreton Hall, Moreton Morrell.** Convincing Palladian house designed by W. H. Romaine Walker and erected 1906. It is of 9 bays with pediments above the 2 bays at either end. Of stone it sits well in its park, having belonged to a previous house on the site. The principal door has an open scrolly pediment. Sober interiors with C17 style plasterwork and carved woodwork. Now an agricultural college. *Pevsner.*

**Moreton Paddox, Moreton.** Jacobethan house built as late as 1909. Shaped gables to the gardens of squares of yew flanking a long canal. To the west, a great window flanking the hall; to the east, a tall Gothic chapel. Exuberant Elizabethan chimneypieces within, backed up by much panelling to evoke the late C16 and early C17. Another room had Adam style decoration. Built for Major Robert Emmet (collateral descendant of the Irish patriot Robert Emmet) and his wife, the former Louise Garland, daughter of a co-founder of the First National Bank, New York City. Demolished 1959. EMMET/IFR.

*Moreton Hall*

*Moreton Paddox*

*Moreton Paddox: hall*

*Moseley Hall*

*New Hall*

*Newbold Comyn Hall*

**Moseley Hall, Moseley, Birmingham.**
Given to the City of Birmingham 1890, for use as a children's home, by Richard Cadbury. It is a handsome building and curiously little-known. Pedimented wings with tripartite windows flank 5 bays in the centre in the middle of which is a porch with 4 pairs of Tuscan columns. Rusticated basement with ashlar above. Long office wing. C18 dovecote of some size with blank arch on each side. Now a geriatric hospital. CADBURY *of North-field*/LG1972; *Colvin; Neale* V (1822); *Pevsner.*

**Moxhull Hall, Wishaw.** An unusual C18 house. In its original form it was of 5 bays—the centre 3 being recessed. Of 3 storeys and of stone it had a top balustrade. But at a later date the space between the wings at ground-floor level was filled in and 2 bay extensions at the same level were made either side of the wings—thus creating a 9 bay front on the ground floor. These extensions had balustrades as well and the bays were divided by pilaster strips. This was the seat of the Hackets and the Noels; but by the early C20 it belonged to H. P. Ryland. The house was demolished *ca* 1920 but the C18 stables remain. NOEL/WCF; *Neale* IV (1821); VCH.

**New Hall, Sutton Coldfield.** A moated house which received its present character *ca* 1870. The best front is to the west where the 1870 remodelling predominates. A 5 storey tower forms the centrepiece, but the grey stone used is medieval masonry. To the north is an Elizabethan range forming a small courtyard—a canted bay in this range lights the banqueting room. The south shows a tower dated 1796 rising sheer from the moat. Inside there is a staircase of *ca* 1640. The building history is far from clear. Early in C20 the house was owned by the Chadwick family, but let to Walter Wilkinson. *Pevsner.*

**Newbold Comyn Hall, Leamington.**
Demolished in 1960s and at the time of disappearance a 5 bay, 2 storey house with a pediment—that was the front to the garden, but the entrance was similar minus the pediment. Sandwiched between these 2 elevations there was probably a much older house. Seat of the Willes family who had owned the property for centuries and who had been great benefactors to the town. WILLES *formerly of Newbold Comyn*/LG1969.

**Newbold Pacey Hall, Newbold Pacey.** An early C19 remodelling of an older house left it as a plain but sizeable building. The grounds are not large, but are well laid out. Seat of Lt-Col J. E. Little. LITTLE/LG1952.

**Newbold Revel, Stretton-under-Fosse.**
Now almost totally engulfed by more modern buildings designed for its needs as St Paul's College. On style alone it is almost certainly a house by Francis Smith of Warwick and it was built for Sir Fulwar Skipwith, 2nd Bt. 11 bay front with recessed 7 bay centre. Red brick with stone dressings and 3 storeys high. Top balustrade with urns and windows with surrounds and brick aprons. The garden front has a pediment above its recessed centre. Much alteration within especially *ca* 1900, but the staircase with its 3 turned balusters to a tread and garlands of the Gibbons tradition in

an overmantel on an upper floor are original. Late C18 chimneypieces in various rooms including 2 of Chambers type on the ground floor. SKIPWITH, Bt/EDB; *Pevsner*; VCH; CL 7 March 1903; *Vitruvius Britannicus* II (1717).

*Newbold Pacey Hall*

*Newbold Revel*

*Newnham Paddox*

*Newnham Paddox: library*

*Newnham Paddox: dining room*

**Newnham Paddox, Monks Kirby.** The huge house of the Feildings, Earls of Denbigh and Desmond, was demolished 1952. Capability Brown added a long 2 storey front to an older house in C18. But this front was first heightened and then almost lost when all was Frenchified by T. H. Wyatt 1870s. Mansard roofs to the pavilions and tall roof over the centre with prominent dormers. Top balustrade. The rooms inside were all done over by Wyatt. Henry Fielding, the novelist, was a cadet member of the family. FEILDING, DENBIGH AND DESMOND, E/PB; *Pevsner*; VCH; Robinson, *The Wyatts* (1980); Stroud, *Capability Brown*.

*Offchurch Bury before partial demolition*

**Offchurch Bury, Offchurch.** Seat of the Knightleys whose heiress married 6th Earl of Aylesford. It was a large "L"-shaped house until a few years ago; but now its oldest part is only represented by re-erected porch arches which are C17. What remains is ashlar and all Gothick. A main front of 7 bays and 2 storeys with canted bays around the corner. Clustered Gothick shafts around the door. Previously in the ownership of the Earls of Aylesford, it now belongs to the Johnson family. FINCH-KNIGHTLEY, AYLESFORD, E/PB; *Neale* IV (1821); *Pevsner*; VCH.

**Oldbury Hall, Mancetter.** The house has gone, but evidence of a much earlier age

*Oldbury Hall*

*Packington Hall*

*Packington: garden front*

survives. That is the large Iron Age hillfort, 7 acres in extent, which enveloped the house and which remains unexcavated. Oldbury was C18 with a giant portico of 4 unfluted Ionic columns. But C19 remodelling had left it devoid of character and encumbered by lumpish additions. Mr A. H. Jackson owned the house 1904. VCH.

**Packington Hall, Great Packington.** Matthew Brettingham enlarged and recased a late C17 house in 1766-72. His client was 3rd Earl of Aylesford and it remains the seat of the 11th and present Earl. But the client in 1693 had been Sir Clement Fisher and he built the surviving Packington Old Hall 1679-80. This older house is an engaging one with its gabled dormers, pronounced quoins and porch with segmental pediment. All the windows have crosses. Some plasterwork of 1680 within. The new house is undeniably grand. Of stone, 9 by 5 bays and 2½ storeys high. On the entrance side the facade is somewhat bland; the garden front, however, is enlivened by giant unfluted Ionic columns which used to be free standing with a loggia behind them. It was filled in in early C19. The outstanding room inside is Bonomi's Pompeian Room—the best scheme of its type in England. This was designed 1782, though not painted by J. F. Rigaud until 20 years later. The entrance hall narrows behind a screen of Roman Doric columns. The staircase with its modest handrail rises the whole height of the building and is top-lit by a glazed circular lantern. More painted work by Rigaud in the drawing-room, little library and in the main room in the north wing. Henry Hakewill designed the interiors of the billiard room and upper library 1828. The very large stables are possibly by William Hiorn. They have a loggia of Tuscan columns and low corner towers with pyramid roofs. Burn designed a conservatory and aviary, but these

*Packington: staircase*

*Packington: hall*

*Packington: Pompeian room*

*Packington Old Hall*

well. The Long Gallery and Hall were created 1925–30. The transomed windows replace 18 Gothick ones and the large hall window to the right of the porch is not original. Some panelling is original and in situ but other panelling was brought in. The famous Yew Garden represents the Sermon on the Mount and has a Multitude Walk, Apostles, etc; it is now said to be largely C19. There are fine iron gates of C18 and C20 and gazebos of *ca* 1680, C18 and C20. FETHERSTON/LG1879; ASH/LG1952; *Pevsner*; VCH; CL 4 Jan 1902 & 9, 16 April 1924.

**Park Hall, Salford Priors.** Designed by William Tasker and built *ca* 1880. Vaguely Queen Anne with its red brick and stone dressings, but put across in a somewhat reckless manner with all too obvious dormers and porches. The house was immediately rebuilt after a fire destroyed it on the eve of occupation Nov 1879. Property of the Marquess of Hertford, it was occupied by his son and heir, the Earl of Yarmouth, 1904; but is now owned by the Espley-Tyas Group Ltd. SEYMOUR, HERTFORD, M/PB; *Pevsner*.

*Packwood House*

have been demolished. The grounds were landscaped by Capability Brown 1751. Packington suffered a very serious fire 1979. FINCH-KNIGHTLEY, AYLESFORD, E/PB; VSA; CL 9, 16, 23 July 1970; VCH; *Pevsner*; *Colvin*; Stroud, *Capability Brown*; Torrington's *Diaries* (1789); *Neale* IV (1821).

**Packwood House, Packwood.** Fetherstons were squires of this place into C20. They built their timber-framed house *ca* 1575. It is covered in a warm apricot rendering which makes an attractive contrast with the long pink brick stables of the 1660s. These exhibit the possibilities of brick for decorative purposes as there are pilasters, cornices, roundels, ovals and window surrounds all in the material. Alfred J. Ash and his son G. Baron Ash carried out their very thorough restoration of Packwood between the wars and presented it to the National Trust in 1941. During the restoration the house received additions as

*Park Hall*

*Pooley Hall*

**Pooley Hall, Polesworth.** Perched on a sharp ridge, giving the appearance of a small castle. Three independent buildings make up the whole; all of brick. The end range has a tower and a spiral stair in the angle; black brick diapering. The principal range in the middle has a big 2 storeyed bay window and a garderobe and it contained the great hall. Part of this range was rebuilt in 1692. The southernmost building was the chapel and has a stair turret on one side. Sir Thomas Cokayne built the house 1509 but it has long served as a farmhouse. VCH; *Pevsner.*

*Pype Hayes Hall*

**Pype Hayes Hall, Erdington, Birmingham.** The late C18 stucco hides a timber-framed building which is probably early C17. The main front shows 4 bay windows of 2 storeys and small gables on the parapet. Pedimented porch of mid-C18. Early C17 panelling and C18 staircase inside. Formerly the seat of the Bagot family and now a children's home. BAGOT/LG 1858. *Pevsner.*

**Radbrook Manor, Preston-on-Stour.** Situated in Gloucestershire until 1935. A block of *ca* 1720 with an outstanding front of 7 bays and 2 storeys was added to an older Tudor building. All windows are segment-headed and the 3 in the centre are flanked by giant pilasters supporting an entablature and pediment containing a cartouche of arms. Large urns decorate both pediment and parapet. The solid parapet with its 4 roundels containing portraits of men's heads is a modern replacement of the former balustrade. The house has been much altered inside. A forecourt entered by bold gatepiers with fine wrought-iron gates faces the entrance. Built for the Lingen family it has spent much of its life as a farm. Mr J. K. Farrow is the present owner. LINGEN, *sub* BURTON *of Longner Hall*/LG 1972.

*Radbrook Manor*

*Radford Hall*

**Radford Hall, Radford Semele.** Jacobean fronting of an older house. One sees the long facade on the road—it is much restored. End gables and mullioned and transomed windows. Hints of its medieval origin lie in the windows left and right of the centre porch. One has 3 lights, the other 4—they indicate the position of the original hall. H. E. Thornley lived here at the beginning of the century; his great-grandson, Mr H. E. J. Marriott, is the present owner. *Pevsner.*

**Radway Grange, Radway.** Of golden stone in a great bowl of a park. This is the gentleman architect Sanderson Miller's own house and it was here that that pioneer of Rococo Gothick transformed a square Elizabethan house into an important landmark of C18 taste. Sanderson Miller, senior, bought the property 1712 and his more famous son succeeded 1737. To the original building he began adding his Gothick frills in the mid-1740s—2 canted bays with lacy cresting to the south and a new front to the east consisting of a central loggia with 3 linked windows above it. Miller added a porch to the west as well and topped it off with an

*Radway Grange*

dated 1744. But dominating the landscape high above the park is the irregular Castle of *ca* Gothick ry within is represented by an alcove in the dining-room and dark grey chimneypieces in various forms of Gothick and Jacobean. Dainty wrought-iron balustrade to the main staircase. Various buildings of interest are to be found in the grounds. Most important is probably the Cottage, asymmetrical and thatched—Miller's very first essay in the Picturesque and mentioned by Swift. It is

Elizabethan gable from the east side. Morley Horder added a wing to the north side *ca* 1900. 1746–47. A mighty octagonal tower is the central feature of a composition made up of gateway, lower tower and bridge. The 1st floor of the main tower contains a room with pretty Gothick decoration. Millers continued in occupation until C20. MILLER/LG1921; VCH; *Colvin*; *Pevsner*; CL 6, 13 Sept 1946.

**Ragley Hall, Arrow.** Robert Hooke design-

ed a house for the Earl of Conway *ca* 1680–90. Much of that house remains today and is represented by the 15 bay front. Originally it had 2 detached wings, but they were demolished *ca* 1780. James Wyatt worked at Ragley from 1783 and it was he who designed the grand portico of 4 unfluted Ionic columns which form the centrepiece of the entrance front. Wyatt added a square attic above the garden front—high above steps and terrace designed by John Tasker 1873—some of

*Ragley Hall*

*Ragley: garden front*

*Ragley: hall*

*Ragley: bedroom*

which has been swept away. The north and south sides have recessed centres with arched windows. Because of the work by James Gibbs at Ragley, it is possible that he tricked up the basement windows with his distinctive surrounds. The great glory of the house is the hall. It is 70' by 40' by 40' and the walls now coloured in flame pink, are articulated by coupled pilasters. Trophies, stucco figures of war and peace, and 2 great chimneypieces with atlantes all build up and enrich this great apartment. More plasterwork is found on the ceiling—the centrepiece being Britannia in a lion-drawn chariot. The work is attributed to Vassali. The study and the billiard room are by Gibbs. The great dining-room with its grisaille overdoors is by Wyatt. The staircases are Victorian and are probably an insertion by Tasker. On the principal one, Graham Rust has recently executed the largest known wall painting. The library has simple bookcases, but retains Hooke and Gibbs decoration. More of Wyatt is found in the Red Saloon and Blue Drawing-Room. Large semi-circular stables and grounds by Capability Brown. From the Conways, Ragley passed to the Seymours who became Marquesses of Hertford in late c18. The 3rd Marquess was used as the model for the "wicked Marquis of Steyne" by Thackeray in *Vanity Fair* and for the "Marquis of Monmouth" in Disraeli's *Coningsby*. His son, the 4th Marquess, was the great c19 collector, whose works of art now form the nucleus of the Wallace collection. The present Marquess has courageously fought to maintain Ragley. SEYMOUR, HERTFORD, M/PB; *Pevsner*; *Colvin*; VCH; CL 1,8 May 1958; Robinson, *The Wyatts*.

*Ragley: library*

**Salford Hall, Salford Priors.** Large irregular building. The north entrance front with its profusion of shaped gables is dated 1602 on its porch; mullioned and transformed windows as well as c18 sashes. The south elevation is earlier with chimneystacks, gables and some half-timbering. c16, c17 and c18 alterations within. In c17 the Alderford and Stanford families lived here. Benedictine nuns who migrated from France in Revolution times made Salford their home 1807–38 and it is still apt to be called The Nunnery. In early c20 it was the property of C. T. Eyston, a younger son of the Berkshire Eystons, but used as a farmhouse. It is approached through an early c17 gatehouse of stone, rubble and timber framing. EYSTON *of East Hendred*/LG1965; CL 16 Dec 1911; VCH III.

*Salford Hall*

*Sheldon Hall*

*Sherbourne Park*

**Sheldon Hall, Sheldon, Birmingham.** Red and black brick with stone dressings makes up the centre of this manor house now surrounded by suburban housing. To this C16 block a cross wing was added to the west and 2 cross wings to the east in C17. These later additions are roughcast and probably timber-framed. Mullioned and transomed windows. Chimneystacks of *ca* 1600. Late C16 wood panelling and staircase have been removed, but timber-framed partition to the screens passage and C16 stone fireplaces remain. *Pevsner.*

**Sherbourne Park, Sherbourne.** On an eminence and commanding a fine view, the house stands next to the notable All Saints Church designed by Sir George Gilbert Scott at the expense of the owner of the property. It is early C18 of 5 bays and 2½ storeys with giant pilasters and a hipped roof. The best thing inside is the mid-C18 staircase with carved tread-ends and 2 turned balusters to a step. Seat of Mr C. M. T. Smith-Ryland, Lord-Lieut of the county. SMITH-RYLAND/LG1965; *Pevsner*; VCH.

**Shuckburgh Hall, Upper Shuckburgh.** Shuckburghs have long been seated here. However, their half-timbered house received a drastic overhaul 1844 at the hands of H. E. Kendall. He left it looking a cross between classical and Italianate, so it comes out as Mixed Renaissance. All a bit nobbly but strangely fascinating and gaining interest all the time. The Victorian church of St John Baptist lies close to the house and forms an effective group in a lush park with cedars skilfully disposed. Large number of monuments to the Shuckburghs therein including 2 by Flaxman. SHUCKBURGH, Bt/PB; *Colvin*; *Pevsner*; VCH.

**Shustoke House, Shustoke.** Late C17 house of brick. Tall with bays and 3 storeys. Cross windows. Inside an C18 staircase with 3 turned balusters to a tread. Seat of the Croxalls,

*Shuckburgh Hall*

Shustoke was demolished *ca* 1950. CROXALL/LG1937.

**Stivichall Hall, Stivichall.** Sober house of 5 bays and 3 storeys built for Arthur Gregory and designed by Henry Flitcroft between 1755–60. Of stone ashlar the original entrance front had a pedimented entrance door and Venetian and lunette windows above it. A 1 bay pediment interrupted the parapet and crowned the slight projection of the centre bay. Later 2 bay extension in keeping made the house lop-sided. The last Gregory died childless 1909 and the estate passed to his cousin, Hon Alexander Hood, who assumed the additional surname of Gregory. The Hall was sold to Coventry Corporation 1927 and was demolished by stages, finally disappearing *post* World War II. The stables had gone too by 1964. GREGORY-HOOD/LG1952; VCH VIII; *Colvin*; *Warwickshire History* I (3) (1970).

**Stoneleigh Abbey, Stoneleigh.** Two great buildings side by side represent the growth of the house which is basically a Cistercian abbey of C12 with the grand Georgian house of 1714–26 on the original west range. Evidences of the Abbey now rest on the footwalls of the south aisle and the vaulted undercroft of the dormitory which is the substructure of the Elizabethan east wing. The C14 gatehouse of the Cistercian Abbey does survive. At the dissolution, Stoneleigh was one of the first to go and it was granted in 1538 to Charles Brandon, Duke of Suffolk, and sold by his heirs to Sir Rowland Hill and Sir Thomas Leigh. Sir Thomas married Hill's niece and

*Shustoke House*

the Leighs have been here since 1571. The north-east corner of the house is *ca* 1600. But the main range is the magnificent block designed by Francis Smith and built in the reign of George I. It is Smith's finest work. Of dark grey stone it is 15 bays long and 3 storeys high crowned by a balustrade. The ground-floor windows have segmental pediments, those on the 1st floor triangular ones. Some fine rooms inside of the highest quality. The saloon, built as the entrance hall, comes first. Yellow demi-columns divide the room which has a rich display of juicy plasterwork. Wall panels, door surrounds, chimneypieces, overmantels are rich and varied and startle the visitor with their quality and variety. The fine

*Stoneleigh Abbey*

*Stoneleigh : staircase*

staircase has 2 twisted and 1 fluted baluster to each tread, but the wall panels and ceiling are of the 1760s. The chapel with its original fittings faces south and in other rooms there are early Georgian panelling with giant pilasters. On the 2nd floor is a suite converted for Queen Victoria and Prince Albert and decorated throughout, including the furniture, in white and gold. More dates come to the surface when other parts of this huge building are examined. C. S. Smith who designed the stables 1814 also designed a long gallery on the north side. There is a late C18 conservatory with arched windows and Doric pilasters. Stoneleigh features as "Sotherton Court" in *Mansfield Park* by Jane Austen, a cousin of the Leighs. Lady Violet Powell describes Queen Victoria's visit to Stoneleigh in her biography of her grandmother, *Margaret, Countess of Jersey*, whose childhood home this was, when even the pig-sties were painted. Stoneleigh,

*Stoneleigh: saloon*

*Stoneleigh: dining room*

now the property of 4th Lord Leigh, is the site of the British Equestrian Centre. LEIGH, B/PB; *Pevsner*, CL 28 Oct 1899 & 5 May 1906. VCH.

**Stoney Thorpe Hall, Southam.** Heavily restored house with fragments of its former self. Mullioned and transomed windows, gables and porch point to the C17; a C16 carved chimneypiece is to be found inside. Fine, well-wooded park. Seat of the Chamberlaynes. CHAMBERLAYNE/LG1969; VSA; *Pevsner*; VCH.

**Stretton Manor, Stretton-on-Fosse.** Cotswold style house of 1836 incorporating parts of C16 and C17. Originally a quadrangular house. Now owned by Mr William Townsend. *Pevsner*.

**Studley Castle, Studley.** Extraordinary building designed by Samuel Beazley 1834 for Sir Francis Goodricke, Bt. The architect specialized in theatres and seems to have given vent to some of his theatrical flair when putting Studley together. All is symmetrical and rather monumental in scale. One's eye is fixed by the huge central lantern which dominates all. Actually it is the top part of the hall inside and its octagonal sides are filled with windows of stained glass. The hall has a wooden balcony around the base of the tower and is a huge room as also are the dining and drawing rooms. Polished oak abounds inside—staircase, doors, floors, etc, make it seemingly endless. From the beginning of C20 the house has

*Stoney Thorpe Hall*

*Stretton Manor*

*Studley Castle*

belonged to the Lady Warwick Agricultural College for Women, so the grounds still contain the splendid things one would expect and set off the Norman/Gothic pile of stone in the centre. GOODRICKE, Bt/EDB; *Colvin*; *Pevsner*; VCH.

**Temple Grafton Court, Temple Grafton.** This large brick and half-timbered house of 1876 is situated in a well-wooded park. Formerly the seat of the Gregg family, Temple Grafton became an hotel 1953 but has now been converted into flats. GREGG/WCF; *Pevsner*.

**Thickthorn Lodge, Kenilworth.** Mild-mannered Tudor Gothic job of *ca* 1830. Battlemented. Once twice the size but more stringent times brought down half of it in 1950s. A fanciful gatehouse guards the approach. George Beard owned the house 1904. *Pevsner*.

**Tidmington House, Tidmington.** The C18 refronting of an early C17 house has resulted in a facade both charming and distinctive. 2 sharp gables with a smaller one on the recessed 3 bay centre in between. In the centre gable there is a lunette window and below that a Venetian window on the 1st floor. The 2 wings are joined by a Tuscan colonnade. 1 bay pavilions extend the facade to the right and left; 3 original gables survive at the back. Property of Mr Thomas Beecham, 2nd son of the conductor. BEECHAM, Bt/PB; *Pevsner*.

*Temple Grafton Court*

*Thickthorn Lodge*

*Tidmington House*

*Umberslade Park*

**Umberslade Park, Tanworth-in-Arden.**
Tall and very sober stone house built for
Andrew Archer, brother of the celebrated
architect Thomas Archer. Because of this
connexion it tends to disappoint. 9 bays long
with a recessed 5 bay centre and quoins,
moulded window surrounds and top
balustrade—nothing more. The years of

building can be fixed as *ca* 1695–1700. Of that
date little or nothing survives inside. But some
plasterwork of *ca* 1740s is to be found as well as
a figure of Venus in the entrance hall which is
dated 1702. The low wings, porte-cochère and
colonnade were added by W. H. Bidlake for G.
F. Muntz in C19; at the same time there was
internal alteration of an undistinguished kind.

The grounds contain lakes and an obelisk put
up by 1st Lord Archer 1749. Lodges joined by
an arch to the north-east. ARCHER, ARCHER,
B/DEP; MUNTZ/LG1972; *Colvin*; VCH; *Pevsner*.

**Upton House, Ratley.** Transformed by the
architect Morley Horder for 1st Viscount

*Upton House before alteration*

Bearsted ostensibly to contain the latter's splendid collection of pictures which, with the house, he gave to the National Trust. Before Horder it must have been sober indeed. Basically a building of 1695, it is of 9 bays with a recessed centre now crowned by Horder's open segmental pediment. The garden front is even plainer—just a long block of 9 bays with thin centre doorway. The canted bays at either end of the house are mostly Horder. The only original feature inside is the principal stair with bold balusters. Before the Samuels owned it Upton was the seat of the Jenkins and Motion families. MOTION *formerly of Stisted Hall*/LG 1952; SAMUEL, BEARSTED, V/PB; JENKINS/WCF; *Pevsner*; CL 10 Sept 1904 & 5, 12 Sept 1936.

**Walsh Hall, Meriden.** Large timber-framed house of C15 and C16. Irregular with brick ranges as well. There are additions of the late 1930s and some internal features, such as a C16 chimneypiece with a lozenge frieze, have been brought in. Until its restoration, Walsh was used as a farmhouse. *Pevsner*.

*Walsh Hall*

*Walton Hall*

**Walton Hall, Walton.** Sir George Gilbert Scott designed this somewhat unimaginative house in 1858–62 for Sir Charles Mordaunt, 10th Bt. It replaced the earlier seat of the family, evidences of which survive in C18 brick stables and stone bath house of *ca* 1750. Of stone, its style is drawn from late C13 or early C14 buildings. Two towers do their best to enliven the entrance front. One is in the angle of the "L"-shaped front and the lesser of the two brings a projecting wing to a halt. On the garden front there is a long colonnade of trefoil arches and there are gables and a canted bay. Colonnade of trefoil arches and gallery in the entrance hall and a staircase with tall windows full of armorial stained glass. The house has lately served as an hotel and is now owned by Mr Danny La Rue, the female impersonator. MORDAUNT, Bt/PB; *Colvin*; *Pevsner*; VCH; *Morris* IV.

**Warmington Manor, Warmington.** A hall house of *ca* 1600 probably built for Richard Cooper. The doorway and the chimneybreast are in their medieval positions. Mullioned windows and 2 gables for solar and service wing. Like most of the houses in Warmington, the Manor is of Hornton stone and is placed directly on the village green, dominating the scene. S. N. Banham lived here *post* World War II. CL 29 Nov 1946; *Pevsner*.

*Walton Hall*

*Warwick Castle*

*Warwick Castle: the Great Hall*

*Warwick Castle: dining room*

**Warwick Castle, Warwick.** Long the seat of the Grevilles, Earls of Warwick, but now in the somewhat different hands of Madame Tussaud's who maintain it perfectly as a major showpiece. Without question one of the most picturesque, as well as one of the most important, castles in the kingdom. On its cliff above the Avon the castle is spectacular while inside the courtyard is more ordered and controlled. Begun as early as 1068 by William the Conqueror its building history became a steady progression through the centuries, the greatest period being in C14. Caesar's Tower, Clock Tower, Guy's Tower are all of that date. In C15 followed Bear and Clarence Towers. The main living quarters are in the south range which rises sheer from the river. Basically C13 it was much altered in C19 by Salvin who worked here 1863–66 and 1872. At the north-east corner is a porch with a complex building history. It was built between early C17 and 1749, when Canaletto executed his celebrated series of views of the castle. Projections and recessions all through the building are of a wide variety of dates and styles. Inside the basement reveals the undercrofts of hall, chapel and staterooms. The Great Hall has a ceiling of 1871 put in after a fire and an important chimneypiece of the same date. The great Dining Room boasts a Georgian ceiling in the Elizabethan style; the chapel is of the mid-C18 and contains an assembly of stained

*Warwick Castle: ante room*

*Warwick Priory*

glass of various periods and from various sources. Much work was done in late C17 and to this period may be assigned the Red Drawing Room and the Cedar Room. Queen Anne's Bedroom shows more late C17 plasterwork with a sumptuous C17 ceiling; even this is outshone by the ceiling in the small Blue Boudoir where there are garlands on the overmantel. Salvin had his own personal fling in the Billiard Room with its open timber roof of *ca* 1866. G. E. Fox designed the library 1871 with Italian Renaissance style bookcases with painted decoration on the pilasters. Stables of 1764–66 and a conservatory of 1784–87 which used to house the famous Warwick Vase now in Glasgow Art Gallery. Brown did the grounds, Mylne did a bridge and Lightoler provided an embattled late Georgian mill. Before selling the castle itself in 1978, Lord Brooke, son of the 7th Earl of Warwick, sold some of its treasures piecemeal, which provoked an outcry. GREVILLE, WARWICK, E/PB; CL; VCH; *Pevsner; Colvin*; Stroud, *Capability Brown*.

**Warwick Priory, Warwick.** Formerly the seat of the Lloyds, this very important early C17 house had a long and attractive entrance front displaying a fine array of shaped gables. Of stone with bay windows strung out along the facade. Later alteration on other fronts. Original 2 storey hall and splendid staircase. However The Priory was almost wholly demolished 1925 and now one has to look to Virginia House, Richmond, Virginia for much of it. Using some of the facade and internal fittings Mr & Mrs Weddell created that house out of Warwick Priory. It is to be regretted that in the rebuilding the house was not put up again in the same form. LLOYD *of Dolobran*/ LGI 1969.

**Weddington Hall, Weddington.** Sometimes known as Weddington Castle because of its castellated and irregular appearance. A large building designed by Lugar for Lionel Place *ante* 1823. Later seat of the Shawes, Weddington was demolished *ca* 1928. SHAWE/LGI 1952; VCH; *Colvin*.

*Warwick Priory: hall*

*Weddington Hall*

*Welcombe*

**Welcombe, Stratford-on-Avon.** On the site of the seat of the Lloyd family, which was a Gothick confection of late C18, Henry Clutton designed a new house 1867 for Mark Philips, MP, the Manchester cottontot. It is large, of brick, with a great flurry of shaped gables. Big service wing on the entrance side and another wing added to the south in C20. Staircase aping C17 pierced strapwork leading to an upper colonnade and a black marble chimneypiece in the hall. The Combes, friends and companions of Shakespeare, lived at the pre- Georgian house. On the death of the bachelor cottontot, Welcombe passed to his brother Robert Philips, MP, whose elder daughter Caroline married Sir George Trevelyan, 2nd Bt, the Victorian statesman. It became a seat of the Trevelyans and was the childhood home of

*Wellesbourne Hall*

*Weston Park*

the great historian G. M. Trevelyan. Now an hotel. PHILIPS *of The Heath House*/LG1965; TREVELYAN, Bt, *of Wallington*/PB; *Pevsner*; *Neale* IV (1821); Girouard, *The Victorian Country House* (1979).

**Wellesbourne Hall, Wellesbourne.** Associated with the artist and writer Mrs Delany who made fireplaces with shellwork here *ca* 1760. Other work of the same period and later at Wellesbourne includes an Adamish plaster ceiling. But it is a William and Mary House of *ca* 1700 of red brick and stone dressings. In the hall there is a gallery and staircase with twisted balusters, though much of this may be recent work. The builder of Alveston House (*qv*) was probably responsible for Wellesbourne too. The Georgian conservatory tacked on to the house has been taken down. Mrs Delany's sister, Anne Granville, married John D'Ewes of Wellesbourne 1740; their son took the surname of Granville, as did his nephew, the ancestor of the present squire (who now lives at Chadley nearby). The Granvilles were originally a West Country family which produced the famous Elizabethan seadog Sir Richard Grenville (or Granville) of the *Revenge*. GRANVILLE/LG1969; *Pevsner*; VCH; Lees-Milne, *English Country Houses: Baroque* (1970).

**Weston Hall, Bulkington.** Stone house of *ca* 1600 with 3 gables to the entrance. Recessed 3 bay centre; mullioned and transomed windows. C19 wing to left with inset doorcase. Owned by the Haywood and du Barry families in C18 and C19, Weston became the property of Col Leyland after a period as a school. Since 1970 it has been an hotel. *Pevsner*.

**Weston Park, Long Compton.** Enormous house by Blore for Sir George Philips, 1st Bt. Built in Jacobean style 1827, replacing a C16 house destroyed by fire, it presented irregular but grand facades to all sides except to the garden where the long stone house was united by an oddly proportioned central tower with even odder turrets at its four corners. Large and impressive rooms inside with some decoration by Pugin. The house was demolished 1933. Sir George Philips's eldest daughter married 2nd Earl of Camperdown (the name of whose Perthshire seat, Gleneagles, was appropriated by an hotel); but on the death of 3rd Earl 1918, Weston was left to the Warriner family who still own the estate today. PHILIPS *of The Heath House*/LG1965; HALDANE-DUNCAN, CAMPERDOWN, E/PB1933 and *sub* CHINNERY-HALDANE *of Gleneagles*/ LG1972; VCH.

*Weston Hall*

*Weston Park: drawing room*

*Weston Park: dining room*

*Weston Park: library*

**Whitacre Hall, Nether Whitacre.** Onetime seat of the Jennens family, but now a farmhouse. A moated Jacobean affair approached through a brick gatehouse, with a shaped gable, of the same date. *Pevsner*; VCH.

**Whitley Abbey, Whitley.** On demolition 1953, when the house was little more than a ruin, the oldest surviving parts appeared to be early C17. Before its C19 enlargement, Whitley was a stone house on an "E"-plan with curvilinear gables. Soane submitted plans for alterations to the Hoods 1808 and about this time its name was changed from Whitley Hall to Whitley Abbey. Soane enlarged the hall; and its beamed ceiling was supported by square classical columns and he gave the house a vaulted drawing room. Also due to Soane were the dining-room and library as well as new wings to the east and west. There was a fire 1874 and after it the house was altered and partly rebuilt by the new owner, E. H. Petre. A chapel and ornamental water gardens were created at this time. The Tate family was known to have been on this site in late C16. They sold it 1627 to the Bowaters. Whitley passed to the Hoods through the marriage of Jane Wheler to Henry Hood (later 2nd Viscount Hood) in late C18. The 4th Viscount sold the estate to E. H. Petre 1867 and the latter's son, O. H. P. Turville-Petre, parted with it 1920. Belgian refugees occupied the house in World War I after which it remained empty and eventually became derelict. A fine modern co-educational school designed by Arthur Ling now enjoys the old site. It was

*Whitacre Hall*

built in 1955–57 and is one of the best of Coventry new schools. HOOD, HOOD, V/PB; PETRE, *sub* PETRE, B/PB; *Colvin*; *Pevsner*; VCH; *Neale* III (1820).

**Wolston Priory, Wolston.** Attractive front of rust coloured stone and an interesting medley of mullioned and mullioned and transomed windows. All irregular with the altered 3

*Whitley Abbey*

*Wolston Priory*

storey porch on the extreme right. But the back shows two timber-framed gables and inside the screens passage is still clearly marked. *Pevsner*; VCH.

**Wolverton Court, Wolverton.** Former timber-framed farmhouse of C16 and C17 revamped and extended by Sir Clough Williams-Ellis *ca* 1912. His somewhat eclectic taste has resulted in an addition of free Queen Anne style. Of stone, this afterthought is of 3 bays and 3 storeys with large urns on top. Mr P. R. Clarke is the present owner.

*Wolvey Hall*

**Wolvey Hall, Wolvey.** A rebuilt house of 1889 which contains a very good staircase partly of 1677. It has an openwork balustrade with interconnected volute-like shapes. H. F. J. Coape-Arnold bought the house towards end of C19 and was responsible for the virtual rebuilding of the late C17 house. His granddaughter, Mrs G. E. Burbidge, owns the house today. COAPE-ARNOLD/LG1952; *Pevsner*.

**Wootton Hall, Wootton Wawen.** Built 1687 for the Smyths, this rather grand house with its swagger facades of apricot stone is now dangerously close to a caravan site. 9 by 9 bays with a slightly abrupt pediment, its monumental quality is enhanced by a pronounced modillion cornice and pediments over the ground floor windows. The west side is

*Wolverton Court*

*Wootton Hall*

*Wroxall Abbey*

enlivened by a giant Venetian window inserted C18. Behind is a large Roman Catholic chapel built 1813. Giant wall pilasters and Greek Doric columns flanking the altar dominate the interior. G. H. C. Hughes owned Wootton in 1904; it is now used as flats. *Pevsner*; VCH.

**Wroxall Abbey, Wroxall.** Famous as the seat of Sir Christopher Wren who bought the house 1713. Wrens continued to live here until well into C19 when they married into the Hoskyns family. The house that the famous architect bought was Elizabethan with shaped gables and had been built for the Burgoyne family, who sold it to Sir Christopher. In the mid-C19 the estate was to come into the possession of James Dugdale of Liverpool and for him Walter Scott of Liverpool designed the rather soulless mansion that enjoys the name of the old house. Late Gothic and Tudor serves as a somewhat loose description of the building. It is dated 1866 and is totally asymmetrical. Inside there is stained glass by T. Drury on the staircase and a chimneypiece with granite columns in the drawing-room. Gatepiers in the garden wall are said to have been designed by Wren and they flank iron gates designed by Sir Clough Williams-Ellis. Dugdales continued to live here until quite recently, but the building is now used as a school for girls. HOSKYNS, Bt/PB; DUGDALE/LG1965; *Pevsner*; VCH: *Neale* IV (1821); Hall, *The Baronial Halls and Picturesque Edifices of England* (1848).

# WORCESTERSHIRE

THE SWELLING Malvern Hills provide the most dramatic piece of natural scenery in Worcestershire. The Teme valley is a place of great beauty yet other parts of the county are somewhat flat—giving way here and there to gently undulating countryside. In the south-east Worcestershire receives a sharp nudge from the Cotswolds sprinkling that corner with houses of hot golden stone.

Like its neighbour Herefordshire it is a county rich in timber-framed houses—some of them having dramatic displays of close-studding such as Mere Hall and Huddington Court both of the 16th century. Besford Court, Eastington Hall and Salwarpe Court are other rewarding examples of spacious timber-framed gentry houses of the same period.

Brick houses started to become more established by the mid-16th century and Grafton Manor and Madresfield Court, both subjects of 19th-century rebuilding, still show crow-stepped gables and important elements of the originals. The most extraordinary house of the 17th century is Westwood Park. It is a tall brick hunting lodge with later diagonal wings which made it into one of the largest houses in the county. Woollas Hall, of and dated 1611 has a very fine wooden chimneypiece typical of a number of such chimneypieces throughout the county. The finest wall paintings survive at Harvington Hall. They date from the late 16th century and even outdo the splendid display at Dowles Manor which is contemporary.

Carolean architecture came late to Worcestershire and Severn End has a Dutch gable of 1673. Generally the 17th century can be considered as a rather thin time for country house building in the county but the 18th century provided a burst of building which somehow made up for the inadequacies of the previous hundred years. Hanbury Hall of 1701 seems the very essence of the English country house with its beautifully balanced facade of soft red brick. Thornhill's painting inside lifts it to a very high rung indeed in the hierarchy of the English house. Worcester developed its own school

of architects in the early 18th century and brick houses with pronounced quoins, such as Drayton and Clent, originated from this source.

The greatest Baroque house in the county was Hewell Grange. It would have ranked as one of the most important Baroque houses in England had it survived, with its low powerful silhouette enlivened by Corinthian pilasters and Cundy's later portico. Francis Smith built Ombersley Court in 1723 with a superb interior and there were lesser offshoots of the Baroque movement such as the rustic Tutnall Hall and the more sophisticated Overbury and Kemerton Courts nearby.

Croome Court and Hagley Hall both of the 1750s are major houses curiously designed by a gardener and high priest of the Gothic Revival respectively. Both houses are unusually rich in garden buildings. James Stuart's Temple of Theseus at Hagley in 1758 can claim to be the first Greek Doric temple front in Europe. A charming late 18th-century house is Craycombe; while the early 19th century provides dramatic contrasts with the sizeable Greek Spetchley Park and the now vanished Lea Castle, a castellated confection which would bear more investigation. Blore's Pull Court of the 1830s/40s is an ambitious Jacobean style house taking us into the reign of Victoria. Daukes's colossal rebuilding of Witley Court (about 1860), followed by Hardwick's Madresfield (from 1863) to the monumental new Hewell Grange by Bodley and Garner (1884), gave the county huge houses for peers with seemingly limitless funds.

Losses in Worcestershire are headed by old Hewell Grange. But others such as Clent House, Park House, Lea Castle and Witley Court (now a shell) provide a small group of rich and diversified buildings which the county could ill afford to lose. Kyre's charming 18th-century interiors, now largely stripped away, are a grievous loss. Few long established families remain: Lechmeres, Coventrys, Lytteltons, Berkeleys are still here—others like the Pakingtons are represented through the female line.

# Principal Bibliography

CL    *Country Life*

Colvin    Colvin, H. M.: *A Biographical Dictionary of British Architects 1600–1840* (1978)

DEP    *Burke's Dormant and Extinct Peerages* (1883)

EDB    *Burke's Extinct and Dormant Baronetcies* (1841)

IFR    *Burke's Irish Family Records* (1976)

LG    *Burke's Landed Gentry*, 18 edns (1833/37–1972)

PB    *Burke's Peerage and Baronetage*, 105 edns (1826–1970)

Pevsner    Pevsner, Nikolaus: *Worcestershire* (1968)

RFW    *Burke's Royal Families of the World*, 2 vols (1977–80)

VCH    *The Victoria History of the County of Worcester*, 4 vols (1901–24)

VSA    Burke, Sir Bernard: *A Visitation of Seats and Arms of the Noblemen and Gentlemen of Great Britain and Ireland*, 2 vols (1852–53); 2nd series, 2 vols (1854–55)

WCF    *Walford's County Families*

**Abberley Hall, Abberley.** By Samuel Daukes for J. L. Moilliet who died before it was completed 1846. Finished for his son James Moilliet. A large Italianate house resembling Barry's vanished Mount Felix, Surrey. Tall asymmetrical tower in the angle of the main block and service wing. Deep porte-cochère. Main facade to the garden where it is long and low with top balustrade and projecting verandah on columns. Comfortable rooms within including an entrance hall with a screen of Ionic columns at one end, and a library with bold bookcases and a chimneypiece with paired columns above. Most startling of all is the 161 ft clock tower which faces the house, but which is some distance from it. This is a landmark for miles about. It is composed of red rock-faced stages with a top of buff stone. The octagonal uppermost stage is flanked by polygonal angle buttresses ending in pinnacles. Oriel windows lower down on each side. The whole structure strongly evokes the clock tower of Eaton Hall, Cheshire, which is earlier and by Waterhouse. It was designed as a memorial to the father of J. J. Jones of Oldham who bought the estate 1867 and it contains 20 bells which can play 42 airs. J. P. St Aubyn designed the tower and it was built 1883–5. By 1928 A. M. Kilby owned the house, but it was let to Gilbert Ashton, the cricketer (*see* LG1969), who ran a preparatory school here—a purpose which it still serves. MOILLIET *of Abbotsleigh*/LG1898; JONES/WCF; Girouard, *The Victorian Country House* (1979); *Pevsner*; VCH IV.

*Abberley Hall*

*Abberton Hall*

**Abberton Hall, Abberton.** A brick skin hides a timber-framed building. There is a great stone chimney-breast, dated 1619, and a range of stout 3 star chimneys of brick. Black and white stables. Sweeping views from house. Formerly the seat of the Laslett family, it was owned by Alline Bushell 1924, but the property of Capt J. M. Gibbon by 1928. LASLETT/LG1886; *Pevsner*; VCH.

**Abbey Manor, Evesham.** This seat of the Rudge family was probably built as late as 1840. Tudor-Gothic with 5 widely-spaced bays—the 1st and 5th projecting. All is battlemented with pinnacles on the projections. Central porch. There is an extension to the north-west of one storey—again with pinnacles—and on the south side there is a 2 storey bay window. To the south-east is a long and irregular conservatory still battlemented. Library with castellated bookcases, and in the

*Abbey Manor*

dining-room a curiosity—above a bogus and elaborately carved chimneypiece and within a carved frame, there is a large square opening looking into the conservatory. The house is on the site of the Battle of Evesham and there is an obelisk in the grounds to commemorate the event. A folly, called the Leicester Tower, and an icehouse further dress the grounds. Recently for sale. RUDGE *of Evesham*/LG1952; *Pevsner*.

**Arley Castle, Upper Arley.** The castle stood on high ground and commanded a view of the Severn Valley and the forest of Wyre. Two distinct builds formed the composition of Arley. To the south was a 2 storeyed block erected in C16 and extended in the reign of James I. This was the Dower House of the Lytteltons of Hagley (*qv*). But to this older part, there was added, 1844, an enormous Gothic castle consisting of a high square tower, huge lower towers flanking a great gateway and a monumental wing stretching away at the rear. The addition brought about a complete refurbishment of the older house and nothing apart from 2 staircases—one Elizabethan, the other Jacobean—was suffered to remain. However, early C17 woodwork was reused in the old block and the library could be considered a successful evocation of the earlier age. In the newer range, detail in the rooms was kept to a minimum and no outstanding chamber was to be noted. On the death of 2nd Lord Lyttelton 1779, Arley passed to his sister Viscountess Valentia. Her son, 2nd and last Earl of Mountnorris, added to the earlier house and transformed it into Arley Castle. Robert Woodward bought the estate from Lord Mountnorris's nephew 1852. Arley was demolished *ca* 1960. LYTTELTON, COBHAM, V/PB; ANNESLEY, VALENTIA, V/PB; WOODWARD/LG1952; VCH III.

**Astley Hall, Astley.** Jacobean-style house of the 1830s or later. Symmetrical 5 bay block with mullioned windows. 3 shaped gables on parapet and projecting porch of the Grafton Manor (*qv*) type. Later incongruous additions on the south side. Built for the Lea family who remained here until it became the home of 1st Earl Baldwin of Bewdley (formerly Stanley Baldwin, the Prime Minister), who died here 1947. Bequeathed to the City of Birmingham to be used as a school. LEA/LG1972; BALDWIN OF BEWDLEY, E/PB; *Pevsner*.

**Badge Court, Elmbridge.** Timber-framed house built for the Talbots probably in early C16. All close studding with diagonal struts as well. Recessed centre at back with chimneybreast and diagonally set stacks. In late C16 inherited by the Wintours. Now a farmhouse. WINTOUR, Bt/EDB; *Pevsner*; VCH III.

**Beckford Hall, Beckford.** Large Jacobean house with high flat front of 7 even gables. Fenestration renewed in Victorian times with extensions of the same date. Beckford stands on the site of a priory of Augustinian canons founded 1128. Buttresses of this ancient building survive in the cellars. The house has now become flats. Once the seat of the Wakemans, it was the property of Capt H. A. Case after World War I. The grounds boast an

*Arley Castle*

*Astley Hall*

*Badge Court*

*Beckford Hall*

*Besley Hall*

*Besford Court*

avenue of box trees said to be several centuries old. WAKEMAN, Bt/PB; CASE/LG1937; *Pevsner*.

**Beoley Hall, Beoley.** The principal front is a rebuilding of 1791 by John Sanders. 2 storeys, 3 wide bays with a robust porch of 4 Tuscan columns. Tripartite windows with blank segmental arches either side. Pretty vase with garlands on parapet and reliefs of Pompeian or Wedgwood type further enliven the facade. All this is tacked on to a 3 storey house which is late C17 or early C18—thus it is a building of considerable size. Inside there is a staircase which rises behind a screen of 2 columns and it is top-lit by a circular skylight. There is a large room with a honeysuckle frieze in the Adam tradition. The bow windows at the side which were part of the 1791 revamping have been heightened. Beoley was the seat of the Sheldons, but in 1788 it was sold to Thomas Holmes. Later owners included the Hornby, Mole and Jones-Langston families. In the 1920s it was still owned by Mrs Cheape, daughter of Richard Hemming who bought the house 1888. SHELDON *of Brailes House-*/LG1898; HEMMING (*now* CHEAPE) *of Bentley Manor*/LG1894; JONES-LANGSTON/WCF; *Colvin*; *Pevsner*; VCH IV.

**Besford Court, Besford.** Good on two counts: the work of *ca* 1500 is matched by very fine work of 1912 by Randall Wells. The west front is of typical close studding of the late C15 and early C16 with a gateway over which is an oriel and gable of *ca* 1600. There is a timber-framed wing running east from the north end and the south side of the front range continues with 2 gables; then there is the work by Wells. His neo-Tudor front at Besford is praiseworthy. He created 3 canted bays on the ground floor with 2 1st-floor oriels above in carefully chosen relation to those below. The chapel is Romanesque and a slavish imitation of that style. On entry one is carried through to a passage with cloister-like openings to the left revealing timber studding of the east range. Then a total surprise: a Lutyens-type staircase sweeping upwards to the 1st floor. At the end of the passage there is a courtyard with cloister on the ground floor and gallery above. In the main hall there are bold transverse stone arches across—a motif used by Norman Shaw at Adcote, Shropshire (*qv*). Besford belonged to the Besford and Harewell families before being inherited by the Sebrights. It was reconstructed deliberately to serve as a Roman Catholic home for mentally defective children. SEBRIGHT, Bt/PB; *Pevsner*; VCH III.

**Bevere House, North Claines.** Notable, above all else, as the home of Dr T. R. Nash, author of *The History of Worcestershire* (in which an engraving of the house appears as a frontispiece). It was built for the Doctor *ca* 1760 and its architect was Anthony Keck. Bevere is the best house in an area of sober and prosperous C18 houses. Of 5 bays and 3 storeys, it has a porch of 4 Ionic columns with a Venetian window above it. At the top there is a tripartite lunette window and a 3 bay pediment. The grounds contain a bridge with charming C18 railing. After the Nashes, it was the seat of the Curtlers. NASH/LG1875; CURTLER/LG1937; *Colvin*; *Nash*; *Pevsner*; VCH III.

*Birtsmorton Court*

*Birtsmorton before restoration*

**Birtsmorton Court, Birtsmorton.** Much of what one sees today is a C20 restoration for the Bradley-Birt family. Birtsmorton is an exceedingly picturesque house of considerable variety and situated in a wide moat. The earliest part seems to be a C14 arch of stone on the north side, and the range to the east of it may be as old. The hall is in the south range with a screens passage and a big fireplace which is represented outside by a broad chimney-breast. The best room is the parlour which has panelling with Corinthian pilasters and a ceiling with beams and plasterwork. Much of the house was the subject of an earlier revamping *ca* 1580 and the structure, plan and details, particularly of the hall, point to that date. The solar cross-wing is basically medieval, but its brick skin is almost wholly C18 and C19 brickwork. Originally the seat of the Nanfans, it later became a farmhouse. Restored early this century, it now belongs to Mr N. Dawes. *Pevsner*; VCH; CL 3 May 1902.

*Birtsmorton: hall*

**Blackmore Park, Hanley Castle.** Grand Jacobean style house of *ca* 1860, built for the Hornyold family. The usual shaped gables with a long straggling wing to the right of the main building. Interiors in keeping. All done in a safe neo-Jacobean way, but uninspired. Large porte-cochère. Thomas Hornyold, a zealous Royalist, helped Charles II escape after the Battle of Worcester 1651. He himself was taken prisoner, Blackmore was disparked and his estates were sequestered, a large quantity of his timber being felled. The estates were partly restored, but without compensation, at the Restoration when Gen Monk described him as the greatest sufferer by the rebellion in Worcs. In 1859 Blackmore passed by inheritance to the Papal family of Gandolfi who took the surname of Hornyold. The house was demolished 1925. HORNYOLD/LG1969; VCH III.

**Bockleton Court, Bockleton.** Large neo-Jacobean house which is now a school. Designed by Henry Curzon and built 1866–69. Formerly seat of the Prescott family. PRESCOTT/LG1952; *Pevsner*.

*Blackmore Park*

*Bohun Court*

*Bockleton Court*

**Bohun Court, Worcester.** Enormous Gothic house of the 1860s. Prominent tower on entrance side and huge bay windows on all fronts. Demolished 1925.

**Brand Lodge, West Malvern.** Designed by Ernest Newton. A semi-circular porch forms the centrepiece of the building which has cross-gabled wings. There are polygonal bay windows in the middle of each of these wings. *Pevsner*.

**Bretforton Hall, Bretforton.** Stuccoed neo-Gothic house said to be as late as 1830. Battlemented tower, ogee-headed windows and a convex porch of Roman Doric wooden columns. *Pevsner*.

**Bretforton Manor, Bretforton.** Seat of the Ashwins. Attractive stone house ranging from early C17 to late C19. There are 5 gables—one is dated 1605, but there is even one with the date 1877. ASHWIN/LG1972.

**Bricklehampton Hall, Bricklehampton.** Another Italianate villa so typical of its date which is 1848. Inevitable asymmetrically placed tower with open-top stage. Plentiful supply of round-headed windows and the whole building rendered and painted white. Built for the Woodwards, it was later the seat of the Elgers and was in the ownership of John Hinshaw 1928. Sold 1972. WOODWARD *of Arley Castle*/LG1952; ELGER/WCF; *Pevsner*.

**Broome House, Broome.** Interesting C18 house with an older front of 3 widely-spaced bays—the outer bays of which are square with battlements. Over the centre bay, though, there is a big ogee gable with a quatrefoil in it. Then there is a porch with battlements and an ogee arch. The other worthwhile front is of 5 bays and 2½ storeys with semi-circular porch; a 3 bay pediment on this side above a Venetian window and tripartite lunette. Both fronts probably 1760–70. J. A. Holder lived here 1928; but by 1970s it belonged to the late W. H. B. Hatton. *Pevsner*.

*Bretforton Manor*

*Bricklehampton Hall*

*Broome House*

**Broomfield Hall, Broomfield.** Late Georgian house of 5 widely-spaced bays and 3 storeys. Pediment over central 3 bays. Tough porch of paired Doric columns. Demolished 1950s.

**Chateau Impney, Droitwich.** An extraordinary evocation of a Louis XIII chateau set down in Worcestershire. Towering, of dressed red Fareham brick and Bath stone. The main facade to the garden with tall pavilion roofs with an extravagant array of dormers in all sizes. The date: 1869–1875; the architect: Tronquois of Paris, assisted by a local Droitwich man, R. P. Spiers. It was built for John Corbett whose wife was French. Inside the best feature is the spacious staircase. The former conservatory has an iron roof and iron apse. Many additions have been made to suit its present use as an hotel. CORBETT/WCF; *Pevsner*; VCH III; Girouard, *Victorian Country House* (1979).

*Chateau Impney*

*Broomfield Hall*

*Clent House*

*Clent: stables before conversion*

**Clent House, Clent.** Dated 1709, of plum brick with quoins at the angles and prominent keystones above the windows, Clent was a grand squire's house of the Worcester school of architects. 9 bays and 3 storeys. The centre 3 segmental-headed bays were recessed and included the re-used Jacobean front door with crisply carved arcades of blank arches. Beneath the parapet were panels of brick above the windows and a wing with cross-windows projected to the right. It was actually an early C18 rebuilding of an older house; evidences of the earlier structure showed themselves at the back, while inside there was one room of C17 panelling. The staircase was early C18, but the Victorians had simplified other interiors to the point of their being featureless. Contemporary with the rebuilding is the fine stable-block now converted into a house. Lately the home of Mr C. A. Norris, it is of brick and has 11 bays of cross-windows. The 3 bay centre is crowned by a pediment, and a slender but prominent cupola forms the centrepiece of the long roof. Clent itself was built for the Amphletts and demolished 1935. AMPHLETT *of Wychbold/* LG1972; *Pevsner*; VCH III.

*Clent: panelled room*

*Cofton Hall*

*Cofton Hall*

**Cofton Hall, Cofton Hackett.** The great surprise of this house is its extremely fine late medieval hall. Outward appearances are deceptive as the main part of the building is a plain 6 bay 3 storeyed house of the early C19. The hall is hidden behind an ashlar-faced block which probably received its outer layer in C17. The hall measures approximately 40′ × 20′ and has 9 hammerbeam trusses and thin queen posts over. The arched braces are cusped with shallow curves between the cusps. The end bays probably date from the time the exterior was covered with ashlar. Nothing has been published of the many excavations on the site. Pilasters and a pediment accentuate the C18 stables which have 2 projecting wings. W. E. Dodd owned the house 1928. *Pevsner*; VCH III.

**Cookhill Priory, Inkberrow.** At first sight an oddly irregular mid-C18 house on to which is tacked a late C18 Gothick chapel. The chapel is battlemented and has a quatrefoiled roundel. Cookhill's history is, however, much older. It began life as a Cistercian nunnery in late C12. Of the church, parts of the east and north walls exist, notably the very large blocked surround of the east window. The north wall contains the east jamb of a north arcade, probably towards a chapel. This fragment became the chapel 1783. The present house dates mainly from 1763 and it is built on the nuns' quarters of the late C12 foundation. Sir Nicholas Fortescue, Groom Porter to Henry VIII, was granted the site 1542 and his descendants

*Cookhill Priory before C20 addition*

*Cookhill Priory*

*Cookhill: hall*

*Cotheridge Court*

*Cookhill Priory: showing chapel*

created most of the building as it now appears. An exception to this is the 3 bay addition to the right of the entrance. This is C20 but built in keeping with the mid-Georgian block. Doric pilasters flank the door and it has a segmental pediment. Ranging behind the C18 house and chapel is a long brick building—probably C17 and basically timber-framed. Inside, a good contemporary staircase of 2 balusters to a tread, and with carved tread-ends, rises out of the entrance hall. Good chimneypiece and doorcases. The dining-room is in the older part of the house and has a heavy-beamed ceiling and inglenook fireplace. Above the house, and like it enjoying magnificent views of the Malverns, is a ruined C18 gazebo. In C20 the house was acquired by the Antrobus family. FORTESCUE, *sub* FORTESCUE-BRICK-DALE/LG1972; ANTROBUS, Bt/PB; *Pevsner*; VCH III.

*Cotheridge: rear elevation*

**Cotheridge Court, Cotheridge.** A front of 1770. But that date must refer to the centre recessed bays which are 5 in number. On the projecting wings there are Venetian and tripartite windows of such coarse detailing that they might be early Victorian in order to match up. The side and back of the house are a surprise as they are C16 timber-framing with close studs, and inside there is an Elizabethan staircase with square balusters. Long the seat of the Berkeley family, Cotheridge has now been converted into flats. BERKELEY/LG1952; *Pevsner*; *Nash*; VCH IV.

**Craycombe House, Fladbury.** The home of Francis Brett Young and the house in which many of his more notable novels were written. Designed by George Byfield and built *ca* 1791 for George Perrott of the East India Company (and of the same family for whom Perrott House, Pershore, was built), it is ashlar-faced and 5 by 3 bays in size. The ground-floor windows are set in blank arches and the parapet is crowned by 3 urns—the middle one being the fattest and most prominent. The main emphasis is on the entrance door which is

*Craycombe House*

*Croome Court*

tripartite with Corinthian pilasters and over all a giant lunette with fan glazing. Round the corner is an original large urn in a niche with an inscription "*Solus vivat que jucunde*". This is flanked by a bay window and a second doorway similar to that at the entrance. Dainty, reticent interiors. Tall rooms with pretty friezes and occasional restrained plasterwork panels. Over the staircase, which has a thin iron balustrade, there is a circular skylight. The grounds show some splendid cedars; in a wood there is a 5 bay orangery with round-headed openings. Before the Youngs bought the house in 1930s, it was the joint property of G. H. C. Butler and Mrs R. G. Hall. *Colvin; Pevsner;* VCH; CL 6 July 1940.

**Croome Court, Croome d'Abitot.** Of golden Bath stone in an extensive, if somewhat flat, park. Capability Brown transformed a marshy landscape into a suitable setting for the great house of the Earls of Coventry; later, Robert Adam peppered it with garden buildings. Brown was, it appears, mainly responsible for the design of the house which was begun 1751. But in 1752 he wrote to Sanderson Miller, architect of Hagley (*qv*), of the house: "Whatever merits it may in future boast, it will be ungrateful not to acknowledge you as the primary author". Hagley, with its corner towers, is remarkably similar, so perhaps Miller did indeed execute a first design for Croome. The entrance front is correct Palladianism—of 11 bays, piano nobile and square towers rising an extra storey to be crowned by pyramid roofs. Pediment over the

*Croome: greenhouse*

3 centre bays. A 2 armed open staircase rising to the front door which has Tuscan columns and a pediment. The garden front provides greater excitement. Here there is a grand tetrastyle portico of unfluted Ionic columns and there are Venetian windows in the corner towers on the piano nobile. Top balustrade and linked chimney-stacks. The west side has a canted bay 2 storeys high. The east side gives way to the large brick service wing which has pedimented entrance arches. There have been

alterations to the interior since it ceased to be a private house in the late 1940s. The entrance hall and the saloon which leads out of it are rooms untouched by Robert Adam who designed the remainder of the state rooms. The hall has a screen of 4 Roman Doric columns. The saloon has a deep coved ceiling with 3 panels and a magnificent pedimented doorcase to the garden. A sumptuous frieze runs around the room. Of Adam's rooms the finest was the long gallery with niches for

*Croome: gallery*

*Croome: rotunda*

statues which have now been removed. The sumptuous chimneypiece in this room has caryatids holding a garland. A tapestry room with all its original furniture has now been re-assembled in the Metropolitan Museum, New York. Adam's bookcases survive in the south-east library which is lit by one of the Venetian windows on the garden front. The cantile-vered staircase has an iron balustrade. In the grounds nearby is Adam's greenhouse with its temple facade, an arch of an underpass called the Dry Arch Bridge, the Punch Bowl gates with 2 low fat urns, a grotto and the Rotunda which has a coffered dome inside and pedim-

ented windows with garland plaques above. On an island is the summer house with Corinthian columns in antis. More garden buildings lie outside the present park, includ-ing the Panorama Tower, the Gothic Ruin and the Park Seat. Notable lodges at the Worcester and Pershore entrances. The Coventry family bought the estate 1597 and it was the 6th Earl of grounds. Croome was sold 1948 and has latterly been in institutional use. COVENTRY, COVENTRY, E/PB; *Colvin*; *Pevsner*; Stroud, *Capability Brown*; Lees-Milne, *Age of Adam*; CL 25 April 1903 & 10 April 1915.

**Dormston Manor, Dormston.** Partly timber-framed with brick infilling. Can be dated *ca* 1600. Close studding below, square panelling above. Good chimneypieces and staircase with imposing newels. Now a farm-house. *Pevsner*.

**Doverdale Manor, Doverdale.** Formerly the rectory. A handsome 5 bay 3 storey house of early C18. Windows with keystones and a fine staircase with three balusters to a tread and with carved tread-ends. Pronounced quoins. The house is another typical product of the Worcester school of architects. Brig-Gen A. E. W. Colville lived in the house between the wars. COLVILLE, *sub* COLVILLE OF CULROSS, V/PB.

**Dowles Manor, Dowles.** Hardly touched by time, Dowles remains a very complete example of an unspoilt Elizabethan manor house. Central hall with living room wing and kitchen wing both with cross gables. It has a stone ground-floor and timber-framed upper storey with close studding. Fully preserved decorative wall paintings are the main internal features of the house. Largely arabesques, they appear in the hall, drawing-room and corre-

sponding rooms above. An Elizabethan overmantel from Bewdley finds a place in the former kitchen. Surrounded by woods, the house lies in an enviable position remote from the world. J. S. Elliott owned the house 1928. *Pevsner*; CL 16 March 1945.

**Drayton House, Belbroughton.** A hand-some brick house of 7 bays and 2 storeys. Probably early C18. Keystones above the windows and handsome doorcase. Bought early C19 by Henry Brinton, the founder of Brintons of Kidderminster, the carpet manu-facturers. Lady Stocks, the educationalist, was a member of this family. Owned in 1970s by the Justicz family. BRINTON/LG1972; *Pevsner*.

**Eardiston House, Lindridge.** Former seat of the Smith of Eardiston Bts, now longtime residents of Australia. Next to the road, but enjoying a wide prospect of valley and hills to the south. A rambling and generally undistin-guished house of *ca* 1830 and earlier. However, each of the 4 bays left and right of the Tuscan porch carries a pediment. All is stuccoed. George Wallace purchased Eardiston, from the Smiths, 1866. His descendants still held the house between the wars. Now divided into flats. SMITH, Bt, *of Eardiston*/PB; WALLACE/WCF; *Pevsner*; VCH III.

**Earls Croome Court, Earls Croome.** Fairly large timber-framed house of C16 to C17 with a centre and two cross-gabled wings. Transomed windows of 5 lights, close-set studs, but in the centre concave-sided lozenges. 3 identical gables with close-set studs on another side of the building. Long the property of the Coventry family and now the seat of the present Earl of Coventry. COVENTRY, E/PB; *Pevsner*.

*Doverdale Manor*

*Drayton House*

*Earls Croome Court*

*Eastington Hall*

**Eastham Grange, Eastham.** Designed by Sir Walter Tapper 1910. Free Tudor style, of brick with one big straight gable and another half-hipped. Mrs Cottingham lived here 1928. *Pevsner.*

**Eastington Hall, Longdon.** Important timber-framed house of *ca* 1500. Built round 3 sides of a square it has close set studs and a prominent star chimneystack. To the east it has a bargeboard with vine trails and an oriel window. Moulded beams in the hall. Mlle de Montgeon lived here 1928. *Pevsner.*

**Elmley Lovett Lodge, Elmley Lovett.** Large, irregular and wholly half-timbered house said to have been built 1635 for the Townshend family. In due course it became the seat of the Forresters. It was demolished *ca* 1890. An c18 dovecote survives. vch iii.

**Elms (The), Abberley.** Probably mid-c18. A centre block of 5 bays and 3 storeys with top balustrade and a central Venetian window on the 1st floor. Lower 2 storey wings projecting forward either side of the main block, thus creating a "U"-shaped building. Important as it contains fine fittings (*e.g.* doorcases, chimneypieces, etc) from Norton Priory, Cheshire, which was demolished 1928. These were brought here by Sir Richard Brooke. Bt, whose family had owned Norton for several hundred years. The Elms is now an hotel. brooke, Bt, *of Norton Priory*/pb.

**Glasshampton, Astley.** Built for Thomas Cookes Winford *ca* 1705 by John Watson (described as architect of the house on his

tombstone in Astley Church). Large, rectangular mansion of the kind associated with the Smiths of Warwick. Rusticated pilasters at the angles and at the angles of the 3 bay centre which probably projected slightly ahead of the 2 bays either side. On the death of the last Winford it passed to a distant relation, Rev D. J. J. Cookes, who ordered a complete restoration of the property. In the ensuing feast

celebrating the renewal of the structure, 1810, the house caught fire and was totally consumed. Cookes obviously commissioned a new stable-block at the same time as the restoration. This is of brick with angle towers with pyramid roofs and a centre with pediment and cupola. Now it is converted to the novitiate of the Society of St Francis of Cerne Abbas. winford, Bt/edb; *Colvin*; *Nash*; *Pevsner.*

*Glasshampton: stable block*

*Grafton Manor*

**Grafton Manor, nr Bromsgrove.** David Brandon's over enthusiastic restoration of the 1860s must have swept away much of the original C16 house which would be of the greatest interest today. However, important parts do remain, notably the porch and the south window of the Upper Parlour. The porch is composed of coupled Roman Doric columns carrying a tryglyph frieze—these flank the entrance—and on the upper floor 3 pilasters frame 2 tall cross-windows and carry a pediment which contains a roundel. Roll-moulded mullions with a fluted band as the transom are the outstanding features of the parlour window, which also carries a frieze and

pediment over it. Long inscription in the frieze. John Talbot gave the house its memorable parts 1567; he was altering a house which dated from the earlier years of that century. The general appearance now is of a large "L"-shaped house with stepped gables connected to the equally over-restored chapel of the perpendicular period. This has a gallery with ogee arches which dates from C1800. Formerly the seat of the Bourne family, Grafton is now owned by Mr J. W. Morris. BOURNE/WCF; *Pevsner*; VCH III.

**Hadzor House, Hadzor.** Built for the Galton family, it remained their property until

quite recently. As one sees it now, it is a late-Georgian revamping around a mid-Georgian core. The basic date is 1779—the general refurbishment by Matthew Habershon dates from 1827. This made it into the 7 bay, 2 1/2 storey building. On the entrance side there is a 3 bay pediment and a porch of Greek Doric columns. On the garden front there is a pediment surmounting pilasters on the upper 2 storeys. Inside the best feature is the staircase with iron balustrade. The former conservatory, with its pretty iron columns, has been converted into a chapel. Hadzor is now a school. GALTON/LG1937; *Colvin*; *Pevsner*; VCH III; CL 17 Aug 1901.

**Hagley Hall, Hagley.** The outer suburbs of Birmingham spread relentlessly toward the seat of the Viscounts Cobham and one wonders how long it will be before the park is encircled by an outright thrust of suburbia. A major landmark in the Palladio-Inigo Jones tradition, Hagley still holds its own largely on account of the superb restoration after the very serious fire of 1926. Designed by Sanderson Miller, better known as an C18 Goth than a classicist, it was built 1754–60. The client was 1st Lord Lyttelton, the politician, whose biography was written by Dr Johnson. The resemblance to Croome (*qv*) is striking and that house owes something to Miller, though precisely what remains elusive. 4 corner towers are the most noticeable feature in common and, as at Croome, the entrance front is of 11 bays with a central 3 bay pediment. Hagley, however, stands high on a substantial basement of smooth rustication and the entrance is reached by a large open staircase in 2 arms. The 1st floor is treated as a half-storey and pyramid roofs crown the higher corner

*Hadzor House*

*Hagley Hall*

towers. The side elevations are of 5 bays and the garden front is a repeat of that on the entrance side save for the fact that a pedimented window is in place of the pedimented doorway. Miller was an accomplished gentleman-architect, but a "committee of taste" was formed for consultation at the birth of Hagley. The members consisted of John Chute of The Vyne, Hampshire, Thomas Prowse of Axbridge, Somerset, and Thomas Lennard Barrett of Belhus, Essex. Inside there is splendid Rococo plasterwork. This is first met with in the entrance hall which has niches with statues and a magnificent chimneypiece (with atlantes and a satyr and cupid above in a rustic relief) by James Lovell. Vassali signs this relief. A tunnel-vaulted recess, which is coffered, leads out of the back of the hall and receives corridors running from the north and south. The former saloon (now the dining-room) lies at the back of the entrance hall and overlooks the garden front. Here there is a splendid Rococo ceiling and garlands and trophies on the walls—representing music, acting, hunting, painting and war. The library has pedimented bookcases with busts and a handsome chimneypiece. The gallery has a screen of columns at either end and a fine Rococo ceiling. James Stuart executed medallions here; in the tapestry room are original tapestries designed in the Mortlake factory. Apart from the stables of 9 bays and a pediment, Hagley, like Croome again, is rich in park buildings. Most notable of these is the Temple of Theseus by James "Athenian" Stuart. It is dated 1758 and is the earliest example of the Grecian revival anywhere in the

country. Other features in the grounds include an obelisk and the Prince of Wales's Column. The most picturesque ornament is undoubtedly the castle with 4 corner turrets. Only one of the towers is complete and the remainder of the building is deliberately ruinous. Of this structure Walpole made his famous remark that it had "the true rust of the Barons' Wars". The Rotunda still exists while other buildings in the park have disappeared. 5th Lord Lyttelton succeeded by special remainder to the Viscountcy of Cobham on the death of the 3rd and last Duke of Buckingham and Chandos 1889. A passion for cricket has been one of the most notable characteristics of the Lytteltons, though perhaps their best known player, 10th Viscount Cobham, sometime Governor-General of New Zealand, never actually got into the Eton XI. His son, the 11th Viscount, now owns the house. LYTTELTON, COBHAM, V/PB; *Colvin*; *Pevsner*; CL 16 Oct 1915, 2, 16 Jan 1926 & 19, 26 Sept 1957; VCH III; Hussey, *English Country Houses: Early Georgian* (1955).

**Halesowen Grange, Halesowen.** Basically early Georgian, but with a south front of the later C18, the house is of brick and has stone dressings. It is of 5 bays and 2 storeys. The facade is enlivened by giant angle pilasters, an upper-middle window flanked by pilasters and a doorway with half-columns and a segmental pediment. Sometime home of the Lords Burgh. LEITH, BURGH, B/PB; *Pevsner*; VCH III.

**Hallow Park, Hallow.** Replacing an C18

house which, in turn, replaced an even earlier structure which was host to Queen Elizabeth 1575, the present building is early C20 and is dominated by its 8 colossal chimney-stacks. Now a Dr Barnardo's Home.

**Ham Court, Upton-on-Severn.** Built for the Martin family of Martins Bank in 1772 and designed by Anthony Keck. An "H"-shaped house, with the link being of 3 storeys and 5 bays flanked by long, low wings of 2 storeys, 7 bays with pediments on the side elevations. Pretty staircase of wood and attractive rooms with good doorcases and chimneypieces. Typical dainty cornices of Keck's. Ham contained a notable collection of furniture and pictures, but all was dispersed before the house succumbed to demolition 1925. The Martins became Bromley-Martins and latterly married into their distant cousins the Holland-Martins of Overbury Court (*qv*). BROMLEY-MARTIN/LG 1965; *Colvin*.

**Hanbury Hall, Hanbury.** Built for the Vernon family and always their property until acquisition by the National Trust 1960, Hanbury is a very English house of 13 bays and 2 storeys. A central cupola crowns the building which has a pedimented 3 bay centre flanked by giant columns on pedestals. 3 bay wings with quoins project either side of the 5 bay centre. William Rudhall signed drawings for the house, but it is likely that he was only the builder; Talman has been suggested as architect because of similarities to his work at Thoresby, Chatsworth and Drayton. Other

*Ham Court*

*Hanbury Hall*

*Hanbury: staircase*

fronts of the house are as composed as the front—apart from the back where all is haphazard. The entrance opens into the hall into which the staircase descends at the left end. This is the great glory of the house, as the large square open well is painted all over with large figure scenes and the artist was Sir James Thornhill. The scenes are flanked by painted fluted pillars in perspective and walls and ceiling are connected by a flying figure. Thornhill also painted 2 ceiling panels in the dining-room where there is fine Rococo wood carving of *ca* 1750 on the chimney overmantel. A Jacobean overmantel from Tickenhill Manor (*qv*) is found in another ground-floor room. In the grounds is the orangery of *ca* 1740 of 9 bays with a 3 bay pediment. The pavilions and forecourt of the house are Victorian. VERNON, Bt/PB1940; *Pevsner*; VCH IV; CL 4, 11 Jan 1968; Lees-Milne, *Baroque*.

**Hanley Court, Hanley William.** The 7 bay centre dated from the early years of C18, but the 2 bay wings which flanked it and projected

*Hanley Court*

forward probably came with the general rebuilding of *ca* 1750. At the same time a pediment was erected over the middle 5 bays. Still later, possibly early C19, the wings were tied together with a colonnade of Ionic columns. There was provincial work of high quality inside. Fine doorcases, chimney-pieces, panelling and plasterwork of mid-C18 were attractions for a demolition firm *ca* 1930. The staircase too was finely carved with 3 balusters to a tread and carved tread-ends. Linked with the house by a one-room pavilion with a high round-headed window was the large stable-block, which remains in excellent order as part-house and part-farm buildings. To one side is a high arch surmounted by a tall cupola and a clock with face and workings from a recently-demolished church in Yorkshire. The centre of the stableyard is planted with some rare shrubs and trees. Until demolition Hanley belonged to the Wakemans who inherited the property from the Newport family. WAKEMAN, Bt/PB; VCH IV.

**Harborough Hall, Blakedown.** Half-timbered house with projecting porch. Inside Jacobean ceilings and 2 priest-holes. Bold central stack with star topped chimneys. *Pevsner.*

**Harvington Hall, nr Kidderminster.** The appearance of Elizabethan brick hides what is in large part a late medieval building of timberframing. Eminently picturesque and placed in a moat, the building is entirely

irregular and all the more attractive because of that fact. The Pakington family inherited Harvington 1529 and John Pakington did a considerable amount of work here *ca* 1560-75. The north end of the entrance range is probably mid-C17 at the earliest while the principal range on the south side contains the hall which was probably there in C15. Most of the windows in this range are mullioned. An unexpected alteration occurs on the north range where a giant basket arch carries the gables—an alteration of 1701 as dated on a rainwater head. The Throckmorton family owned Harvington in C18 and when their taste took them to Coughton Court, Warwicks (*qv*), they took the original staircase with them, so what one sees now is a replica. The house has a profusion of priest-holes—said to be the most remarkable collection under one roof. These range from a trap-door beneath the chapel to a hiding-place whence one could descend by rope to the moat. The Elizabethan wall paintings in the house are the finest in the county. Their source lies in Flanders and there are exquisite arabesques on the first and second floors. Harvington now belongs to the Roman Catholic Archdiocese of Birmingham. PAKINGTON, Bt/EDB; PAKINGTON, *sub* HAMPTON, B/PB; *Pevsner*; VCH III; CL 4, 11, 18 Aug 1944.

**Henwick Hall, nr Worcester.** Views of this house on old Worcester porcelain show a 5 bay, 2½ storey house. The centre was accentuated by attached columns on the 2nd and 3rd

*Old Hewell Grange, showing Cundy's portico*

*Harvington Hall*

storeys surmounted by a pediment. Long demolished.

**Hewell Grange, Tardebigge.** In a park by Humphry Repton stands this huge house built 1884–91 by Bodley & Garner for 1st Earl of Plymouth (of the 2nd creation). Hewell is of red sandstone and dominates its surroundings by the sheer bulk of its size. Said to have been inspired by Montacute, Somerset, it is considerably less successful, for it strikes one as a combination of Jacobean and Early French Renaissance styles. On the entrance side, long wings come forward to embrace the visitor. A cupola and porte-cochère provide accents to the 3 storey wall of stone. On the garden front there are towers with turrets and a loggia on the ground floor. Bay windows and shaped gables everywhere. But all this does not prepare one for the great shock inside which is the 2 storeyed hall with colonnaded galleries on 3 sides—the whole room decidedly Renaissance and much more marked than one would expect from a view of the outside. The visitor has been transported suddenly and without warning to Italy. Limestone columns of the screens make a heady display. The hall takes up at least half the interior space of the building. The staircase looks *ca* 1700, but its detail remains Jacobean. Detmar Blow and Billerey provided the wooden ceiling to the chapel and the paving there of marble and lapis lazuli is by Farmer and Brindley. A great garden in the early Jacobean English Renaissance style faced the south front, but all this has now been swept away as Hewell is now a reform school. Fragments of the earlier house (for which the park was designed) remain. It was a large square stone building of 2 storeys with a

*Old Hewell Grange*

*Hewell Grange: new house under construction*

*Hewell Grange : hall of new house*

*Hewell Grange : garden front of new house*

balustrade. Almost certainly designed by Thomas Archer for the Earls of Plymouth (of the 1st creation), its elevations were relieved by pilasters and prominent window surrounds. Thomas Cundy added a huge portico of tall Corinthian columns 1816 and probably made internal alterations as well. 4 lodges by Cundy at the main entrance remain. WINDSOR, PLYMOUTH, E/DEP; WINDSOR-CLIVE, PLYMOUTH, E/PB; *Colvin; Pevsner;* VCH III; Stroud, *Humphry Repton; Neale;* CL 6 Dec 1902, 15 Aug 1903.

*Hillhampton House*

**Hillhampton House, Great Witley.** Brick, of 7 bays and 2 storeys. The centre bay forms a tower in which the entrance is situated and it is given an added storey. The 2-bay wings are surmounted by straight gables. All this represents an C18 refronting of an older house and evidences of the earlier structure are found at the rear of the building where there are buttresses. Evidences of C17 work are found in one or two rooms within. Wreaths of plasterwork of that date are to be seen on ceilings in 2 bedrooms. Lately the home of Sir Tatton Brinton, MP. BRINTON *formerly of Drayton House*/LG 1972; VCH II.

**Hindlip Hall, Hindlip.** Large early C19 house of white brick. The principal block is of 2½ storeys with a 3 bay pediment and a porch of unfluted Ionic columns. But this is extended by 3 bay, 2 storey wings which, in turn, are tacked on to 3 bay, 1½ storey outer wings. The house replaced a large earlier building dating from the time of Elizabeth I; this was destroyed by fire in C18. It was built for John Habingdon, cofferer of Queen Elizabeth's household, and was noted as the meeting place of Henry Garnet, the Jesuit, and Oldcorn, conspirators in the Gunpower Plot. Garnet, Hall, Owen and Chambers, all conspirators, were captured at old Hindlip Hall Jan 1606. The well-known brewing family, the Allsopps, bought the estate in C19 and they were partly responsible for enlarging the wings of the house 1867. It was from this estate that they took their title when ennobled 1886. The house is now a police training college. An early C19 lodge heralds the approach from the main Worcester road. ALLSOPP, HINDLIP, B/PB; *Pevsner;* VCH IV.

**Holdfast Manor, Queenhill.** A brick house of late C17. 7 bays with hipped roof and wooden cross windows. The home of Thomas Bolland 1928. *Pevsner.*

**Holt Castle, Holt.** Holt stands high above the river and close to the church and is an interesting combination of medieval work plus the more civilized hand of C18. First, one is met by the bold C14 tower with small decorated windows and a 2 bay rib-vaulted entrance; it is a powerful piece and dominates the whole

*Hindlip Hall:* C16 *house*

*Hindlip: early* C19 *house*

building. The tower stands in front of a C15 hall which has C18 panelling. To the right of the entrance in the tower is a chamber with 3 slit windows, and, to the left, a straight staircase in the thickness of the wall. The C15 hall range was "L"-shaped with a solar wing projecting to the east. In the early C18 the part between the hall and the wing was filled in with a spacious and elegant staircase. Some floral ceiling stucco and a fine wooden handrail in this apartment. Other ground-floor rooms show C18 fielded panelling. On the 1st floor the solar roof remains and there is an early C19 porch of 2 pairs of Greek Doric columns on the garden front. Warwick, Beauchamp, Wysham, Bromley and Foley were some of the early families who occupied the castle. Latterly it has belonged to Messrs Dewhurst and Arliss in the 1920s and Mrs Pepys Cockerell in 1930s. When occupied by Mr F. J. Harper in the 1960s, it was occasionally open to the public. FOLEY, FOLEY, B/PB; COCKERELL *of The Brook House*/LG 1952; *Nash; Pevsner;* VCH; CL 20, 27 July 1940.

**Huddington Court, Huddington.** Notable on two counts: first, as the most picturesque house in the county; secondly, as a hub of the Gunpowder Plot. For it was here that the Wintours lived until 1658. The house is an early C16 building with many alterations of *ca* 1584. At one time it was a much larger building. Now it is "L"-shaped and in the angle is a highly ornate chimney of brick with various decorative patterns and star-tops. All timbering is close set studs and the windows project slightly in an oriel-like fashion. The best interior feature is the staircase and there is a priest-hole on the 2nd floor. The earlier house probably left the moat which sets off the building and also the spectacular C14 stone frieze of 4 quatrefoils with suspended shields. For many years Huddington was a farmhouse, but it is now restored and is the property of Dr H. D. Edmondson. The grounds now show 2 timber-framed C17 dovecotes, a summer house from Strensham Court (*qv*) and fine C18 iron gates from Yorkshire. WINTOUR, Bt/EDB; *Pevsner;* VCH IV; CL 1 Aug 1936.

*Holt Castle*

*Huddington Court*

**Ipsley Court, Ipsley.** 2 long parallel ranges of
what appears to be a c17 building survive.
These were joined by a cross wing which was
demolished 1724. Joining these 2 ranges now is
a brick wall with small Tudor doorway
probably from elsewhere. The substantial
ranges of what is left show hipped roofs, wide
eaves and cross windows. This was long the
seat of the Hubands—c16 monuments of
whom are in St Peter's Church in the village.
HUBAND, Bt/EDB; HUBAND/LG1952; *Pevsner*;
VCH III.

**Kemerton Court, Kemerton.** The refronting of an earlier house gave Kemerton a
garden front of surprising Baroque elegance.
An unusual facade consisting of 4 planes of 2
bays each with a central plane of 1 bay.
Pilasters divide these planes. The parapet is
swept up in the middle and at the ends. On the
entrance side, close to the by-road, the house
assumes a muddled but not unattractive
appearance. Within there is a good Queen
Anne staircase and panelled rooms. Built for
the Parsons family, it was inherited by the
Hoptons of Canon Frome Court, Herefordshire (*qv*). Sold in c20 to the Darbys and now
the home of Mr Adrian Darby, who is married
to Lord Home of the Hirsel's 2nd daughter.
HOPTON *of Canon Frome*/LG1937; DARBY *of
Adcote and Sunnyside*/LG1921; Lees-Milne,
*English Country Houses: Baroque* (1970).

**Kenswick Manor, Kenswick.** Well-
situated house dating from at least c13,
formerly surrounded by a moat. In the house
there is panelling and an elaborate Jacobean
overmantel from Wichenford Court (*qv*). It
has belonged to the Britten family for much of
this century—the present owner being Brig C.
R. Britten whose mother was a daughter of 1st
Viscount Colville of Culross. COLVILLE,
COLVILLE OF CULROSS, V/PB; *Pevsner*; VCH III.

**Knight House, Wolverley.** A handsome and
sizeable house of *ca* 1760 in brick; 7 bays and
2½ storeys with a parapet. Entrance door with
Tuscan columns and a pediment. Arched
windows in blank arches on outbuildings and a
stable-block with central three-bay pediment.
The house contained very fine chimneypieces,
but these have been removed and it is now
divided into flats. *Pevsner*; VCH III.

**Knightwick Manor, Knightwick.** An early
c18 house of 7 bays and 2 storeys with a hipped
roof. The property of John Walker 1928.
*Pevsner*; VCH IV.

**Kyre Park, Kyre Wyard.** When approaching
from the south and west one would assume that
the house is wholly Georgian; but it is basically
an Elizabethan, Jacobean and Georgian addition to a medieval west wing. "L"-shaped,
the show front is to the south where it is of 7
bays and 2½ storeys. The east front is
similarly windowed, but it lacks the canted
bay, Venetian windows and tripartite lunette.
Early this century, Kyre had c18 interiors,
probably by William Hiorn, of the greatest
prettiness and delicacy. Fine chimneypieces,
doorcases and plasterwork created an except-
ionally charming background for the original
c18 furniture. However, this has all but
disappeared—leaving only the main staircase

*Kenswick Manor*

*Kyre: staircase*

*Kyre Park*

*Lea Castle*

of *ca* 1754 which has 3 balusters to a tread with carved tread-ends. An earlier and lesser staircase survives which might be Elizabethan. Kyre was the seat of the Pytts family and then, through an heiress, it passed to the Baldwyn-Childes. The latter sold up in the 1930s and the house is now a sanatorium. There is splendid planting in the grounds which include a chain of lakes. A medieval dovecote and Jacobean barn complete the picture. BALDWYN-CHILDE/LG1921; *Colvin*; *Pevsner*; VCH III; Hussey, *English Country Houses: Early Georgian*; CL 17, 24 March 1917.

**Laughern House, Martley.** Of 2½ storeys. Mid-Georgian with an ashlar-faced centre flanked by 2 bays either side which are in brick. Tripartite, pedimented doorway in centre with tripartite window above. Pediment at roof level. Restrained interiors. *Pevsner*.

**Lea Castle, Cookley.** Lea disappeared *ca* 1945, but it was probably a building of very considerable interest as it was built for the Payne Knight family of Downton Castle,

Herefordshire (*qv*). Lea dated from early C19 and was irregular and built deliberately as a picturesque structure. Both entrance and garden fronts of the house had asymmetrically placed towers and the whole building was, of course, battlemented. No record is known of the interior. Perched on a long ridge, the land fell sharply away from the garden front. Castellated lodges of *ca* 1850 survive. They flank a tripartite entrance. After the Knights, Lea was owned by the Brown-Westheads. ROUSE-BOUGHTON-KNIGHT *of Downton Castle*/ LG1937; BROWN-WESTHEAD/FR; VCH IV.

*The Leasowes*

**Leasowes (The), Halesowen.** On the site of William Shenstone's house where he wrote essays, letters and poetry. His planting survives today in spite of the house being the centre of a golf club. The house as it is dates from early C19. It is pebbledashed and of 3 bays and has a semi-circular Ionic porch. There are attached side pavilions. Shenstone's Gothick stables have gone, but a fragment of his Priory Ruin still remains. Horace Walpole described Shenstone as a "Watergruel Bard". *Pevsner*; VCH IV; CL 3 Nov 1950.

**Lickhill Manor, Stourport.** Queen Anne house of 3 storeys and 7 bays. R. B. Worth lived here 1928. *Pevsner.*

**Little Malvern Court, Little Malvern.** House and St Giles Church form an impressive group. Both are remnants of a Benedictine priory founded 1171, if not before. The house stands to the west of the original cloisters. The refectory or prior's hall represents the west range of these cloisters and this is the only surviving medieval building in the present house. The north range probably incorporates some of the stone of the original south aisle of the church and is timber-framed at 1st-floor level. This range was restored rather badly in C19. The C19 architect, Charles Hansom, designed the west side of the house in 1860 and also the round tower with conical cap on the south side. The east range, however, contains the most important feature of the building and that is the refectory or prior's hall. A floor has

*Little Malvern Court*

*Little Malvern Court*

been inserted in it, but the entire medieval roof is perfect. It is a double-purlin roof exhibiting cusped wind-braces and open collar trusses. The house underwent an extensive restoration in the late 1960s and much new evidence of early work came to light. Mr T. P. Berington is the present owner and his family—long established here and in the neighbouring county of Herefordshire—inherited it through a marriage with a member of the earlier family seated here, the Russells. BERINGTON/LG 1969; *Pevsner*; VCH IV.

**Madresfield Court, Madresfield.** The initial impact is of a very large and irregular Victorian house set down in a perfect moat. It is spiky and theatrical with roofs and facades of the greatest variety. But in fact there is evidence that the basic house was C15, although there is nothing earlier now than the age of the first Elizabeth. The left half of the south front with its steppped gables might represent work of the second half of C16. Most of what one sees, though, is the work of the highly successful P. C. Hardwick for 4th Earl

Beauchamp, descendant of those earlier Lygons for whom the house was begun in C15. Hardwick worked from 1863 to 1885 on the building. The chapel, completed 1867, was amongst his first work here and the additional storey to the old south wing, in the 1880s, was amongst the last. The inner courtyard provides one of the happiest visual thrills. Here the combination of timberwork, huge Perpendicular windows of the hall and brick infilling, as well as the patterned surface of the courtyard itself provides a rich display of designs and shapes that blend happily together. The tall bell-turret gives a vertical accent in the right place. Grand rooms within—the most notable being the Great Hall with a C15 minstrel's gallery from elsewhere. From elsewhere too are a number of Elizabethan and Jacobean chimneypieces. Another hall dates from 1913 and is spectacular too on account of its skylights, staircase and balcony. The wife of the 7th Earl was responsible for commissioning the interior of the chapel as a wedding present to her husband. It is a very complete example of Arts and Crafts decoration from 1902 until 1923. There are paintings by A. Payne, a triptych by Charles Gere, glass quarries of the screen by M. Lamplough and woodwork by C. R. Ashbee's guild. A few good things are to be found in the extensive grounds—notably a brick dovecote restored by Norman Shaw, a temple with 4 Tuscan columns and a pediment, lodge cottages by Voysey taking the form of a symmetrical pair linked by an archway and yet more work by Norman Shaw in the west and north lodges which are picturesquely half-

*Madresfield Court*

*Madresfield: parts of C16 building*

*Madresfield: north front*

*Madresfield: courtyard*

*Madresfield: hall*

timbered. Madresfield now belongs to the Countess Beauchamp, widow of the 8th and last Earl who died 1979. The late Lord Beauchamp was an Oxford friend of Evelyn Waugh and it is thought that the novelist may have drawn on his experiences of staying at Madresfield in the 1920s in *Brideshead Revisited*. LYGON, BEAUCHAMP, E/PB; *Pevsner*; VCH; CL 30 March 1907.

**Manor House (The), Bredon.** Stone c18 house of 5 bays with a most unusual segmental pediment looping over the 3 bays in the centre. Porch with Tuscan columns and a repeat of the segmental gable as a pediment. Fine tithe barn 124 ft long nearby. The house belonged to G. S. Cottrell 1928. *Pevsner*.

**Manor House (The), Cleeve Prior.** Hidden behind massive yews is this fine late c16 house, built on an asymmetrical plan. High quality detail is evident on the porch and the mullioned and transomed windows. Medallions with busts enliven the facade to the left and right of the porch. There is a priest-hole on the 1st floor and a circular dovecote in the grounds. The Misses Holtom lived here in 1920s. *Pevsner*; VCH IV; CL 26 May 1900.

*The Manor House, Cleeve Prior*

*The Manor House, Hinton-on-the-Green*

**Manor House (The), Hinton-on-the-Green.** Close to the church, it is a Cotswold-style house of *ca* 1600 with straight gables and mullioned and transomed windows. It is approached through a pair of late-c17 pigeoncotes joined by arches.

**Manor House (The), Hollybush.** 3 bays, of brick, with a Venetian window on the 1st floor in the middle. Early or mid-c18.

**Mere Hall, Hanbury.** Mere was built for the Bearcrofts and they remained here until 1977 when it was sold to Mr J. L. Duggin. It is a very pretty building; all timber-framed, it dates from *ca* 1560. The front is light and fanciful and the most charming features are the 5 small gables with finials on the 2nd floor which light a small long gallery. The porch with its barley-sugar columns is late c17. The house is crowned by a large lantern topped by a large golden ball. The close studding, herringbone struts and concave-sided lozenges all contribute to the highly decorative appearance of the facade. Some of the window glazing is c19 and was probably added by the architect M. Habershon. Inside there is a carved chimneypiece in the west wing. The house is embraced by a Georgian forecourt of brick walls with corner pavilions and it used to face a

fine avenue of oak trees, but these have been felled. BEARCROFT/LG1952; *Colvin*; *Pevsner*; VCH III; CL 22 Dec 1900.

**Middle Bean Hall, Bradley.** One is struck by the similarity to Mere Hall (*qv*). Surely this is due to an attempt to copy the attic storey of that house with its many gables and close studding. Here again are the continuous windows in the gables, but at Middle Bean they have been blocked. And whereas Mere is a house of *ca* 1560, this house is a refronting of 1635—date on a rainwater head—of a house of *ca* 1500 of the upper-front-hall type. The porch also belongs to the period of refronting. A farmhouse for a long time. *Pevsner*; VCH III.

**Middle Hill, Broadway.** In a fine position amidst gentle hills, this substantial building is ashlar faced of 5 bays in the rhythm of 2-1-2. Its appearance is deceptive, for it seems to be an early c19 structure, but is, in fact, of *ca* 1725 with an enlargement of *ca* 1780. A large 2-storey bow on the south side. Middle Hill is notable as the home of the famous bibliophile Sir Thomas Phillipps and, at one time, it must have housed part of his enormous collections. He had a private printing press here. The Misses Hingley owned Middle Hill before the last war; it now belongs to Lord Dulverton's Batsford Estates. PHILLIPPS, Bt/PB1872; HINGLEY, Bt/PB1917; WILLS, *sub* DULVERTON, Batsford Estates. PHILLIPPS, Bt/PB1872;

*Middle Hill*

*Mere Hall*

*Norgrove Court*

**Morton Hall, Inkberrow.** Sober, no-nonsense house of 5 bays and 2¹/₂ storeys with a lower left wing. Probably C18 and of brick, but now rendered. The only excitement to relieve the very sober front is a porch of 2 pairs of Tuscan columns. Mrs Kirk lived here 1928. *Pevsner*; VCH III.

**Nash (The), Kempsey.** In spite of alteration *ca* 1900, the house remains as something of interest. The oldest part—the corner where the parlour is—probably dates from the time of Henry VIII. Brick diapers outside and close studding visible within. Also of *ca* 1600 are the fine plaster ceilings of the dining-room and the room above it. In the latter the overmantel has columns decorated with strapwork. Later work is shown in the staircase which is *ca* 1700–10 with slim balusters and carved tread-ends. Octagonal brick piers are to be found in a part of the basement. The general picture one sees on approach is of a many crow-stepped house of brick—long and low. Onetime seat of the Temple family who became Bts 1876. TEMPLE, Bt/PB; *Pevsner*; VCH III.

**Norgrove Court, Webheath.** Long, mid-C17 house of brick with prominent stacks; one facade of rhythmic fenestration, the other totally irregular. All cross-windows; big hipped roof. Inside, one room boasts a splendid stucco chimneypiece with an overmantel of broad strapwork. The staircase has flat balusters. W. W. Impey lived here 1928. *Pevsner*; VCH III.

*Norgrove: staircase*

**Norton Park, Bredon's Norton.** Norton appears Victorian, but it was, in fact, built 1830. Of Tudor style and not particularly distinguished, it belonged to Miss Z. M. Woodhull 1937. CL 14 June 1902.

*Norgrove: chimneypiece*

**Ombersley Court, Ombersley.** Seat of the Lords Sandys. The house is a surprise, for the entrance front of 1812–14 is sober to the point of plainness and it masks the basic building of 1723–26 by Francis Smith for Samuel Sandys,

*Ombersley Court*

1st Lord Sandys (of the 1st creation), Chancellor of the Exchequer and Speaker of the House of Lords. Now there is a 7 bay, 2¹/₂ storey entrance side of the greatest reticence relieved only by a porch of 4 unfluted Ionic columns. The refronting was carried out by J. Webb after John Nash had prepared extensive alterations to the facades 1808. Inside, however, there are fine interiors of the greatest quality and refinement. A 2 storeyed entrance hall greets the visitor. It has a splendid ceiling, probably of 1814, and pilasters and blank niches on the ground floor. A balcony connects the upper rooms at the back. The 3 principal rooms to the west have magnificent wood panelling between pilasters of different orders and splendid doorcases. Fine marble chimneypiece in the saloon. The staircase with its plaster ceiling is of *ca* 1725 as well. Crisply carved balusters, 3 to each step, and treadends. More Webb work of the early C19 is found in the service staircase, as well as rooms flanking the entrance hall. Painted Chinese silk panels and Dufour wallpaper are to be found on 1st and 2nd-floor rooms respectively. The house is approached by way of a lodge of *ca* 1815 which has segmental arches with paterae. The Sandys barony became extinct on the death of the 2nd Baron of the 1st creation and the Ombersley estate passed to his niece, the Marchioness of Downshire, who was created Baroness Sandys with remainder to her younger sons. SANDYS and HILL, SANDYS, B; *Colvin*; *Pevsner*; VCH; CL 2, 9, 16 Jan 1953.

**Overbury Court, Overbury.** House and village evoke a vanished age: all is beautifully maintained and the feeling of a manorial stronghold is still very strong. Situated in an extensive park, the house of 1740 is large. The main front is 7 bays and 3 storeys with a 3 bay centre projection and rusticated quoins of even length. The principal door has unfluted Ionic columns and a pediment. Segment-headed windows on the attic storey which carries a pediment. A 5 bay side elevation to the park with a pedimented doorway with a Gibbs surround. The porch-like projection to the right side which rises to the 3rd floor is an addition of the 1890s. Norman Shaw did work here in 1895, but all has been swept away along with that of Sir Ernest Newton. Inside much has been changed, but the original staircase survives in spite of slight alteration. Handsome stables with 5 bays and slender wooden cross-windows. Hipped roof and lantern. The squire's family is a branch of Martin of Martin's Bank and is also connected

*Overbury Court*

*Park House: entrance front*

with the Bromley-Martins of Ham Court (*qv*). His nephew is Mr T. D. Holland-Martin, the amateur jockey and Jockey Club Steward. HOLLAND-MARTIN/LG 1965; *Pevsner*; *Nash*.

**Park House, Elmley Castle.** A large house, built *ca* 1550 and demolished *ca* 1960, it was extensively renovated in early C18. The entrance front was of 9 bays; the ends came forward. The front door had Tuscan columns and a segmental pediment; it broke forward slightly, too, with the one bay above it and this whole projection, emphasized by quoins at the angles, ended in a round-headed attic window, which broke into the solid parapet. Both the end bays of the entrance and the side and rear elevations carried their original pointed

gables, but all windows had been sashed at the time of the C18 rehabilitation. But it was inside that the C18 gave its greatest richness. Round a square well rose the elegant staircase with 3 balusters to a tread, while above it presided the most sumptuous plaster ceiling. A great wreath of fruit and flowers encircled the centre from which there burst foliated strands to all points of the compass. In the corners there were more panels with swirls encompassing the coat-of-arms of the Savage family, while in the slight cove between wall and ceiling there were shells and swirls of exuberant character. The walls of this chamber were divided into panels with more plasterwork. Formerly the seat of the Savages, the Elmley estate was acquired by the Davies family, with whom it remains, early in C19. DAVIES/LG 1969; VCH III.

*Park House: staircase*

*Park House: garden front*

*Park House: ceiling of staircase*

*Perdiswell: hall*

**Perdiswell Hall, Worcester.** Fine gatepiers with Coade stone reliefs of Navigation and Agriculture are all that remains of Perdiswell which was demolished 1956. The house was mid-Georgian of 5 bays and 3 storeys. Pediment over centre 3 bays and Tuscan porch. Inside a screen of columns at the end of the hall gave way to a gently sweeping wrought-iron staircase. Mrs Kirkham lived here 1928. *Colvin*; *Pevsner*; VCH IV.

**Pirton Court, Pirton.** Much restored, but a large timber-framed house of late C16 with merry decoration especially at one end of the building. It has the appearance of someone trying to be frolicsome with half-timbered detail. A very juicy chimneypiece inside with a semi-circular pediment filled with a shell. In another room there is simple decoration on a Jacobean plaster ceiling. Pirton forms part of the Croome Court estate (*qv*) owned by the Earls of Coventry. COVENTRY, E/PB; *Pevsner*; VCH III.

*Perdiswell Hall*

*Pirton Court*

**Powick Court, Powick.** Demolished in the 1950s at the time when so many country houses disappeared, Powick was late C18 of 3 storeys with bows to the entrance front. Long side elevation of 5 bays, with a 3 bay pediment.

**Priors Court, Powick.** Historically notable as the home of Jane Lane, one of those to help Charles II escape after the battle of Worcester 1651; and even Charles I is said to have sheltered here after the Battle of Naseby 1645. This former property of the Lanes is architecturally notable, too, as a highly picturesque C16 half-timbered house built round a small courtyard. All black and white with tall diagonal brick chimneys and a Stuart or Tudor porch of 4 gables on oak columns. The staircase has turned oak balusters and there is some original panelling. The Goole family were here in C18 and it was the property of Earl Beauchamp in C20. Lately the home of Dr Warwick Jackson. LANE *formerly of King's Bromley*/LG1965; LYGON, BEAUCHAMP, E/PB; VCH IV.

**Pull Court, Bushley.** The best front faces the garden. A centre treated like a gatehouse with 2 Tudor turrets. Between them a shaped gable and to the right and left of this central feature more shaped gables. On the entrance side there are 3 transomed and 3 light windows flanking the entrance itself. The whole building is monumental and a fanfare for Blore who built it 1836–46 for Canon Dowdeswell. The centre has 2 far-projecting wings—parts of which are the same height and other parts of which are lower. These wings are connected by a low screen in the middle of which is a large gateway. High entrance hall with screens at either end—one of which hides the staircase.

*Powick Court*

*Priors Court*

More exuberant rooms elsewhere. The grounds contain an artificial ruin made up from 2 C14 windows from the old church. Dowdeswells continued to live here until quite recently, but it is now Bredon School. DOWDESWELL/LG1937; *Colvin*; *Pevsner*; VCH III.

**Purshall Hall, Elmbridge.** A farmhouse now, mostly of Jacobean brick, but the original 4 bay cruck house survives within. There is an C18 projection with tall narrow windows. It is said to have been a recusant-priests' hide-out.

**Rhydd Court, Guarlford.** In 1863 David Brandon enlarged a house of *ca* 1800 into a large, irregular and featureless building. Rhydd used to belong to the Lechmere family and Mrs Allen-Hoblyn was here in the 1920s. Making up in some measure for the lack of interest provided by the house, there is the chapel attached to it. It is an apsed Gothic building begun by Charles Hansom and completed by Norman Shaw, who failed to leave his own distinguishing mark upon it. Stained glass by John Hardman. LECHMERE, Bt/PB; *Pevsner*; VCH III; Morris, *Seats* IV.

**Ribbesford House, Ribbesford.** The general plan of the house belongs to the period when Leland referred to it as a "goodly manour place", in other words *ca* 1535. But a first glance now makes it appear early C19 medieval. In C18 the 2 turrets which face south were circular; now they are octagonal and the corridor between them is early C19. The hall, entered through a big porch, retains its original moulded beams and a wing still has diapered brickwork. Much alteration has taken place and the house awaits elucidation. The famous philosopher and diplomatist Lord Herbert of Chirbury lived here in C17. Late C19 owners included the Ingram and Lees-Milne families. Ribbesford was sold by A. M. Lees-Milne (who died 1931) and between the wars it was the property of J. T. Brockhouse. HERBERT, HERBERT OF CHIRBURY, B/DEP; LEES-MILNE *formerly of Wickhamford Manor*/LG1965; INGRAM/WCF; CL 19 Jan 1945; *Nash*; *Pevsner*; VCH IV.

**Rous Lench Court, Rous Lench.** Originally a large house built around 2 courtyards, Rous Lench is now an "L"-shaped building, all black and white and highly picturesque. It stands high above an outstanding garden full of arbours, tunnels, terraces and avenues—all in yew. Both the house and garden, as we see them now, are largely a C19 creation. Of the early C16, however, is the west range with the gateway and a notable stone chimneypiece in an upper room. The south range is basically early C17 apart from the projection to the north which is early Victorian. Inside this range, on an upper floor, there is a fine stone chimneypiece from Shaw in the North Riding; this was originally intended for William Randolph Hearst's Californian extravaganza, San Simeon. The C19 refurbishment has left the interior rich in exposed timberwork. An Italianate tower of brick presides over house and garden and commands an extensive prospect. The Rouse family lived here from C14 to 1721. Their handsome monuments fill the church. Rouse Boughtons succeeded thereafter and remained in possession until

*Rous Lench Court*

1876 when it was sold to Rev W. K. W. Chafy. His son retained the house until 1926. Frederick Burn owned the house 1928. A visitor to the house, *ca* 1647, was Richard Baxter who wrote part of his famous hymn "Saints Everlasting Rest" here. ROUSE BOUGHTON, Bt/PB1963; CHAFY/LG1952; *Pevsner*; VCH; CL 16 Sept 1899.

**Salwarpe Court, Salwarpe.** On an older site, this is one of the best black and white houses in the county. Long, low rambling structure of late C15 or early C16 built for Sir John Talbot. Close vertical studding with later brickwork painted to imitate black and white. A projecting bay, supported by brackets, forms the original entrance porch. But the best exterior feature is on the south-west solar side where there is an overhanging upper bay and bargeboarded gable with carved decoration. Most of the original interior has been stripped, but some exposed timbering remains. The house was sold 1780 to Philip Gresley and it later belonged to Rev W. W. Douglas. By the early C20 it had become a farmhouse. Resuscitated since then, it was recently advertised for sale. TALBOT, *sub* SHREWSBURY, E/PB; GRESLEY, Bt/PB; *Pevsner*; VCH.

*Salwarpe Court*

*Severn End*

**Severn Bank, Severn Stoke.** Surrounded by magnificent woods and affording delightful views of the River Severn, Severn Bank is an early C19 house, all stuccoed. On one side there are canted bay windows and an iron verandah; on another is a bow window. This latter side is 3 storeyed, while the former is only 2. The whole house is battlemented and looks like a miniature castle. A. C. Lupton lived here 1928. *Pevsner*.

**Severn End, Hanley Castle.** This is the ancient seat of the old Worcs family of Lechmere, but much of what one sees today is a rebuilding after a disastrous fire 1896. In the rebuilding the enthusiasm for half-timbering prevailed and parts which had been brick before disappeared in the new zeal for making all of closely set studding. The centre of the entrance side with its lively half-timbering is

*South Littleton Manor*

original. Decoration includes concave-sided lozenges and keyed-in ovals—possibly dating from 1660–70 when Sir Nicholas Lechmere, MP, built so much. Original chimney-stacks with star tops. The long wings date from 1673 and are of brick with Dutch gables. In the north wing is the only original plaster ceiling. The house contains the Lechmere stone, a small part of a tombstone possibly dating from C9 or C11. The grounds contain various delights such as the square, 2 storeyed summer house with two stone arches; it is dated 1661. There is also a timber-framed barn of 1658 and a square brick dovecote of 1677. LECHMERE, Bt/PB; *Nash*; *Pevsner*; VCH; CL 24 & 31/7/75.

**Shakenhurst Hall, Bayton.** The C17 house was refronted 1798. Red brick, 2½ storeys; 2 canted bays flank a 3 bay centre which is topped with a pediment. There is an Ionic porch with broken pediment too. Built for the Wigley

family, it was the property of P. H. Gurney, a member of the formidable East Anglian cousinhood, in 1920s. GURNEY *formerly of North Runcton*/LG1965; *Pevsner*; VCH IV.

**Sodington Hall, Mamble.** An early C19 3 storeyed brick house built on the site of an earlier structure demolished 1807. There was once a moat and, in the present entrance hall, there is a panel dated 1606. Parliamentarians burnt the previous house where the Blount family were first heard of in C14. Sir Walter Blount, 1st Bt, was imprisoned at Oxford and in the Tower of London and his estates were confiscated by Cromwell. Some considerable part of the original house probably survived in C18, as Nash refers to it as having the appearance of a house formerly of some strength with 4 drawbridges over the moat. Now the home of the Turner family. BLOUNT, Bt/PB; *Nash*; VCH.

**South Littleton Manor, South Littleton.** Ranging from pre-Reformation at the east end, past the gabled middle parts of the Elizabethans to the rectangular and main entrance block at the west. This block has steep pitched roof surmounted by a belvedere with a prominent weathervane. Either side of this central feature, though, are huge arched chimney-stacks pronouncing the Baroque. It is 5 by 3 bays with wooden cross windows. The date 1721 appears on the weathervane. Narrow entrance hall. Sturdy staircase with twisted balusters and a wreath of plaster decoration on the ceiling of the drawing-room. Formerly a property of the Lees-Milnes. LEES-MILNE *formerly of Wickhamford Manor*-/LG1965; *Pevsner*; VCH IV.

**Spetchley Park, Spetchley.** In place of an older house, John Tasker built the present long building for the ancient family of Berkeley *post* 1811. Of smooth Bath stone, Spetchley has a long south front and a shorter west front, which bears the giant portico of 4 unfluted Ionic columns. The whole is of 2 storeys and is sparing of ornament. On the south side there is a central semi-circular projection with unfluted Ionic pilasters. There are single windows, tripartite windows and long tablets, instead of windows, on the 1st floor. Reticent decoration within. The 3 main reception rooms are all ranged along the south front. The hall has pairs of red scagliola columns and the spacious staircase has a very fine handrail. The chapel is an impressive apartment running the whole height and nearly the whole depth of the house, with the altar wall to the south. This has a blank Venetian motif with a segmental arch. Pretty iron footbridge and a root house in the park. Notable gardens frequently on show. As collaterals of the Earls of Berkeley, the present generation of the family inherited Berkeley Castle, Gloucestershire, on the death of the last Earl 1943. BERKELEY/LG1969; *Pevsner*; *Colvin*; CL 8, 15 July 1975.

*Spetchley Park*

**Springhill House, Broadway.** Notable for its park which, although a somewhat watered-down version of what it once was, still shows vestiges of the hand of Capability Brown who worked here for 6th Earl of Coventry 1763. The present house is plain and ashlar, but this is largely due to the alterations of Gen Hon E. P. Lygon, who bought the place 1830. He added the front behind which the C18 wings remain. This front is quite plain. Stables with cupola. COVENTRY, COVENTRY, E/PB; LYGON, *sub* BEAUCHAMP, E/PB; *Colvin*; *Pevsner*; VCH IV; Stroud, *Capability Brown*.

**Stanford Court, Stanford-on-Teme.** According to VCH, the house destroyed by fire on 6 Dec 1882 was a brick building consisting of a centre and 2 projecting wings dating from the time of James I. But the north front was Georgian, ashlar-faced and 2 storeyed with a bow in the centre. This front survived the fire. The remainder of the house, though, appears wholly Georgian too; so presumably this was rebuilt in 1886–88 in order to conform with the north front. Valuable collections of MSS and pictures were destroyed in the fire. Longtime seat of the Winnington Bts who inherited the

*Stanford Court*

manor from the Salweys in C17. SALWEY *of The Lodge, Overton*/LG1952; WINNINGTON, Bt/PB; *Pevsner*; VCH IV.

**Stockton House, Stockton-on-Teme.** Of brick with a great shaped gable-end, Stockton is late C17. The Miller family owned the house in late C19 and Mrs Eshelby was here in 1920s. *Pevsner*; VCH III.

**Strensham Court, Strensham.** Built 1824 for John Taylor, Strensham was a large ashlar-faced house of 2 storeys in the Grecian taste. To this was added, a few years later, a giant tetrastyle portico of unfluted Ionic columns. It was as deep as it was high—perhaps a trifle too grand for the house. Inside, an elegant staircase with wrought-iron balustrade. Still owned by the Taylors *post* World War I when it was let, Strensham soon fell on evil days and for many years it looked like a stranded hulk as it stood empty beside the new motorway. Mysteriously destroyed by fire Nov 1974, it was demolished soon afterwards as an unsafe structure. TAYLOR/LG1937; *Pevsner*; VCH III.

**Thorngrove, Grimley.** Napoleon's brother, Lucien Bonaparte, Prince of Canino, lived here for several years thereby placing a high historical value on the property. Thorngrove is not an outstanding house, but its design is curious and therefore interesting. Ashlar-faced and of 7 bays, it probably dates from early C19. The oddness in the design is exhibited by the very thin angle pilasters and the weak 1 bay pediment. On the garden front are canted bay windows as well as one big bow.

*Strensham Court*

*Thorngrove*

*Tickenhill Manor*

A 3 arch bridge with cast-iron parapet with lampholders is in the grounds. Following the French connexion, Thorngrove was owned by Sir Herbert Huntingdon-Whiteley, 1st Bt, who died 1936. BONAPARTE/RFWi; HUNTINGTON-WHITELEY, Bt/PB; *Pevsner*; VCH III.

**Tickenhill Manor, Bewdley.** Externally Tickenhill presents an "L"-shaped, wholly Georgian facade of *ca* 1740. Inside, however, there are roof timbers of a C15 hall; it was originally the council house of the Lords President of the Marches of Wales and a royal residence. It is said that both Queens Mary and Elizabeth I sometimes resided here and Charles I is said to have written the letter that set off the Battle of Marston Moor 1644. It became the property of the Winningtons; then of the Tangye family in 1870s and, finally, of the Parker family who sold it recently. WINNINGTON, Bt/PB; TANGYE, Bt/PB; *Pevsner*; CL 19 Jan 1945; VCH III.

**Tutnall Hall, Tardebigge.** Pediment and parapet have gone and the house now assumes a roughed-up appearance; nevertheless it is still reminiscent of the type of place epitomized by Cound Hall, Shropshire (*qv*). Early C18 and red brick with a 3 bay centre and 2 bay ends punctuated by no-nonsense Tuscan pilasters and entablatures embracing 2 storeys and attic. Despite its nobility Tutnall does not appear entirely at odds in its present role as a farmhouse. *Pevsner*; Lees-Milne, *English Country Houses*: *Baroque* (1970).

*Tutnall Hall*

**Wassell Wood, High Habberley.** Brick, rendered and of middle-size; Tudor-Gothic probably of the 1860s. 3 gabled entrance front with projecting porch with prominent pointed arches. A mullioned bay topped with balustrade continues the line of the porch to the right. Dark oak combined with more Gothicry within. Lately owned by Mr E. L. Dudley, having been bought by his family 1934, but recently for sale.

**Weatheroak Hall, King's Norton.** Rebuilt *ca* 1910 and now King's Norton Golf Club. It is, in fact, a late C18 house showing a centre block of 5 bays and 3 storeys with a pediment over the 3 bays in the centre. Links join the main block to lower 3 bay, 2 storey wings. Built for James Mynors, a successful surgeon, Weatheroak remained in his family until C20. The Birmingham Art Gallery has recently acquired a picture depicting Mynors with his family and the house in the background. MYNORS/LG1921.

**Welland Court, Welland.** Simple but elegant refacing of an older building. Mid-C18 and of brick; 5 bays, 2 storeys—the centre bay projecting slightly and crowned by a pediment. Venetian window at 1st-floor level over stone doorway with pediment. Parapet, urns, quoins—all robust yet, at the same time, elegant and agreeable. Now a farmhouse. *Pevsner*; VCH III.

**Westwood Park, nr Droitwich.** On an ancient site, Westwood was founded as early as

*Wassell Wood*

C12, but only after various vicissitudes did it come to the Pakingtons in C16. Sir John Pakington probably began the house after his marriage 1598 and originally it was tall and more or less square and intended as a hunting lodge. Canted bay windows are a feature of this original compact block, as are the shaped gables and diagonal chimneys. But how much of this decoration is of *ca* 1600 or really of 1660–70, when the diagonal wings were added, remains problematical. These wings are extraordinary: they were attached diagon-

ally and yet they were so well done that no change of plan or style is noticeable. The wings, too, show canted bays and shaped gables and their end pavilions boast concave-convex-concave roofs as redone by Sir Reginald Blomfield. Originally they were plain and steep pyramid roofs. The Great Hall occupies two-fifths of the original square, but its decoration is not original. The staircase of *ca* 1670 is, however, spectacular: it runs up in 2 flights separated by a landing and the really startling features are the much higher newel

*Westwood Park*

posts crowned by balls. The Great Chamber has as its show features a splendid wooden chimneypiece of *ca* 1600 and a rich wreath-filled ceiling of *ca* 1675. More plasterwork of the same date is in the wings. The house is approached through a gatehouse which has shaped gables and a broad wooden cupola on top. It is decorated like the house with the armorial mullets and wheatsheaves of the Pakingtons. In C20 the house was bought by 1st Lord Doverdale, but on the death of the 3rd and last Baron (who married an Australian chorus girl), it was sold and eventually became flats. It is unkindly said that the Partingtons were prone to pretend that they were the same family as the Pakingtons. PAKINGTON, Bt/EDB; PARTINGTON, DOVERDALE, B/PB1949; *Pevsner*; VCH; CL 29 Nov 1902 & 14, 21 July 1928.

**Wichenford Court, Wichenford.** Good provincial house of 1670-80. Of brick, 7 by 3 bays, with hipped roof and mullion and transomed cross-windows. Wooden over-mantel inside with Jacobean panels. Long the seat of the Washbournes, it is now a farm-house. WASHBURN *formerly of Little Washbourne and Wichenford*/DFUSA; *Pevsner*; VCH.

**Wick House, Wick.** Long C18 house chiefly remarkable for its high 3 bay centre surmounted by a pediment. Inside a notable early C18 hall with exuberant Baroque chimneypiece. The hall was of 2 storeys and the walls were of high quality panelling. Seat of the Hudsons. Demolished 1950s. HUDSON/ LG1937; VCH.

*Wichenford Court*

*Wick House*

*Wick House: hall*

*Wick Manor*

*Wickhamford Manor*

**Wick Manor, Wick.** Large and picturesque, but a confection of 1923 round a Georgian core. Successful because it groups all the right motifs of timber-framing native to the county. Another property of the Hudsons. HUDSON/LG1937; *Pevsner.*

**Wickhamford Manor, Wickhamford.** House and church overlooking a lake form a highly picturesque group. But the spacious half-timbered manor, with recessed centre and gabled wings, is largely work of C20, although a much smaller C16 building forms the core. All close studding and exposed timberwork within; and one fine C17 chimneypiece. The Lees-Milne family lived here for first half of C20, selling it 1946. Wickhamford was the childhood home of the writer and architectural historian James Lees-Milne and it features in his hilarious autobiography *Another Self.* LEES-MILNE/LG1965; VCH IV.

**Witley Court, Great Witley.** Now in the guardianship of the Department of the Environment, who have strengthened the shell of what remains after the great fire of 1937. On first sight it appears as a huge mid-C19 palace, but it has been the subject of repeated rebuildings. Of the Jacobean house of the Russells there remain the twin towers to the north between the long wings added 1683 by Thomas Foley. It was Samuel Daukes who turned the house into the triumphant C19 palace we see today. In transforming Witley he retained the early C19 porticos on both sides of the building—that on the garden front being by John Nash. He did, however, add 4 storeyed towers and $2^{1}/_{2}$ storeyed wings with canted bay windows at their ends. Over all is a top balustrade. Daukes's work is, though, in

*Witley Court: entrance front*

*Witley Court: garden front*

keeping with the great chapel of St Michael which dates from 1735 and which adjoins the house. He retained round-headed windows and surrounding blank arches in order to keep the great house in harmony with the chapel, which contains the famous ceiling paintings and glass from Canons, Middx (demolished 1747). High Victorianism is found in the curving 7 bay wing to the left of the garden front, which ends in a pavilion whose ground-floor openings are derived from Michelangelo and Bernini. Beyond this wing is the now roofless 13 bay orangery. Nesfield laid out the grounds and among the more remarkable features of these is the Perseus Fountain by James Forsyth, which displays lively Baroque abandon, and the Triton Fountain, with four tritons blowing their shells. Records of the interior of the house are scanty, but old photographs reveal huge rooms in the French taste. The Foley family held the estate until 1835 when it was bought by 11th Lord Ward (created 1st Earl of Dudley 1860). Sir Herbert Smith, Bt, the carpet manufacturer, was the owner at the time of the fire. The Dowager Queen Adelaide occupied the house 1843–46. FOLEY, B/PB; WARD, DUDLEY, E/PB; SMITH, Bt, *of Kidderminster*/PB1959; *Colvin*; *Pevsner*; VCH III; CL 8, 15 June 1945.

**Wolverton Hall, Stoulton.** Plain, early C18 rectangular block of brick. A main front of 7 bays and 3 storeys—relieved only by string-courses. At each end of the building there are

*Wolverton Hall*

prominent doorcases. The earlier one, with large segmental pediment, is probably contemporary with the date of building, but the later Georgian one, which forms the entrance, is composed of Tuscan columns and a broken pediment. Lower, later additions at this end. Built by the Actons to replace an older house of considerable size, it is now the property of Mrs Trevor Dawson whose father, Mr W. A. Acton, made it over to her 1965. The Actons inherited the property from the Cookseys who

were seated at Wolverton in medieval times. ACTON/LG1972; *Pevsner*; VCH III.

**Woodmanton, Clifton-on-Teme.** Plain brick house, built 1827, which replaced an ancient manor house dating from at least 1332 when licence was given to crenellate. The old moat was partly filled-in when the present house was built, but remains of a circular tower are to be seen; and, most notable of all, the former chapel (now a farm building) still

*Woodnorton*

exists. It is timber-framed and has an interesting roof which is a wagon vault. It is one of the few examples of a rafter roof with curved ashlar pieces and originally supported by a wholly timber-framed substructure. Onetime seat of the Wyshams, it was the property of D. A. Wright 1928. *Pevsner*; VCH III.

**Woodnorton, Norton.** Large and lacking in character, Woodnorton appears Victorian, but possibly contains earlier parts. The chapel dates from 1865 and work was done as late as 1897. The interest of the house lies in the fact that it belonged to the Duc d'Aumale and afterwards to the Duc d'Orleans, his grand-nephew. The gates, now somewhat stripped of their original ornament, are said to have come from Versailles via Orleans House, Twickenham. Woodnorton was taken over by the BBC *ca* World War II and is still used by the Corporation's engineering training department. It was badly damaged by a fire some years back. FRANCE/RFWi; *Pevsner*.

**Woollas Hall, Eckington.** Longtime seat of the Hanfords, but now divided into flats. A very picturesque and high gabled house of 1611 with an irregular facade. A 3 storey porch punctuates this facade and it has an arched

entrance. 2 hall windows with transoms and little gables appear to the right of the porch, while to the left there is a bigger and higher gable above different floor levels. Shaped screen walls frame the facade. Inside there is a screens passage behind a screen with handsome Ionic pilasters; another room has a chimneypiece with thin columns and blank arches above. Stables with mullioned windows below and in the gables. *Nash*; *Pevsner*; VCH III; CL 25 Aug 1906.

**Wyre Piddle House, Wyre Piddle.** Drastic rebuilding *ca* 1840–50 gave the house its present appearance with straight-headed windows in the style of *ca* 1500 with hoodmoulds and bargeboard gables. However, Wyre Piddle is basically a house of *ca* 1625–50. Thomas Sheaf lived here 1928. *Pevsner*; VCH III.

*Woollas Hall*

# Sources for Illustrations

*Where there is more than one source on a page, the credits start with the picture furthest to the left and nearest the top of the page and work down each column (a, b, c, d, e, etc)*

Simon Bailey, page 131a; R. A. & W. L. Banks, 12c, 17a, 43a, 45d, 47d, 53a; Banks & Silvers, 110a; Mrs Egbert Barnes, 83c; Batsford, 49a, 174; Hon Lady Betjeman, 107b; Birmingham Public Library, 146c,d, 150c; Mrs L. F. P. Bletchly, 67a; Richard Booth, 149a; Chesshire, Gibson & Co, 195f; John Chivers & Son, 132c; Brig A. Clive, 51a; Lady Mary Clive, 63a, 69b; Gerald Cobb, 86b, 178b, 191a; C. E. Colbourn, 135c; R. J. Collins, 191b, 199ce, 204b, 212c, 214a, 225b, 228a, 229a; Sir John Cotterell, Bt 23a, 28abcd, 56c, 139b; *Country Life*, 23b, 66a, 74, 75c, 87b, 91b, 97a, 126a, 200a, 205b, 206, 207b, 213a, 214b; J. R. Snead-Cox, 10a; Lt-Col H. R. H. Davies, 223a; Betty Countess of Denbigh, 163bce; Richard Dennis, 26b, 43c, 84a, 93c, 108b, 121a, 132de; Denton Clark & Co 121c; Capt Thomas Dunne, 29b; Edwards, Bigwood & Bewley, 157c, 185b, 192b, 202b; A. B. R. Fairclough, 42c; J. K. Farrow, 168c; A. T. Foley, 58b, 59ab; John German, Ralph Pay, 80c; Miss E. H. Harding, 130b; C. C. Harley, 24c; Capt R. H. de L. Hulton-Harrop, 100d; Hereford Public Library, 31a, 57b; Major H. R. Holden, 114b; E. G. Holt, 7a; Simon Hopton, 13ab, 14a; F. G. Howell, 32b; Kidderminster Public Library, 215b; Knight, Frank & Rutley, 20a; Misses Grosvenor-Launder 27a, 33b; Peter T. Leach, 86a, 93b, 103a, 112a, 216a; *Leamington Spa Courier*, 148c,

158b, 183a, 188; Ian Leith, 30c, 47a, 60d, 69c, 104c; Michael Marshall, 56a, 179bc; E. Holland-Martin, 207a, 222a; C. Monkhouse, 80a; N. J. Moore, *frontispiece*, 31d, 37a; Mrs Mary Morgan, 47c; Musicians Benevolent Fund, 22ab; C. A. Norris, 196b, 197ab; Marquess of Northampton, 140b; Mrs D. Oglander, 76b; Mrs J. H. Oram, 18a, 68a; Lord Ormathwaite, 16b; Trevor Parker, 15ab; A. V. Powell, 195c; Hon Diana Pritchard, 125a, 128cde, 129d, 131d, 133abc, 137b, 138b, 139cd, 141bc, 142cd, 143c, 154a, 155c, 156bcd, 157cd, 160a, 162a, 167c, 168abc, 172ac, 176bc, 177ab, 186b, 187c; Cecil Reilly, 203a; D. T. Rice, 58a; Alistair Rowan, 48d, 80de, 176a; Savills, 163d, 233b; Derek Sherborn, 9b, 24b, 184a; Shrewsbury Public Library, 96c; Lt-Cmdr R. M. Simpson, 11d, 12a; Strutt & Parker, 220c; Sir Edward Thompson, 90a; Major J. H. N. Thompson, 115a; Brig H. Vaughan, 168e; Bernard Walsh & Co, 19b; Miss O. I. W. Lee-Warner, 62b; Lt-Col M. H. Warriner, 184b, 185acd; W. D. Webber, 63b; Mrs J. H. G. Wells, 16a, 55ab; Lady Alston-Roberts-West, 125bc; and C. J. Wingfield, 106ab.

The remainder of the photographs in the book are drawn from the collections of the author and the National Monuments Record.

# Index

*Families connected with the houses are listed under their surname (in capitals) alone; compound surnames appear under the last. Illustrations are indicated by italic numerals.*

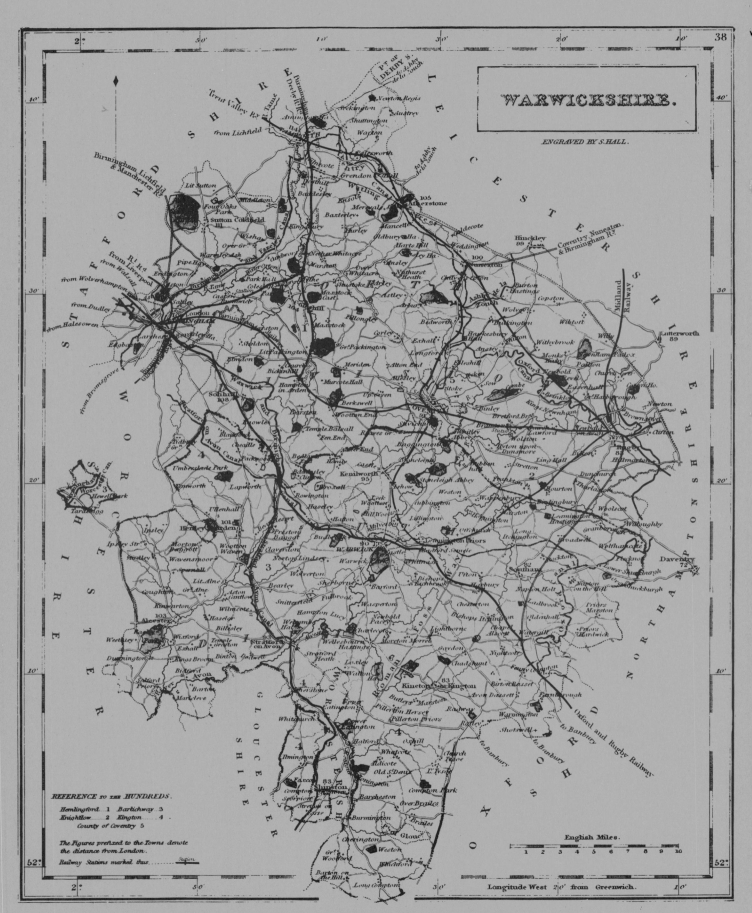

# WARWICKSHIRE.

ENGRAVED BY S. HALL.

REFERENCE to the HUNDREDS.

Hemlingford....1    Barlichway...3
Knightlow.......2    Kington.......4
                County of Coventry 5

The Figures prefixed to the Towns denote
the distance from London.

Railway Stations marked thus........

English Miles.
1 2 3 4 5 6 7 8 9 10

Longitude West 2° from Greenwich.

London, Published by Chapman & Hall, 186 Piccadilly.